THE ROAD
TO LINDI

THE F
TO L

HULL BOYS

The 1st (Hull) H

Garriso

East Africa and

R

Ubique

There is a word you often see, pronounce it as you may
"You bike," "you bykwee," "ubbikwe" – alludin' to R.A.
It serves 'Orse, Field, an' Garrison as motto for a crest,
An' when you've found out all it means I'll tell you 'alf the rest.

Rudyard Kipling

Reveille Press is an imprint of
Tommies Guides Military Booksellers & Publishers

Gemini House
136-140 Old Shoreham Road
Brighton
BN3 7BD

www.tommiesguides.co.uk

First published in Great Britain by
Reveille Press 2013

For more information please visit
www.reveillepress.com

ISBN 978-1-908336-56-9

Cover design by Reveille Press

Typeset by Graham Hales

Printed and bound by
Print-on-Demand Worldwide, Peterborough

Contents

List of Abbreviations and Definitions

A.C.I.: Army Council Instruction
Formal Orders issued by the War Office.

A.S.C.: Army Service Corps
"The unsung heroes of the British army in the Great War – the A.S.C., *Ally Sloper's Cavalry*. Soldiers cannot fight without food, equipment, and ammunition. In the Great War, the vast majority of this tonnage, supplying a vast army on many fronts, was supplied from Britain. Using horsed and motor vehicles, railways and waterways, the A.S.C. performed prodigious feats of logistics and were one of the great strengths of organisation by which the war was won". (Chris Baker, http://www.1914-1918.net/asc.htm)

B.E.F.: British Expeditionary Force
A highly mobile section of the British Army intended for deployment on active service in an overseas theatre of war.

D.C.M.: Distinguished Conduct Medal.
A military award to recognise gallantry within the other ranks created in 1854.

F.O.O.: Field Observation Officer
The officer assigned to occupy the forward observation post (F.O.P.) of the artillery battery. The officer would report the fall of shot, range, and movements of the enemy, and make sketches of the terrain and targets, carrying out reconnaissance when required. The F.O.O. would be connected to the gun battery by field telephone. However, semaphore signaling could be employed where connections could not be maintained.

H.M.S.: His Majesty's Ship
Classification prefix of ships belonging to the British Royal Navy.

H.M.T.: Hired Military Transport
A prefix classification of shipping that covered those ships

requisitioned for use by the British military, e.g. H.M.T. *Huntsgreen.*

I.W.M.: Imperial War Museum

L.O.C.: Lines of Communication

"Lines of Communication" was an army term used to describe what today we might call the army's logistics: the supply lines from port to front line, and the camps, stores, dumps, workshops of the rear areas". (Chris Baker, http://www.1914-1918.net/asc.htm)

M.C.: Military Cross

A military bravery award, created in 1914, for commissioned officers.

N.C.O.: Non-Commissioned Officer

An officer in the army who has not been granted a commission. Normally promoted from the ranks, typically this rank covers Sergeants, Corporals but also Warrant Officers (WO), Quartermasters (RQS / BQS) and Regimental or Battery Sergeant Majors (RSM / BSM).

O.C.: Officer Commanding

The senior officer of a sub-unit within a larger formation, e.g. Captain B. E. Floyd, Officer Commanding, the Hull Heavy Battery, within the R.G.A. or Artillery Group.

R.A.: Royal Artillery

The Royal Artillery is a Corps within the British Army. It provides the firepower for the infantry, using a range of different caliber guns and howitzers. During the Great War, with the exception of the Royal Horse Artillery, it was organised into two main elements.

R.F.A.: Royal Field Artillery

The Royal Field Artillery: the most numerous arm of the artillery, the horse-drawn RFA was responsible for the medium calibre guns and howitzers deployed close to the front line and was reasonably mobile. It was organised into brigades. (Chris Baker, http://www.1914-1918.net/asc.htm)

R.G.A.: Royal Garrison Artillery

The Royal Garrison Artillery: developed from fortress-based artillery located on British coasts. From 1914 when the army possessed very little heavy artillery it grew into a very large component of the British forces. It was armed with heavy, large calibre guns and howitzers that were positioned some way behind the front line and had immense destructive power. (Chris Baker, http:// www.1914-1918.net/asc.htm)

R.M.S.: Royal Mail Steamer
Classification prefix for ships used for the transport of mail between countries in addition to passenger transport, e.g. R.M.S. *Durham Castle*

R.N.A.S.:Royal Naval Air Service
The air arm of the Royal Navy, administered by the Admiralty. In 1918, the Royal Air Force was formed by the amalgamation of the R.N.A.S with the air wing of the Army, the Royal Flying Corps (R.F.C).

S.M.S.: Seiner Majestät Schiff
German translation of H.M.S, used by the Prussian Navy and Imperial German Navy.

S.S.: Steam Ship
A prefix classification for civilian vessel denoting the means of propulsion.

List of Illustrations

13

List of Appendices

1. The Nominal Roll of Battery Officers
2. Officers' Awards
3. The Nominal Roll of the 1st (Hull) Heavy Battery R.G.A.
4. The Nominal Roll of the 1st (Hull) Heavy Battery (1st Depot) R.G.A.
5. Men Discharged from 1st (Hull) Heavy Battery R.G.A.
6. Men Discharged from 1st (Hull) Heavy Battery (1st Depot) R.G.A.
7. Men Discharged following appointment to an Officer's Commission
8. Men Mentioned in Despatches
9. The Roll of Honour of Those who Died
10. Battery Members Listed on the Hull Rolls of Honour
11. Men Released from Military Service

List of Maps

Foreword

TIME dulls memory, particularly about disagreeable and tragic subjects such as wars. The residents of Hull and its environs are fortunate that Rupert Drake has, over several years, very diligently researched and compiled information on the 1st (Hull) Heavy Battery, Royal Garrison Artillery, during the First World War. The result of Rupert's research, inspired by his grandfather Jack Drake's involvement, is this extremely well-illustrated book, that traces the wartime journeys of Hull artillerymen out to the tropical jungles of East Africa, where death was more likely to come from disease than from the German enemy, and then to the Western Front, where the combat was intense.

These Hull artillerymen were on the whole well educated lads, and the excerpts from their diaries and letters that Rupert has obtained are fascinating. Here one gets a sense of how England was in 1914, with trades such as farrier and blacksmith being proudly practised, and also how the horse was such an important part of both rural and urban life. Some of the Hull boys did not return, and today you can visit their graves or memorials in very well tended cemeteries in East Africa and France; for this we must thank the Commonwealth War Graves Commission for performing an excellent but relatively little-known overseas maintenance task.

Please do not only read this book yourself, but encourage others, especially schoolchildren and students, either to read it, or be guided through it. This story contains many interesting facts about geography and tropical medicine as well as about colonial and military history. But most of all this book portrays how groups of young men from around Britain and its then Empire, black men, brown men and white men, responded to the call of wartime service, and how they bonded together through good times and bad.

Thank you, Rupert, your years of careful and conscientious research have resulted in a unique, relevant and very readable piece of local history.

Harry Fecitt MBE TD

Preface

A S a boy in the 1960s my father would take me on Sundays to visit my grandparents. My grandmother would dominate the proceedings, regaling her temporary audience with literary extracts, poems, rhymes and tales of her Edwardian schooldays in Deptford, South East London along with stories handed down by her father, a seaman in the Victorian Royal Navy. Throughout this family ritual, my grandfather Jack would sit in his wooden chair reading and silent, sometimes excusing himself to take a pipe of tobacco, only occasionally adding to the conversation, making pots of strong sweet tea, when requested by grandmother, and most visibly to us children by making up a table for a game of whist come teatime: he was a man of few words.

My knowledge of my grandparent's world was therefore much influenced by my grandmother's recollections and her mention on many occasions of her brother William being killed in the Great War. My grandfather's involvement in that same war was taken very much for granted as he had survived whereas my grandmother's brother had died. Grandfather's war was condensed into a cover-all statement that "he was in East Africa with the R.G.A. [Royal Garrison Artillery]". This until my teens was the limit of my knowledge despite my own father having a long-time interest in the Great War and indeed having visited the Western Front battlefields throughout the 1960s and 70s: my grandfather's story remained elusive.

Being a child, my concentration wandered as my grandmother spoke; my eyes would settle on the two, framed, embroidered postcards permanently displayed on the walls of their modest parlour. One celebrated the New Year 1918, the other simply said R.G.A. with a depiction of a gun and the word Ubique [Latin: Everywhere], which I found intriguing. My grandmother's brother, William McDonald, who died that same year with the 33rd Division artillery, in a field near Hallebast crossroads, Ypres, during the German spring offensive, I later learned, sent the first postcard, from Belgium. The other framed postcard of the gun was a reminder of my grandfather's service. It was many years later, after my grandmother's death, that he revealed a little more of his story.

Prologue

IN the late summer of 1914, with Britain already at war with Germany, Horatio, Lord Kitchener of Khartoum, who had been appointed Secretary of State for War on 5th August, with great foresight, set out to recruit a new army to face what he recognised as a formidable foe that would take some years to defeat. The British army that at the outbreak of war comprised ten infantry divisions would eventually consist of around fifty-nine active divisions by the end of the conflict. It would, in addition, include hitherto unknown branches of arms such as aircraft, tanks, and gas that were the new weapons of warfare of the industrialised combatants. The Royal Artillery, whose technological development and growth would ultimately facilitate winning the war, grew alongside the infantry divisions to surpass the Royal Navy in manpower, employing in excess of half a million officers and men at the cessation of hostilities. The Corps underwent an almost six-fold increase in manpower from its 1914 strength but a sixteen-fold increase in the number of weapons it employed.

It is the experiences of one unit of the Royal Garrison Artillery, the heavy guns, which this book aims to illustrate, from their formation, and during their service in German East Africa and later the Western Front during the Great War of 1914–1918. It is hoped that it may give the reader some contrasting perspectives of the Royal Garrison Artillery's role in this conflict, and record for posterity a history of this unit, and most importantly the men who served therein. Indeed few histories have been written of artillery units, certainly few in recent times. Most histories that exist were compiled almost immediately following the war by the officers of those units, with little contribution made by ordinary soldiers. The easier access now afforded to the National Archives, the Royal Artillery library and use of the internet have allowed for detailed research to be considered, bringing together many hitherto unknown sources of information that would otherwise have been lost as successive generations lost touch with their forebears' war service.

The action of the 11th (Hull) Heavy Battery R.G.A. and its successor, the 545th Siege Battery R.G.A., is also the wartime experience of my grandfather, Jack, who served throughout the war with the Royal Garrison Artillery in these batteries until he was demobilised in March 1919. In reading this narrative of the events described, we share in some of the experiences of my grandfather and his comrades and hopefully garner some knowledge of the war as a whole. This book is not by any means a complete history of the campaigns referred to in the text, this has been written more comprehensively by other historians, more expert in their field, than the focus of this book allows. Key events have however been explored or described to place the battery's operations in context.

Jack was born at Brandywharfe, North Lincolnshire in 1890, the eldest son of George Drake and Elizabeth his wife. George was a farmer and coal merchant in Snitterby and Brandywharfe, close to the River Ancholme in North Lincolnshire. A few years prior to the First World War, George moved from Snitterby, having rented a small farm at Goxhill near the Humber estuary.

Jack invested his savings, earned in service to other farms, for a share in the new venture along with his father. They were able to make a modest but comfortable living growing barley and vegetables for sale across the Humber in the growing city of Hull: Jack playing a major part in the farming effort, encouraged and mentored by his father. Jack's two brothers were too young to be of help except for controlling the rabbit population with George's tired but serviceable shotgun.

In December 1914, following the outbreak of war, Jack enlisted in Hull, Yorkshire, rather than into other nearby army units being formed in Lincolnshire. The paddle-driven ferry across the River Humber from New Holland to Hull's Victoria Pier, along with the various sloops and keels that plied their trade along the estuarine shores, made for easy access to Hull from Goxhill. The journey could be further aided by using the short rail route to the ferry wharf. The route to enlist would be familiar to Jack, as Hull was the main market for their farm produce; he would have made the journey many times before.

Jack Drake (author)

Due to his skills with horses, and a few others, he was, upon enlisting, posted to the 1st Hull Heavy Battery, Depot Company (originally known as the Hull Heavy Battery until the formation of the 2nd Hull Heavy Battery) still being formed at the East Hull Barracks on Holderness Road. Jack being literate and imbued with the excitement of the occasion kept very brief notes in his pocketbook: this has fortunately survived. Jack in his writings stuck to the most basic facts, which made for a very short diary, lacking day-to-day detail, but it had been a wholly important and sufficient guide for the compilation of this history. Within the general narrative I have intertwined parts of Jack's pocketbook and those of his comrades, with diary entries of others contemporary with events, along with Jack's own verbal recollections. It is hoped that this gives the reader a sense of vibrancy rather than viewing his experience in isolation: additionally it describes the occasions that Jack did not feel sufficiently enthusiastic about to record in his diary. It should be remembered, Jack's experience was not in isolation: he was only one of nearly 300 men in this artillery unit, all from different backgrounds, social classes, and occupations that experienced similar circumstances once in the British Army.

Jack, it would appear, was not over-enthused with army life and would probably have preferred to stay home on the farm. The national emergency and the pressure brought to bear by a wave of patriotism on the young men of Britain during these early months of the war motivated him and thousands of others to enlist. He wrote in a letter to his parents in 1917, in which he explained:

> I wish I could have helped you longer, but it wasn't to be. I
> hadn't much choice had I?

Jack had dutifully left the farm to enlist, as many others of his acquaintance had. From the available evidence, it seems that Jack made a reliable soldier; he was not mentioned in despatches nor awarded any gallantry medals, but did his service uncomplainingly as many thousands of others did. One of many young men of the cities, towns and villages of Britain, he was propelled from civilian life into the largest and most technologically advanced conflict the world had then known, a conflict that still dominates much of our modern life due to the social impact and the changes it engendered.

Following the war, Jack spent some years in the Territorial Army, and spent his working life as a farm labourer. He survived, but lost the little farm that, with his father he had worked hard to maintain. The untimely illness and death of his father George in 1917 (while Jack himself was stricken with fever in Morogoro hospital), resulted in the farm being sold and the proceeds being used to maintain his mother and younger brothers and sisters. In later years Jack worked for the Upper Witham Inland Drainage Board, cycling many miles around the county of Lincolnshire to fulfil his duties. During the Second World War he was, along with many other men who had served in the previous conflict, a member of the Home Guard. His time after retirement in 1955 was spent grave digging and grass mowing with his scythe for bacca money. He had a large vegetable and cottage garden; his rhubarb patch could conceal one whole platoon of the Home Guard! He continued working in some small way into his late seventies.

Jack did not elaborate greatly on his wartime experiences, but what he told me when asked, was enough to stir my interest and answer what limited questions I had as a young man, that is now my further research. In 1977, he went to hospital for a urinary disorder (a lifelong problem resulting from blackwater fever). The doctor told him he should have come sixty years previously but that option was not available then. Whilst at hospital he met another man with a similar complaint, reading a magazine article, and they got chatting:

> I was sitting alongside a chap at the County Hospital waiting
> for an operation. I picked up a copy of a magazine and there

was a picture of Dar Es Salaam. I said I was there when we captured it, and then this chap said he was there as well.

Harry Downs

Harry Downs 1977   *Jack Drake 1977*

I asked which mob he was with and he said the RGA and I was too. Then we found we had (both) joined up in Hull in 1914 and had been with the Hull Heavy Battery.

Jack Drake

Then he asked me if I was Sgt. Downs. I said I was, and he told me that he had been in my section.

Harry Downs

When I saw the picture I said I knew Dar es Salaam. We got talking and he said he was Sgt. Downs, and then I knew him. He remembered my name as well. I thought it rather funny to meet him, because he is the first one I have met of that regiment since I was demobbed in 1919.

Jack Drake

Jack lived in fairly good health until, nearing his ninety-third birthday, he died. Throughout the years he had kept his medals, cap badge, shoulder titles, and his pocket book. A twenty-Heller coin, minted by the German administration in Tabora when the German colony's currency was in short supply, had been his souvenir. The pocket book was lost when Jack's house was cleared following his death. Twenty years later I located a copy in the United States of America having found and contacted a long-lost cousin who had had the foresight to photocopy it many years previously. From this my direction and research interest was rekindled, resulting in this modest, but hopefully useful history of the 1st Hull Heavy Battery, Royal Garrison Artillery, its successors, and the Hull men it comprised during the Great War of 1914–1918.

Acknowledgements

IN this narrative I am indebted to the contributions made by Denis Hopkin, the grandson of Section Sergeant Joseph "Dan" Fewster, who provided the first substantive information for this book. To Francis and David Floyd, Edward Nannini; the generosity and personal recollections, photographs and papers of Mary Rimington, the daughter of Charles Townend Rimington, is notable alongside contributions by Jean Chandler and Hillary Dixon, the family of Jim Dixon, for providing a detailed diary, maps and photographs. To the family of the late John D'Olier in Kenya, my gratitude for the photographs provided.

My thanks also to: John McBain, Derek Cowbourne in Canada and Donald and John in England, Garner and Kenneth Ledran, Robert Colbridge, Lynda McKinder, John Brocklehurst, Alan Burnham, Denis Medforth, Ronald Tuton, Eric Prynn, Fred, Phil, Brenda and Betty Skern, Geoff Frost, Maurice Lydon, Mrs J. R. Mckee, J. P. Roydhouse, Mrs J. Stancliffe the daughter of Tom Roydhouse, Mrs. P. Sprowson, Elsie Jacobson, Elsie Binley, Mr C. Brockwell, D.S.M., and David Elsom.

To the late Ben Masterman and his wife in assisting with identifying individuals in photographs, fellow researcher Charles Dinsdale for passing on his extensive local knowledge and locating archive information on my behalf, to Harry Fecitt for sharing a passion for East Africa and taking the time and making the effort to photograph the graves in Dar es Salaam and Voi on my behalf, Richard Flory of California for his encyclopaedic knowledge of artillery officer's service, Richard Pullen for sharing his research, and Bob Hutchison for proof-reading and punctuation corrections. To the many families who responded to my mail enquires, and to those who contributed many of the photographs included in the book.

Mention is also warranted for the assistance given by the South African Museum of Military History, directed by Major J. L. Keene and his staff. Major Keene provided copies of the war diary of Captain F. E. Jackson and that of C. S. Thompson, permitting the use of extracts for this work. The copyright is held by the SAMMH. Further assistance was appreciated from the staff at the Royal Artillery Museum, James Cavell Library at Woolwich and also at the Imperial War Museum, Photographic Archive at Lambeth. To the members of the Great War Forum for numerous calls for assistance and information which were so willingly answered.

Finally, my thanks to Karen Dyer and Steven Mwenda at African Eden Safaris, in Arusha, who uncomplainingly allowed me the use of their safari vehicles on numerous occasions when visiting Tanzania for my research.

Introduction

FOLLOWING Jack's enlistment into the army and training, his first service overseas was during Lieutenant General Jan Smuts' campaign against German East Africa, the country now known as Tanzania. The overriding feature of this campaign was the high incidence of disease, which saw casualties from illness exceeding those from enemy action by a large amount. Jack and his comrades suffered severely throughout their time in East Africa with malaria, blackwater fever, and enteric fever (typhoid) that would continue to affect their health in later years. Jack who suffered both malaria and blackwater fever required medical treatment for several years following the war. Many troops died or were debilitated from the tropical ailments that found ready hosts in the Europeans: in many cases men were hospitalised within a few weeks of arrival in East Africa.

It has been estimated that in excess of one third of all troops in East Africa were permanently unfit for duty during the rainy season. With a higher incidence of malaria, this proportion increased considerably.

The consequence of this was that many troops were repatriated to Britain or to the large hospitals that had been established for this purpose in South Africa. Such debilitation had a considerable effect upon their ability as a military force, and it necessitated a considerably enlarged medical establishment and associated logistics.

For any individual, the East African campaign, and that in Mesopotamia, posed the highest risk of contracting an illness of any other theatre of war. For the Hull Battery, 1917 proved the most demanding with a high proportion of those troops that remained in East Africa being repatriated to hospitals in South Africa and England.

Apart from Jack having frequent attacks of malaria, other causes of discomfort existed. Jack's particular enemy was not so much the Germans but something equally formidable, the Jigger (Chigoa) flea. This tiny insect inhabited the sandy ground that was to be found around the army camps. The female would make a bite wound under the toenails or on the feet of the troops, before burrowing into the flesh to lay her eggs. The egg sac would grow, gradually but painfully, forming into an enlarging cyst inside the toe. The most effective method used to remove the offending parasite entailed a knife, needle or pin, applied before the egg sac had fully developed. Carelessness would cause the sac to burst with the potential of serious infection occurring.

Equally common and troublesome were ticks, in particular those that were to be found living in the soil near the walls of native huts and other structures. These creatures survived by attaching themselves to their host by biting into the flesh and sucking their blood. The transfer of bacteria from the mouthparts of the tick to the blood stream of the host causes the onset of relapsing fever. Once infected, headaches, joint pains and fevers are symptomatic; in some severe cases it may result in death. Due to the primitive conditions that existed in the army camps in East Africa many of the troops were affected by this pernicious malady.

Another interesting recollection by Jack was how, with the transport difficulties and shortage of medical supplies, the army doctors used puff-balls as part of their treatment regimen. This fungus grows naturally in East Africa, and it was the spores that the puffball encapsulates that were used to apply to the dressings of open wounds to help staunch the flow of blood. The use of fungi (and puffballs in particular) for medicinal use has been a long tradition: both the Greeks and Romans recognised it and more recently it was used by the Plains' Indians of North America.

Wildlife added further interest to the lives of the troops; the army's use (in some areas now recognised as the world's premier game reserves) of mounted infantry and animal-drawn transport which comprised hundreds of oxen, mules and horses, resulted in many incidents. Rhinoceros, hyenas, and crocodiles were common, close encounters with lions were more frequent. The Hull men, who were fearful of the lions that prowled the darkness around their camps, spent many sleepless nights listening to the roar of the lions and the cackling of hyenas. Large fires intended to keep the lions away cast shadows in the surrounding bush and the picket guards, isolated on the camp perimeter, had an unenviable task. On one particular occasion, a night with many lions on the prowl, the Hull men sat back-to-back in a defensive circle, their rifles ready, awaiting an attack, their bravery returning with the dawn of the new day.

High mortality in the horses, donkeys and other domesticated animals used by the army for both food and transport was caused by the bite of the tsetse fly that occurred in belts across the country. Mules, due to their breed, were slightly more resistant to this affliction; this was further aided by the Veterinary Corps administering arsenic. All the draught animals suffered loss of condition through hard work and poor feed. Upon the death of the afflicted animals, which could occur within fourteen days of infection, their carcasses provided easy pickings for the many lions, hyenas, vultures and flies that multiplied in proportion to the increase in carrion available. During the advance through the Pare Mountains the sergeant of the 134th Cornwall Heavy Battery, who had charge of the battery section ammunition column during that time stated, perhaps with slight exaggeration, that on average he lost one draught animal for every mile of the march. Brigade General Brits, whose 2nd South African Mounted Brigade shipped 1,000 horses from South Africa aboard the H.M.T. *Hunscliffe* in April 1916, was severely affected by the effects of the tsetse and suffered the loss of fifty horses a day. Sergeant Joseph Dan Fewster, a former employee of Hull Breweries, whose battery section was attached to Brits' column in mid July 1916, wrote:

> Britts' Mounted Men which left M'buyini in all their glory
> are no longer mounted, because all their horses are dead.

These, bluebottle-encrusted, bloated carcasses fringing the roads became known to the troops as 'Brits' Violets', the flies rising as billowing smoke when disturbed. The tsetse fly belts were known to the British: the Germans had mapped these areas and avoided them in settling the colony in previous years, and this knowledge now prevented the loss of animals. Super-ficially it would appear that little heed was taken of this information by the allies; it proved to be a very costly decision. General Sir Jacob L. van Deventer, who commanded the 2nd South African Division in German

Joseph Dan Fewster

East Africa, lost 250 horses and sixty mules from a combination of horse sickness and lack of water during his advance from Arusha to Lolkisali, a distance of 35 miles. Dead animals and Germans killed in the numerous skirmishes had already polluted the waterholes that were available; the remaining horses refusing to drink. Jack recounted how the battery, on one occasion being short of water, used these polluted waterholes for their immediate needs.

Because of the loss of such a large number of animals, the mounted troops and cavalry were reduced to marching until replacement mounts could be acquired from South Africa. The Union eventually shipped 1,000 mounts per month, India contributing other draught animals. The impact on the lines of communication rapidly became apparent with the result that the troops were sustained in the most basic manner and their ration allowance reduced to one quarter of their norm. Horse-feed in the form of hay and oats, being particularly bulky, took precedence over other supplies. This situation led to the use of human porters, thousands of whom were employed, their number increasing throughout the campaign. To further illustrate the severity of the impact caused by the tsetse fly on the animals, a return for Deventer's 2nd Division written on the 23rd May 1916, whilst his division was beleaguered at Kondoa, showed that he lost 1,639 horses out of an establishment of 3,894 since the beginning of April.

At the outbreak of the war, the world's motor vehicle industry was in its infancy making many of the vehicles that were shipped to East Africa, illsuited to the arduous conditions to be found there. In this vast country where, in pre-war years, motor vehicles could be counted by the handful, few roads had been established outside of the major towns.

Travel throughout the colony was reliant on the existing slave and caravan routes that in many cases had existed for centuries. As Smuts' army advanced, rough roads were cut through the bush to allow for the resupply of the troops; the number of vehicles this employed and the urgency of this requirement prevented completion of the roads for some time. Tree stumps and rocks remained in place until they could be removed by explosives. The vehicles proved to be unreliable, suffering many breakdowns, and breakages of components as a result of the condition of the unfinished roads. The consequence of these factors led to the unavailability of many vehicles until they could be repaired, which compounded the transport problems caused by the loss of horses and oxen.

The transport situation led to a general shortage of food which contributed seriously to the declining health of the men and animals alike, making recovery from illness more difficult than would otherwise have been the case. In order to relieve this situation and to supplement the paucity of supplies, where possible, produce was acquired from the local population with recompense to suppliers made by promissory notes.

> … giving receipts which will ensure payment for all cattle and food commandeered from the inhabitants who are trading freely in eggs and fowl.
>
> Jacob van Deventer

Initially, for strategic reasons, the British army discouraged the shooting of the wild game that flourished in their area of operation. Shooting wild game for sport became, briefly, a court martial offence. It is however apparent that considerable amounts of game were hunted for meat: as the logistical problems escalated it became inevitable particularly amongst the South African troops who, in comparison, were poorly catered for. Captain Fred Jackson, Brigade Signals Officer of the 1st South African Mounted Brigade, describes the perils associated with allowing troops to go hunting:

> Lots of men are out game shooting and bullets flying in all
> directions, it is positively dangerous to go into the bush and
> sounds like a miniature battle.

The Germans had little compunction about sourcing their needs
by hunting game, and successfully supplied most of their troops'
meat ration in this manner in addition to commandeering their
requirements from the local population. As the Germans retreated,
they consumed or destroyed the food resources in the areas through
which they passed. This left nothing of value for the remaining
population who, in consequence, endured famine conditions.

Much of the war materiel was sourced and transported from
outside of the East African territories, predominantly South Africa.
Once landed at Mombasa everything was transported overland
by a combination of rail, motor lorry, ox carts, and porters. As the
allied force advanced further south into the German colony the
lines of supply became increasingly vulnerable to attack. The use
of additional infantry regiments to guard the roads added to the
logistical requirement and increased the burden on the medical
facilities as these, mainly Indian troops, succumbed to disease and
general malaise from the unfamiliar diet. The enemy patrols, often
present in considerable strength, could move unobserved behind
the allied lines and outposts, hidden by the dense bush which
benefited the attacker more than the defender. Lieutenant General
van Deventer, who would eventually take command in East Africa,
summarised the terrain and the difficulties it engendered in his final
despatch to the War Office:

> Diverse are the physical features of the East African theatre,
> ranging from the uplands of Aruscha to the swamps of
> the Rufigi, and from the 9000 passes of the Livingstone
> Mountains to the deadly coast belts of Kilwa and Lindi, yet
> there is one feature that, as an obstacle to military operations
> varies little – the bush. It stretched over nine tenths of the
> country. Its extent was reckoned in hundreds of thousands
> of square miles. It enormously increased difficulties
> of movement, made the accurate timing of combined
> operations almost impossible, and magnified tenfold the
> normal fog of war.

Smuts' campaign, in which the Hull Heavy Battery played a part, achieved the strategic objective of capturing the main rail routes and harbours of the German colony along with the major part of the territory, at which juncture Smuts expected the Germans to surrender. The enemy, however, had not been defeated and with no further strategic plan, beyond his expectations, Smuts' campaign floundered. The particularly heavy rains in early 1916 which had been wrongly predicted by local sources, coincided with Smuts' initial advance into the German colony: but they were surpassed by the winter rains that were the heaviest recorded for nine years. The lack of transport vehicles, the impassable roads, and the vast tracts of flooded countryside prevented movement of any kind. Holding a defensive line along the north bank of the Mgeta River, the army could do little: malaria and malnourishment claimed many casualties.

After the capture of the coastal belt, mountain ranges and the central railway, with no further strategic gains to be made, the focus of the campaign remained the undefeated body of the enemy force, which proved as agile and evasive as it had previously demonstrated, withdrawing into the vast watershed of the Rufigi River and beyond. This phase of the campaign lasted throughout 1917 with the German forces being gradually eroded and culminating when they crossed the border into Portuguese East Africa (Mozambique) in November 1917. Von Lettow, and the remnants of his officers and men, surrendered nearly one year later in November 1918 at Abercorn in Northern Rhodesia (Zambia), several days after the armistice in Europe was agreed. The nature of this final phase in the East African campaign made the allies' use of the remaining European troops impractical; leaving the final years of operations dominated by the colonial and empire soldiers of the Baluchis, Kings African Rifles, Gold Coast and Nigerian regiments, all of whom, it was quickly recognised, were more suited to the climate than the "white man".

The sixty-one officers and men, the remnant of the Hull Heavy Battery, landed in England in early 1918. After a period of leave, the battery was re-designated as the 545th Siege Battery Royal Garrison Artillery. Captain Floyd, the Officer Commanding throughout the East African campaign, became personally involved in relocating the previous members of the battery with whom he had served in East Africa for the formation of the new battery. Many of the men had been repatriated to hospital from East Africa and had subsequently been posted to depots and training bases in England, or had been drafted to artillery units on the western front where, sadly, some of the men died.

The war had brought significant developments in the artillery weapons and gunnery techniques, about which the battery had to learn; the previous experience in East Africa using obsolete guns in a campaign reminiscent of the Victorian colonial era would henceforth seem distant. The battery, after retraining at Lydd, one of the R.G.A. Siege Training Schools, embarked for France in late July 1918. In the three and a half months from landing in France to the cessation of hostilities on the western front in November, the battery wore out the barrels of its new field guns. It had fired in the order of 6,000 rounds during the German withdrawal from the Lys Salient and during the battles of the Hindenburg Line and beyond, during which actions Jack was wounded in the scalp by shrapnel. The armistice found the battery near the French town of Le Cateau, before it moved to the village of Saulzoir, in the valley of the River Selle. The battery was demobilised in March 1919 at Saulzoir.

Part 1

Chapter 1

The 1st (Hull) Heavy Battery R.G.A.

Let us start with Jack's words:

1914/
Dec. 14th – Joined the 1st Hull Heavy Battery at the City Hall, Hull.

THE East Riding Territorial Association, presided over by Charles Henry Wellesley Wilson, 2nd Baron Nunburnholme and Lord Lieutenant of East Yorkshire, formed the 1st (Hull) Heavy Battery RGA and ammunition column as part of Kitchener's New Army, having received sanction from the War Office on the 7th September 1914. The foundations had been laid at a meeting between Lords Kitchener, Roberts, and Nunburnholme along with Colonel Lambert White that would result in the formation of the first heavy artillery battery for Kitchener's New Army. The War Office, who could not immediately administer, manage or finance the simultaneous raising of multiple units, handed the initial responsibilities of founding and funding the new units to local councils, businesses, corporations and existing Territorial Associations. Through this arrangement the responsibility for training, feeding, clothing and accommodating the new units was borne locally until the War Office, already overwhelmed with demands, could accept and equip these units. It was by this mechanism that the 1st Hull Heavy Battery of the Royal Garrison Artillery was to be formed.

A Hull Corporation tram that provided free passage to City Hall for volunteers (Hull Archives KINCM:2008.4056)

Recruitment in Hull had commenced immediately war was declared using the existing Pryme Street recruiting office. The high number of volunteers for all branches of service proved this office inadequate for the needs of raising a large army. Wenlock Barracks where the 1st Hull Battalion of the East Yorkshire Regiment would be raised was the first alternative to Pryme Street followed by the East Hull Barracks on Holderness Road. A more centralised office was required so Lord Nunburnholme approached the City Corporation for assistance and was granted the use of Hull City Hall, thus when staffed and equipped it became the Central Hull Recruiting Office.

Enticed by military bands, rousing speeches and patriotic fervour dispensed from the balcony of the hall, with the further assistance afforded by free transport on the specially provided recruiting trams, volunteers now flocked to the new office. Douglas Boyd who would enlist many of the men for the 1st Hull Heavy Battery R.G.A. and other Hull-raised units, was formerly an employee of

Hull Corporation but had been appointed the recruiting officer at the request of Lord Nunburnholme.

Recruits for the 13th (Service) Battalion of the East Yorkshire Regiment
(author)

Commissioned with the rank of Lieutenant in order to fulfil his military duties, Boyd opened the City Hall office for enlistments on the 6th September 1914. The office would later be considered to be one of the most efficient and successful in the country raising in excess of 75,000 men for all branches of service throughout the war. Douglas Boyd's son, Hubert, would be one of the early recruits to the new artillery battery. At sixteen years of age and having recently left Hymers College he would be amongst the youngest of the recruits and would become the battery trumpeter.

> A communication has been received from the War Office to the effect that recruits appearing before their commanding officer in a good suit of clothes, a good pair of boots and overcoat will on such being approved receive an allowance of 10/-. When proper uniforms are provided, the recruit will have his clothes parcelled up and sent home free of cost.
>
> *Hull Daily Mail* 15th September 1914

Lord Nunburnholme, raised the 10th, 11th, 12th and 13th (Service Battalions) of the East Yorkshire Regiment, arming them for drill purposes with Winchester repeating rifles acquired in America at his own expense. His wealth arose from the family-owned, Hull-based shipping company, Thomas Wilson Sons & Co Ltd, at that time the largest privately owned shipping line in the world. Additionally to raising the 1st (Hull) Heavy Battery, Nunburnholme would also form the 2nd and 3rd (Hull) Heavy Batteries R.G.A., later renumbered as 124th and 146th Heavy Batteries R.G.A. respectively and the 32nd Divisional ammunition column.

Summary of Recruits
Raised in the 15th Recruiting Area.

					Population of Hull and E. Riding 444,780
Regular and New Armies	Area (Except Hull)	1002		To 26th April, '15	
	Pryme Street, Hull	2936		do.	
	City Hall "	6855		do.	
	East Hull	215		30th Sept., '14	Office Closed
	West Hull	1917		31st Jan., '15	do.
	Walton Street "	1097		19th Sept., '14	do. [Frontiersmen, &c.
	Specials Area	140		Approx :	Motor Drivers, Flying Corps, Sports Bn.,
	Waggoners' Reserve	1010			Were Registered prior to the War
	National "	115	15287	26th April, '15	For service outside East Riding
Territorial Force	East Riding Units	3726		31st March, '15	
	North " "	572		do.	Located in East Riding
	Officers	90	4388	Approx :	
Royal Navy	Regulation Navy	176		31st March, '15	
	Re-engagements	161		23rd April, '15	Ex-Royal Navy
	Reserve for War	2375		do.	Mine Sweepers, &c.
	Specials	195		do.	Patrol Ships, &c.
	Officers	50		Approx :	
	Coast Watchers	40	2997		From Hull only
			22672		
Volunteer Training Corps	East Riding		2400		Estimated 3 Battalions at 800 each
For firms producing munitions of war.			No Record		The Area outside Hull have put forward the names of about 400 skilled workmen

Beverley 26th April, 1915.   R. SAUNDERS (Major), Recruiting Officer 15th Rec. Area.

Hull's contribution to the war effort

On the 12th September 1914, the command of the 1st Hull Heavy Battery, now under formation, was assigned to Captain John Claybourn Williams RNR, a forty-four-year-old veteran of the merchant fleet and a commissioned officer in the Royal Naval Reserve since January 1906. He had established his home in Hull, given his employment with Thomas Wilson Sons & Co Ltd, having originated in the North Yorkshire coastal town of Scarborough. Williams' assignments had taken him to Norway and the Baltic, strongholds of Wilson's trans-emigration trade and ready markets for Hull's exports and import needs, particularly timber, as is still the case today. Upon formation, now having a commanding officer, the 1st Hull Heavy Battery was headquartered at the East Hull Barracks adjacent to East Park on Holderness Road, where Jack would later, upon his enlistment, undergo his basic training.

Captain Williams, the sole authoritative figure at this time, took the daily battery parades in his naval uniform, with the permission of the Admiralty.

> Over 80 specially picked men have been enrolled for Hull's Heavy battery and Captain Williams RNR late of the Wilson liner Aaro has been appointed temporarily in command. Captain Williams has just returned from taking the Austrian Ambassador from England on the Aaro. His appointment will give great satisfaction. Captain Williams is well pleased with the men that have enrolled. Their headquarters will be the East Hull Barracks and they will do daily drill in East Park.
>
> *Hull Daily Mail*, 15th September 1914

The new battery was intended to be a very smart unit, drawing on the engineering and professional expertise found in the East Hull area. The city was both excited and proud to be able to raise such a prestigious contribution to the war effort, a feeling which continued for the duration of the war for all three Hull artillery batteries.

Hull, in the early part of the twentieth century, was a rich city founded on shipping, grain and seed imports, and the milling of

Arthur Cowbourne (second from right, second row seated) and recruits for the Hull Heavy Battery in East Park on the 15th September 1914 (Cowbourne)

grains and oilseed. The large fishing fleet centred on St. Andrew's Dock and the associated engineering and service industries it spawned made Hull a vibrant city. Thomas Wilson Sons & Co Ltd, Reckitt & Sons Ltd; Smith & Nephew and Joseph Rank Ltd, of Hovis flour fame, were already well-established and large corporations. The Wilson-owned, Admiralty approved, Earles' Shipbuilding & Engineering Co. Ltd, which had supplied a flotilla of boats for the relief of General Gordon whilst he was besieged in Khartoum, was a significant employer in the city. Many smaller engineering, ware-housing and transport companies existed alongside a growing manufacturing industry based upon the processing of imported raw materials. It was a cosmopolitan city with workers from all regions and of many different nationalities and until the outbreak of war had been the major port for the transmigration of people from Scandinavia and northern Europe to the newer world of North America. It was also a city of fine civic buildings; libraries and colleges, picturesque avenues and public gardens. Respectable middle class residences were juxtaposed with the terraced streets of the working majority. The city of Hull was one of the richest cities in the Kingdom and its third most important port, but like many a city, one of stark social contrast.

Hull street scene in 1906 with the City Hall (author)

It was due to the opportunities of commerce in Hull that Jack, with George his father, had found good fortune in moving to Goxhill. Their previous holding at Snitterby in Lincolnshire had entailed a long weekly cart journey to Lincoln, the nearest large town, to sell their goods. In Hull, a growing city, they found ready retail markets for their vegetable crops and wholesale sales for barley and grains without the significant and time-consuming labours of getting there. New Holland, and its ferry terminal, was but two miles away from their farmstead. The ferry landed its varied animal and human passengers onto the Victoria Pier, close to the market areas of the city.

The paddle steamer ferry from New Holland in Lincolnshire berths at the Victoria Pier, Hull (author)

The new artillery unit, which set high entry criteria, would take longer to establish than anticipated. The majority of the early recruits came from the urban parishes of Sculcoates, Cottingham and Holy Trinity and the remainder, particularly drivers, from the rural villages of the East Riding, Holderness and the north shore of Lincolnshire. It was the difficulty in acquiring the drivers that caused some concern given the demands of agriculture at that time, and the requirements of other army units formed simultaneously competing for similar skills. It would not have been possible for the army of 1914 to train so many new recruits to this task at short notice; the farm boys' existing experience was of high importance in mobilising the army and the many units involving horse transport. Similar constraints existed for motorised transport units where the technology was far beyond the experience of most of the population.

> East Hull may not appear from the returns from their recruiting centre to have shown up well, but it must be remembered the bulk of the East Hull young men have either been recruited at the City Hall or the Wenlock Barracks. Hull people are advised to keep a look-out for the Hull Heavy Battery, which is now being formed, for it is going to be a smart section. The headquarters will be the East Hull Drill Hall and Captain J. C. Williams, RNR of the Wilson Line has been appointed acting commanding officer. The battery when complete will comprise a major, captain, four lieutenants, non-commissioned officers and 220 men with four 4.7" guns. Only picked men, such as mechanics and drivers of good physical standard are being enrolled and they include all classes, university men, doctors and workers. This morning over 100 paraded and went through physical and foot drill in fine style, and if the battery can turn out as anticipated next week, the citizens will see something to talk about. Captain Williams is at the East Hull Barracks now practically all day, and would be recruits should apply there.
>
> *Hull Daily Mail*, 17th Sept. 1914

The early recruits showed promise and it seemed Captain Williams was getting the quality of men he desired. Archibald John Tweddell, a twenty-one-year-old Cottingham man, enlisted on the 15th September 1914. Given Tweddell's qualifications, Captain Williams, who was present, gave immediate acceptance. Archibald, known as Jack to family and friends, had done well at Holderness College, Withernsea before attending Caistor Grammar School in Lincolnshire where he captained the 1st XI football team. He had then undertaken a course at Hull Technical School in order to gain entry to the merchant service as an officer, in which he succeeded. Gaining a position with Macvicar, Marshall & Co of Liverpool, he had sailed on 20th November 1913 aboard the S.S. *Frankmere* as second mate from Liverpool to the Gulf of Mexico, returning to Barry Docks, South Wales on 2nd February 1914 where he was paid off. Archibald then took a third officer's position with Thomas Wilson Sons & Co Ltd (the company of Lord Nunburnholme) in his hometown port of Hull, undertaking two voyages on their behalf, the latter ending on the 12th September 1914, three days before he enlisted.

Gunner William Brocklehurst (right) at his family home 26, Plane Street. William's brother Jim wears the uniform of the East Yorkshire Regiment (Brocklehurst)

Similarly, Sheffield born and grammar school educated, Herbert George Pinder, who had made a trade as a cutlery manufacturers' agent in Hull, had enlisted on the 3rd October. At nearly thirty-eight years of age he had some previous military service having enlisted previously in February 1901 and served as Trooper 25306 in the 66th Company (York's) Imperial Yeomanry in South Africa. This earned Herbert the King's and Queen's South Africa medals before he left the service in 1902. Although now requiring glasses, Williams accepted Herbert when he appeared before him at East Hull barracks, posting him to the ammunition column being formed as part of the battery.

On the 20th October 1914, a twenty-five-year-old painter and decorator appeared at East Hull Barracks to enlist. Having undergone a medical examination, and being described by the examining officer as "fit", he was posted to the battery with approval from Capt. Williams. Gunner 213, Walter Henry Maslin, had previously served six years in part of the Northumbrian Brigade, Royal Field Artillery, a Territorial Army unit based at Wenlock Barracks in Hull. His experience would be invaluable in forming the new battery and in later years he would play a major part in the battery's development. In recognition of his experience he was quickly promoted to acting sergeant.

Captain Williams fulfilled his appointed role of building the battery until the appointment of 2nd Lieutenant John Loe McCracken R.G.A. on the 2nd November 1914. Williams returned to the naval reserve list on the 5th November 1914 having been appointed Lieutenant Commander; a year later he was appointed to the command of the armed boarding steamer H.M.S. *Royal Scot*. By the end of hostilitics he had gained the rank of acting Commander eventually retiring from the sea in 1933 after being elected Assistant Elder Brother of Trinity House in Hull. Williams died two years later. The S.S. *Aaro*, Williams' old vessel, built in 1909 by Earle's Shipyard in Hull was torpedoed in the North Sea during 1916 with the loss of three lives. Thomas Wilson Sons & Co Ltd; part of Ellerman Wilson Line Ltd. from 1916, lost in the order of thirty-nine vessels due to enemy action during the conflict.

McCracken was promoted Temporary Captain on 29th December 1914. He had joined the Royal Artillery at Woolwich as a boy in 1891, had served in the South African campaign rising to the rank of bombardier before being invalided home in 1901. A series of home postings brought him further promotion and at the outbreak of the war in August 1914 he was a Battery Sergeant Major. The shortage of officers for Kitchener's new armies saw McCracken promoted from the ranks to become a 2nd Lieutenant, on 2nd November, quickly followed by the rank of Temporary Captain in order to command the 1st Hull Heavy Battery. Walter Maslin was further promoted during McCracken's command attaining the rank of Battery Quartermaster Sergeant, McCracken himself relinquishing this command on the 25th May 1915 when his term of service expired.

Dec.15th – First days drill in the East Park, Hull, continued until 1st May 1915.

Jack Drake

By the middle of December, the Hull Heavy Battery had completed enlistment for its authorised war establishment. The War Office had however given thought to the question of reinforcements for the local infantry battalions currently being raised nationwide for Kitchener's New Army. It was decided that additional ranks would be enrolled to provide this reserve; this was communicated in an Army Council Instruction issued on the 13th December 1914. This A.C.I. also applied to locally raised artillery units.

> The question of providing reinforcements for local battalions has been under consideration and the following system is approved. Each local battalion will now recruit in excess of the War Establishment up to a total strength of 1350 all ranks, and the additional 250 men will be organised as a 5th (Depot) company of the battalion. This depot company will have an establishment of officers and NCOs similar to that of a company of the Service Battalion. At a future date, not later than two months before the battalion is likely to take the field, orders will be issued for the formation in the same way of a 6th (Depot) company. These depot companies will for the present be quartered and trained with the battalion. When the battalion embarks for service overseas these depot companies will remain in this country to form the reserve unit, which will train and supply its drafts. In the case of the Hull Heavy Battery, and other similar units, which may be raised under local arrangement the same principal will be followed by forming an additional section. If it can be arranged these depot companies should, at any rate during the present cold weather, be accommodated in suitable buildings or billet.
>
> Army Council Instruction of 13th December 1914

To raise the 1st Depot section of the battery, recruitment continued. A further period of enlistment was instigated in May 1915 to comply further with the arrangements outlined in the ACI to complete the new establishment. This increase in numbers would later facilitate their formation into a larger unit when the battery mobilised for East Africa.

Uniforms and weapons were not available at formation, which saw much improvisation, the men of the various Hull units that were formed by Lord Nunburnholme being distinguished from each other by a coloured armband, the 1st Hull Heavy Battery wearing those of red and blue. Lord Nunburnholme took a keen interest in the units of the East Riding that he had been involved with during their formation, later spending considerable time in the front line with various units. In 1918, Nunburnholme joined the renamed Hull Heavy Battery as a Temporary Captain of the Royal Artillery; but as December 1914 approached he set his thoughts to Christmas:

> On Christmas Eve every officer NCO and man was the recipient of a Christmas card from Lord Nunburnholme. The card consisted of a picture of St George slaying the dragon, and the names of the battalions raised by his Lordship, in Hull, on coloured bands representing the arm badges worn, in the first instance, by the separate Battalions, viz, the 1st, 2nd, 3rd and 4th Battalions East Yorkshire Regiment, and the 1st and 2nd Hull Heavy Batteries. The regimental badge was printed in one corner of the card and in another the words "Wishing You a Happy Christmas 1914". Needless to say, this card was very much appreciated and should serve as a pleasing memento in the years to come.
>
> The *Snapper* (Journal of the East Yorkshire Regiment),
> January 1915

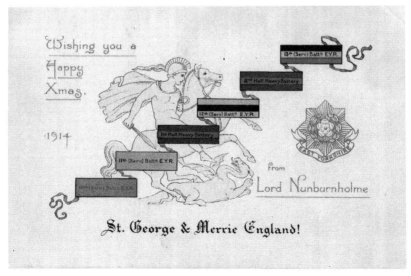

Christmas Card 1914 (author)

Throughout their time training at East Hull Barracks the Hull men had been able to continue living at home. Jack and those from the outlying districts were billeted in Hull. On their first Christmas of the war, they all went home for the holiday. It would be the last Christmas at home for Jack, and many others, until 1919.

Oliver Medforth

Leslie Prynn

The Hull Battery attend the Naval Hospital, Argyle Street, Hull for inoculations in April 1915 (Colbridge/ McKinder)

George Mckee

A section of the Hull Heavy Battery. April 1915 (Colbridge/McKinder)

Chapter 2

11th (Hull) Heavy Battery R.G.A.

1915/ May 1st – Went into camp on Hedon Racecourse, near Hull, given charge of 2 horses and harness. Now 11th Hull Heavy Battery R.G.A.

Jack Drake

THE battery, now sufficiently trained in the rudiments of soldiering, and deemed 'efficient', was accepted by the War Office in May 1915 and taken under its administration. The battery was assigned to the 11th (Northern) Division, the first division formed in the first New Army. Equipment was supplied in the form of four 4.7-inch guns and horse teams in which Jack, a driver at this time, would appear to have had ample opportunity to utilise the skills that he had learned previously on his father's farm and elsewhere.

Hedon racecourse had originally opened in 1888 and gained early success. Its

Gunner John McBain in the paddock at Hedon, the old grandstand to the rear (McBain)

58

popularity had, however, declined by 1910 and the site now provided a suitable location for the on-going training of the battery. Situated adjacent to the railway it had its own station which facilitated the delivery of horses, materials, guns and other heavy equipment required by the battery and other units that would eventually use this location. Circular canvas tents had been erected which would accommodate six men. Horse lines utilising the existing racecourse railings for hitching were easily established, although the rails had fallen into disrepair. These invariably got torn up when the horses' halter leads were tied too short by the novice horsemen in the battery. The old racecourse paddock area and stables were used to accommodate and exercise the horses. The racecourse had previously been used as a temporary aerodrome and would regain this role during the course of the war. In 1929 the Corporation of Hull bought the land in order to establish Hull airport. It was at this site that Amy Johnson the famous aviator, a Hull girl herself, landed the following year.

Top to bottom: Jim Dixon, Bernard Berry, Charlie Rimington, Jim Magee, Harold Masterman and Alfred Towers at Hedon Racecourse (Rimington)

In early June 1915, with Captain McCracken's departure to take up the post of adjutant to the Humber Garrison, the battery command passed temporarily to Lieutenant Colonel H. M. Slater R.G.A. following his invitation to the position by Lord Nunburnholme and Colonel Lambert White. Slater quickly saw in Walter Maslin the talent to become an officer, resulting in Maslin being discharged from the ranks on appointment of an officer's commission following Slater's recommendation of the 3rd July. Maslin the former painter and decorator became a Temporary 2nd Lieutenant on the 13th July 1915.

Masterman, Berry, Rimington, Magee and Tower photographed by Jim Dixon at Hedon May 1915 (Rimington)

Henry Martyn Slater, who started his career as a gentleman cadet at the Royal Military Academy, Woolwich in 1875, was commissioned as a 2nd Lieutenant in the Royal Garrison Artillery in June 1877. A Lieutenant Colonel by 1903, he was further promoted to Brevet Colonel in December 1906 before retiring in 1908. His only previous war service was during the second Afghan War in 1879–80. He was recalled to active duty in 1914 becoming the officer commanding the training brigade at Hedon. Due to ill health, Slater remained in the United Kingdom throughout the war and he dedicated his time post-war to the settlement of soldiers' pension issues and the welfare of the orphans of colonial and dominion war casualties. He died in 1925.

The QF 4.7-inch Howitzer, with which the battery was now supplied, originated from a modified 40-pounder naval gun that had been adapted as a pivot-mounted weapon for coastal defence work and was first introduced to service by the Navy in 1887. A quick-firing design, as its prefix implies, incorporated the projectile and propellant combined by the use of a shell casing. The weapon was originally manufactured by the Elswick Ordinance Company of Newcastle-upon-Tyne. By the turn of the twentieth century this weapon had metamorphosed into an army field gun by the addition of a field carriage and limber. With further development, the gun became capable of firing a 46-pound shell, 10,000 yards. The gun, because of its unplanned evolution, was rather cumbersome with a tendency towards being top heavy. Whilst it had been used in the Boer War and despite its operational inefficiency, it was widely adopted for use by the Territorial Force due to the lack of an alternative weapon or suitable replacement. By the outbreak of the First World War the guns were considered obsolete, but continued to see service until the introduction of the modernised 60-pounder gun which became the standard weapon for Heavy Batteries. Initially, many 4.7-inch weapons were present with the British Expeditionary Force in France and Belgium until the newer designs could be introduced from 1915 onwards. As was the case with the Hull Battery, the weapon was used extensively for training purposes.

A battery subsection take a lunch break near Hedon (Cowbourne)

The newly equipped and uniformed battery was soon to be seen on the roads of East Yorkshire around Hedon undergoing road drill and route marching. Parade square drill, semaphore signal training, and work fatigues occupied the battery whilst in camp. For those joining the battery in the late stages of its formation, courses in sanitation and signalling were initiated with recruits undertaking training in the latter at Tynemouth, a stronghold of the pre-war R.G.A. coastal defence.

The new divisions raised by Kitchener's call to arms made up the New Armies. Initially each division was assigned its own artillery and supporting units. The 1st (Hull) Heavy Battery R.G.A. (now renamed), its depot section and its ammunition column, was attached to the 11th (Northern) Division that had been formed as part of Kitchener's First New Army (K1). The 11th (Hull) Heavy Battery was originally destined for Gallipoli, but on the 1st July 1915 the 11th Northern Division, without their artillery, embarked at Liverpool in order to reinforce the garrison besieged at Gallipoli.

Trawlerman Joseph Brockwell who became one of the battery cooks whilst at Hedon (Brockwell)

During the summer, we were attached to the 11th Division and after being inspected by the GOC of the Division we were ordered for service over-seas, our destination being the Dardanelles. Our Regimental title now became the 11th (Hull) Heavy Battery. Whilst in the midst of mobilisation we had a rather severe outbreak of scarlet fever which placed half the battery in quarantine. This was a big blow to us… Our chaps grumbled because they were firmly convinced that the war would be over before we could get out…The year was drawing to a close before the fever was thoroughly stamped out. I believe the drainage system was blamed for the outbreak.

Joseph Dan Fewster

The 11th (Hull) Heavy Battery R.G.A. was transferred out of the division, in June 1915, and was temporarily assigned for administration purposes only, to the 30th Division artillery.

With the battery now trained, armed and seemingly ready for active service, Slater, whose poor health was to prevent him taking the battery to war, was now replaced. Temporary Captain Basil Edward Floyd R.G.A. joined the battery at Hedon racecourse on the 9th September 1915. Floyd would remain with this battery and its successor, the 545th Siege Battery R.G.A. until the cessation of hostilities, before joining the post-war army of occupation on the Rhine, in Germany.

Major Basil Edward Floyd R.G.A. pictured c. 1923 (Floyd)

Floyd had previously served as a Lieutenant with 116th Heavy Battery R.G.A.. This battery had been formed at Woolwich on the 27th September 1914 and had embarked for France on the 29th at which point Floyd had joined them. Floyd was involved in some of the early actions of the British Expeditionary Force on the Western front; during the 1st Battle of Ypres, with 4th Corps, the 3rd Division and the French 42nd Division at Dickebusch, and later the actions in the Forest of Nieppe, where the King reviewed the battery. Until his return to England to join 21st Siege Battery in August 1915, Floyd would see the battery involved in further action in the Ypres area particularly at Wytschaete and St. Eloi. During an offensive by the German Bavarian Division against the British 27th Division on the 14th and 15th of March 1915, the 116th Heavy Battery fired 550 rounds in twenty-five hours. After a very brief period with 21st Siege Battery, where he was promoted to the rank of Temporary Captain, Floyd returned to England to take up his new command at Hedon. Basil Floyd had originally gained an officers commission in the Royal Artillery in September 1910 after his education at Stonyhurst in Lancashire. Floyd later went up to higher education at Exeter College in Oxford:

Oct. 28th – Left Hedon for Charlton Park, SE

Following their entrainment at Hull's Paragon station, the battery arrived at Charlton Park in south-east London in the early hours of the following day. Their new camp was adjacent to Woolwich Barracks, the Royal Artillery's traditional home, and to Woolwich Arsenal where many of the munitions for the war effort were developed and manufactured:

> We had a good many see us off at the station, but it is a mug's game seeing anyone off when they have horses to entrain. Some of the horses were the very deuce to get into the trucks. We got no grub on the road but got a good dinner when we got there about 2:30 am. The horses got none either.
>
> Charlie Rimington, 28th October 1915

Charlton Park camp was a marked improvement when compared to the conditions experienced by the battery at Hedon. Each man was assigned a proper bed, rather than sleeping at ground level, as they had done previously whilst living in the tents. Meals, being prepared and cooked by women, were of superior quality to that produced in the mobile field kitchens that had, by necessity, been employed at Hedon. On arrival the battery was assigned to wooden-hutted billets, in Number 2 Camp, Charlton Park, where the battery met with other artillery units, including the 134th Cornwall Heavy Battery R.G.A., all batteries concentrated there were to undergo further training.

> The YMCA is a treat – about 10 times bigger than the one at Hedon. There are four other batteries in the camp besides ours but they are southern ones. Our lot rather astounded them when we gathered round the piano and were rattling choruses.
>
> Charlie Rimington, Oct 28th 1915

Those with an interest in education could take French lessons; a recreation room was provided at a church just outside the barrack gates where badminton, table tennis and board games could be played. Entertainment was provided in the form of a weekly music concert:

> Last Thursday night we had one, and a girl of about 24 sang "I wouldn't leave my little Wooden Hut" and two others dating from about the same epoch. It was chronic – worse than some we had at Hedon.
>
> Charlie Rimington, 1st November 1915

The close proximity to the lights and attractions of wartime London were irresistible to the provincial lads from the battery, but they very quickly learned that their army pay did not go very far. A state of impoverishment ensued for many whilst at Charlton: the proximity to Woolwich Arsenal (which provided employment for hundreds of young women) did not help the soldiers' financial wellbeing.

> We hadn't much money left so we went to the free refreshment bar, which has been fitted up in the entrance of Victoria Station for soldiers and sailors. There are sandwiches, cakes etc. laid out on dishes and one helps oneself to them; tea, coffee & cocoa are on tap free also.
>
> Charlie Rimington, 1st November 1915

Their Saturday extravagance was assuaged each Sunday morning by attendance at church parade. Being the first of the New Army artillery batteries to be formed, and thus the senior by unit establishment, the battery took precedence on church parades and similar functions. The following weekend, providing guard and piquet duties could be avoided, ensured further financial hardship.

> … went to London on pass until 12 pm on Saturday – from 2 pm – and we came back absolutely skinned.
>
> Charlie Rimington, 1st November 1915

Charles Rimington (Charlie), in peacetime a schoolteacher, had, upon enlistment, been posted to the ammunition column. Having a natural talent and a love for arts and crafts, he set about decorating the interior of the hut he shared with other members from the battery with intricate stencils of swallows in flight. This transformed a stark timber-planked army hut into Swallowdene, their temporary home-from-home. Seeing further opportunity to pursue his love Charlie took it upon himself to decorate the YMCA hut using the same stencils of flying swallows that he had made, his effort bringing appreciation from the both the YMCA and the other artillerymen.

Charlie Rimington (rear row, centre), Harrison Roydhouse (second row, extreme right), Robert Colbridge (standing front row, left), John Burnham (front row, second from left, arms folded) outside Swallowdene their hut at Charlton Park (Burnham)

The Hull Battery, now under the scrutiny of the regular army artillery, experienced their first taste of real soldiering. Not only did the battery undertake extensive gun drill, but also the necessary morning tasks of feeding and grooming the horses, daily stable cleaning and essential harness and equipment maintenance. It was also required for the battery to provide camp guards, each spell being of twenty-four hours with each section fulfilling this duty in turn, as was also the case with town piquet.

> Our battery compares very favourably with any here. And for riding we can beat them hollow.
>
> Charlie Rimington, 28th October 1915

The proximity of the camp to Woolwich Arsenal had other benefits. The munitions work carried out there employed hundreds of young ladies, who naturally found the presence of the uniformed young men amenable. The soldiers were, therefore, never wanting for companions to take to town for tea or a dance. The battery spent Christmas 1915 at Charlton Park.

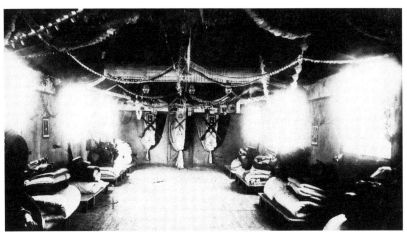

Swallowdene decorated for Christmas 1915.
Swallow stencils can be seen adorning the wall pelmet (Rimington)

In the first week of January 1916, whilst at Charlton, the personnel of the 11th (Hull) Heavy Battery and ammunition column were requested to volunteer for service in German East Africa. Without exception every man did so. Due to this development, Jack and the other drivers from the battery, with some sadness, handed in their horses, to which they had become very attached, to the No 2 Remount Depot at Charlton Park.

> Just a line hoping you are well. I am now going through a course of signalling and gunnery. The Battery is being transferred to a Howitzer siege battery. The horses are being taken from us as we shall have motors instead.
>
> John Burnham, January 1916

Leaving their guns at Charlton, the battery entrained from Woolwich to Denham, Buckinghamshire to create a new formation for operations in East Africa.

YMCA at Charlton Park: Charlie's swallow stencil design adorns the pelmet
(Rimington)

The request for volunteers was made because the army was unable to implement normal leave arrangements in East Africa, so required the consent of the men. The high acceptance of the offer was presumably seen by the men as an opportunity for adventure rather than the prospect of fighting the enemy. The stories of Victorian-era exploration and missionary effort in Africa that had pervaded the literature and lives of Britons may have made Africa seem an attractive destination for the Hull boys, not knowing what awaited them!

Jan. 18th – Left Charlton Park for Denham, Bucks.

Jack Drake

The 11th (Hull) Heavy Battery near Withernsea in the summer of 1915
(author)

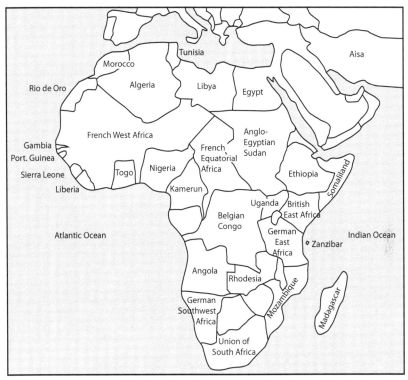

Map showing the the European spheres of Influence in Africa

A GS (General Service) wagon, marked 11th Divisional Heavy Artillery R.G.A., near Hedon in the autumn of 1915 (Colbridge/McKinder)

"Given charge of two horses and harness" – a driver with his charges at Hedon (McBain)

Stable duties at Hedon (McBain)

Battery semaphore training course at Charlton Park. (Rimington)
Back row: Charles Thompson, Arthur Marr, Fred Howlett, Donald McKay, Arthur Frost, Frank Jackson, Charlie Rimington, Jack Redshaw, Charles Jebson, Jim Dixon Second row: Pearson (standing), William Turner, Charles Potter, James Forrester, Alec Robertson, Frederick Geater, Webster, Arthur Cowbourne, Alfred Towers. Third row: Brown, George Ledrew, Sidney Wainright, Lt Anthony Nannini, James Bland, Thomas Reaston, John Peacock, Robert Colbridge, Bernard Berry (standing). Front row: Harold Elgey, Jessie Masterman, Jim Magee, William Ward, Percy Shanks, Albert Burras

Chapter 3

The 38th Howitzer Brigade R.G.A.

U PON the battery's arrival at Denham, the personnel of the 11th (Hull) Heavy Battery R.G.A. were formed into the 38th, 5-inch Howitzer B.L Brigade R.G.A. on the 19th January 1916. The battery, its depot section and ammunition column, were divided to create a second battery for the formation of the brigade, 158th (Hull) Heavy Battery R.G.A., and in addition, a headquarters section, brigade ammunition column and a depot company.

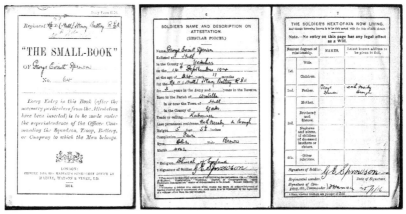

The soldiers Small Book belonging to George Sprowson

As a result of this reorganisation, Major Piercy Neville Graham Reade R.G.A., who had initially been appointed Officer

Commanding of the 158th (Hull) Heavy Battery assumed command of the whole brigade with 2nd Lieutenant Edward Charrington Mackenzie R.G.A. acting as adjutant until the arrival of 2nd Lieutenant Francis Thomas Galloway R.G.A.. Temporary Captain. Basil E. Floyd R.G.A. remained in command of the 11th (Hull) Heavy Battery R.G.A. and 2nd Lieutenant Frank Harrison

George Sprowson in 1942
(Sprowson)

R.G.A., who had gained an officer's commission after joining the battery in Hull as a volunteer, assumed command of 158th (Hull) Heavy Battery in place of Major Reade. Jack remained with the 11th (Hull) Battery.

The total of the men that comprised the new brigade at Denham included those additional men of the depot company that had been raised in Hull under the Army Council Instruction of 13th December 1914. This number of men exceeded the War Office establishment for the original Hull Heavy Battery, but now made the creation of the two batteries of the 38th Howitzer Brigade R.G.A. possible. The reduction of the existing ammunition column and the loss of the battery horses and the subsequent release of the manpower they had employed further facilitated this reorganisation with the result that the new brigade now exceeded its authorised war establishment of 274 men. At this juncture a number of men were transferred away from the brigade, especially those with a less than perfect record sheet, but also those whose skills would be of limited further use in a motorised unit. To this end, Gunner James Skern was transferred. A farrier in civilian life, he had been an obvious recruit for the new Hull Battery whilst at Hedon. He was posted to the Royal Field Artillery where his shoeing skills could be fully employed. Skern eventually served in Salonika. The replacement of the ammunition column with motorised transport and the provision of supplementary drivers provided by the Army Service Corp completed the establishment of the new brigade. Denham, during this period, was a temporary camp of timber huts near to the

James Skern (Skern)

town of Uxbridge; it later became a pilot training centre for the nascent Royal Air Force. Jack, with mobilisation imminent, took the opportunity to have his photograph taken in Uxbridge.

The period from the formation of the brigade until its mobilisation saw the arrival of many requirements and supplies amongst which were tropical clothing from the Royal Army Clothing Department at Pimlico, and deliveries of gun stores from Woolwich. Guns and limbers arrived at Uxbridge station; their collection by the battery with their FWD lorries causing great interest amongst the local population as they drove along the main streets of Uxbridge and Denham at 15 miles per hour, their maximum speed. The origin of the guns was from the Territorial Force, 1st/ 4th Home Counties Brigade, Royal Field Artillery, at Fareham, part of the 44th Divisional Artillery. This brigade had recently been redesignated as the 27th Divisional Ammunition Column. It was their now redundant guns that Sergeant Dan Fewster and a detail of gunners of the 11th (Hull) Heavy Battery travelled to receive and entrain at Fareham Station prior to their despatch to Uxbridge.

The BL 5-inch howitzer, with which the brigade was now equipped, was a breech loading design as suggested by its name, and that of the Brigade, was manufactured by Vickers Maxim & Sons. The Army introduced it in 1896 for firing shrapnel shells in support of infantry against what were expected to be hostile native hordes in small colonial wars. The gun was reaching obsolescence by 1908 having been previously employed to good effect in the second Boer War and most effectively at Omdurman in the Sudan against the Mahdi's forces. There, along with the newly introduced Maxim machine gun, the howitzer is credited with much of the success in that action. Prior to the outbreak of war in 1914, the howitzer became the mainstay of the Territorial artillery units and saw service throughout the First World War with the Royal Field

Artillery, a shortage of other suitable weapons made its continued use unavoidable. It had a capability to fire a 50-pound shell some 4,500 yards or, when using a 40-pound shell (introduced later in the war), the range was increased to 6,500 yards. Despite its poor range to weight ratio, the guns were considered, and later proved, suitable for deployment in East Africa utilising both of the available types of ammunition. Simple in design but lacking the finesse of later weapons, the 5-inch howitzer became noted for its fierce recoil, the result of its short barrel and equally short recuperator stroke, necessitating the removal of the gunsight at each firing to prevent its damage. At the outbreak of war and the subsequent British mobilisation many of these guns crossed to France with the Royal Field Artillery howitzer units, and in addition, a large number were supplied to Russia to bolster the Tsar's army in their efforts on the eastern front.

Additional motor transport of the Army Service Corps joined the brigade from Catterick. The vehicles were a combination of FWD lorries, Napier cars, and a Ford Model T car for the use of the officer commanding the brigade. A number of Douglas and BSA motorcycles were also provided for the battery signal sections and headquarters to aid communications within the brigade. The Army Service Corps provided two days' motorcycle riding instruction for the battery non-commissioned officers. With embarkation imminent, leave was arranged, the first brigade section departing for home on the 25th January. Outstanding stores arrived at Denham, and for each of the eight howitzers of the brigade, fifty rounds of ammunition and gun cotton was delivered from Woolwich. Jack went on embarkation leave with the second brigade section having received his inoculations against typhoid and cholera. Leave was arranged in such manner as to exclude the travelling time from the entitlement:

Jan. 27th – Went home on leave for 48 hrs.

Jack Drake

The decision to use motorised vehicles as the primary transport for the battery was founded on the unsuitability of horses for use in East Africa, a point the South African government failed to fully appreciate when sending mounted brigades there. The motor lorries supplied to the 38th Howitzer Brigade were FWD Model B's, manufactured in Clintonville, Wisconsin by the Four Wheel Drive Auto Company (FWD). In what was, at that time, a relatively new industry, these lorries were among the first four-wheel drive vehicles readily available. The lorries had undergone assessment for some years by the US army during the war against Mexico, this relatively successful application contributing greatly to their selection for service by the British army. The outbreak of hostilities in Europe provided a ready market for this innovation resulting in the purchase of the model by several allied governments. The truck could carry a load of three tons and travel at a maximum of 15 miles per hour powered by its twin cylinder 50-horsepower engine and three-speed gearbox; its wheels were of cast iron shod with solid rubber tyres. The FWD lorries had the ability to tow the brigade howitzers when travelling at a reduced speed, and, in addition, to carry a full load of ammunition and battery supplies. Their major weakness, which would become apparent in East Africa, was their weight; at three and a half tons unladen it was found that they exceeded the bearing capacity of the African soils when either wet or dry which resulted in the trucks floundering.

> Feb. 1st – Mobilized for East Africa as the 38th Brigade (8 x 5" Howitzers).
>
> Jack Drake

With mobilisation of the brigade imminent, a series of experimental route marches are made in the Buckinghamshire countryside accompanied by the motor lorries towing the guns. The combination of new motorised technology and their unfamiliarity caused understandable anxiety in Captain Floyd who could foresee problems ahead. The personnel, composing former farm boys, professions and trades people, were unaccustomed to motorised transport and it was a new experience for officers and men alike. The final days in England saw the brigade undergo further training and gun drill, stores were drawn from bond and packed in battery sections before being loaded onto the motor transport and departing Denham for Avonmouth accompanied by a number of N.C.O.s and men. On arrival at Avonmouth, the lorries, men and stores were embarked aboard the tramp steamer S.S. *Anselma de Larrinaga*. The lorries, guns, stores and personnel remaining at Denham depart for the railway station for onward travel to Devonport.

> Feb. 6th – 12 o'clock midnight entrained at Denham station.
>
> Jack Drake

Travelling via Westbury, in Wiltshire, a brief stop was made for a mug of coffee to be issued to each man; as morning approached a further stop in Exeter allowed the Mayoress of the city to provide a breakfast bun for each and arrange the filling of their water bottles with hot sweetened tea. The battery, refreshed by their last halt, arrived at Devonport where, throughout the ensuing day they completed the loading of guns and stores upon their transport vessel.

> Feb. 7th – Arrived at Devonport, embarked on HMT *Huntsgreen* formerly a German ship named "The Derflinger".
>
> Jack Drake

H.M.T. *Huntsgreen*, upon which the battery embarked, was originally the North German Lloyd Company vessel named

H.M.T. Huntsgreen (author)

Derfflinger. Built in Danzig, its homeport was Bremen. On the outbreak of hostilities, the British, in Port Said, impounded it. With a new crew, and renamed, the ship would, henceforth, operate as a troopship. Following the war the British government resold H.M.T. *Huntsgreen* back to its original owners; the vessel was eventually scrapped in 1932.

The 38th Howitzer Brigade R.G.A., and other contingents that were embarked aboard H.M.T. *Huntsgreen,* were to join with the existing forces of Lieutenant General Jan Christian Smuts that were already operational in British East Africa. Smuts was the newly appointed General Officer Commanding for British operations in East Africa, replacing General Horace Smith-Dorrien. By reinforcing his two existing divisions, Smuts planned to undertake an offensive into German East Africa.

A picture of Jack taken in Uxbridge a few days before embarkation for East Africa (author)

The 11th Hull Heavy Battery R.G.A. pictured following the formation of the 38th Brigade in January 1916. Captain Floyd sits behind the sign, 2nd Lieutenant Nannini to his right; Jack back row, third from left. McKee, Tuton and Storry rear row 5th – 3rd right (Tuton)

Chapter 4

The Outbound Voyage

Feb 8th – Sailed from England, had a snowstorm in the channel, 2 destroyers escorted us until dark, at night I saw the lighthouse on the French coast, I'm not sure of the name. I felt homesick if not seasick.

H.M.T. *Huntsgreen* departed Devonport at 8 a.m. on the 8th February 1916, passing the lighthouse at Ushant on the French coast and moving into the Bay of Biscay. The sea was rough and the majority of the troops were seasick. For many men, despite originating from a maritime port, this was their first experience at sea, including Jack.

It was rotten; the sea once or twice came over the promenade decks. I was sick twice and then turned in, had a pretty good night. Sick as a cat.

Jim Dixon, 8th February 1916

A routine of daily drill and lectures was started along with periodic medical inspection and further inoculations.

Paraded at 9, physical drill afterwards, buzzer practice near the fore gun which is manned by one or two Navy men the rest of the gun crew being made up of our men. Machine guns of motor machine gun section posted in various parts of the ship. After practising a little, place got rather smelly as we were just behind sleeping place of dogs, which are coming with us to smell for water, I believe, also for rats.

Jim Dixon, February 11th

Sir John Willoughby acted as the Officer Commanding for the on board contingent of troops. Willoughby, who had become infamous some years previously for his involvement in the Jameson Raids into Matabeleland, was now en route to command No. 1 (Willoughby's) Armoured Motor Battery. This unit had been formed privately in February 1915, it was equipped with four Leyland armoured cars. It was accepted by the Army as No. 322 Company, Army Service Corps, and sent out to East Africa. Following its service in East Africa, the unit was disbanded upon its return to England in July 1917.

Conditions below getting pretty rotten. Find it much better to stay on deck whenever possible.

Jim Dixon, February 10th

The long and often monotonous days of the voyage were punctuated by mealtimes. A predictable menu of indifferent quality was provided. Typically, breakfast comprised porridge, bread and margarine, and a mug of tea. The midday meal of canned beef stew and potatoes was more substantial, whilst in the evening bread and jam was served. To preclude the risk of scurvy whilst at sea, lime juice was provided at midday. As the climate warmed, efforts were made to provide leisure facilities for the troops. Two large canvas seawater baths were erected on the ship's decks, one fore and one aft. At nearly 3 feet deep they provided the opportunity for the troops to swim and find respite from the heat of the tropics, but the motion of the ship created waves that surged to and fro with some vigour, adding to the entertainment for the troops.

Feb. 11th – Passed Madeira Island, we were now getting into the warmer climates the sea was practically calm since leaving the Bay of Biscay.

Jack Drake

An auxiliary cruiser off St. Vincent photographed from H.M.T. Huntsgreen (D'Olier)

Feb. 14th – Called at St Vincent, Cape de Verda Islands for coal, water and provisions, and posted 2 letters.

Jack Drake

H.M.T. *Huntsgreen* anchored in Mindelo harbour to take on coal. Lighters brought the coal alongside the vessel, where native labour

The coal wharves and lighters in Mindelo harbour, St. Vincent, Cape Verde Islands. Ships continued to coal here until 1952 (author)

was employed to raise the coal sacks aboard using hand windlasses, an arduous task. Dust hung in the tropical air as thousands of coal sacks were hauled on board and emptied into the ships stokehold below. St. Vincent was an established Royal Navy coaling station and was regularly resupplied by colliers from England. The Navy, from around 1912, had in part converted its fleet to burn oil for the ships boilers, but there still remained a large number of vessels that were fired by coal, predating mechanical stokers their boilers were stoked manually using shovels.

> Not being allowed to land, it was not very enjoyable, except for the fact that we got bananas, oranges and coconuts sold to us from boats. The fruit was not cheap by any means, oranges being 14 for 1/– and the nuts 4d each.
>
> Charlie Rimington, February 26th 1916

Still at anchor, troops whiled away their time leaning overboard and looking at the many colourful and unknown types of fish that they could see in the clear waters. A further distraction, which proved expensive, was throwing coins into the water for the native boys to dive for and retrieve. By the time the ships left Mindelo the men had exhausted their limited supply of silver coins and spent their last copper coins in this pursuit.

> We have seen all the usual things one comes across in these waters, two sharks, flying fish and three waterspouts. All we saw of the sharks by the way was their dorsal fins – I think that's the word – sticking up like a triangle.
>
> Charlie Rimington, 18th February 1916

Captain Floyd and his officers, challenged by the sportsmen of Mindelo, went ashore for a day. Forming a team, the officers enjoyed a brisk game of cricket without distinguishing themselves. In the evening, when once more aboard the ship, a concert was arranged with performances by the island's most promising singers and entertainers, including the wife of the British Consul. The finale to the evening was sounded by the troops with enthusiastic renditions of 'Rule Britannia' and 'God Save the King'.

Feb. 19th – Left Cape de Verda islands was out of sight of land until 3rd March.

Mar. 3rd – Saw the Table Mountain about 6 o'clock in the morning, sea quite calm in rounding the Cape.

Mar. 5th – In sight of land from the Cape, passed Port Elizabeth in the night, in the morning saw East London in the distance.

Jack Drake

Nearing Durban, Willoughby ordered a guard to be mounted aboard the ship; Sergeant Fewster, Corporal Danby and Corporal Berry took charge of the seventy-five men of the ship allotted to the guard. Willoughby's precaution was well founded, despite South Africa having elected to join with the allies, and was in the process of mobilising troops to both Europe and East Africa; there was a pro-German faction within the country that, despite suppression by the government in December 1914, could still have posed a threat to British interests there.

Mar. 6th – Reached Durban put in Harbour for coal & water & provisions, went on shore all the troops had a good reception by the people, the best of everything was given to us.

Jack Drake

The arrival in Durban had been anticipated with some excitement and relief by the troops. Following their departure aboard *Huntsgreen* from Devonport, almost one month early, this was their first opportunity for a sojourn ashore.

Granted shore leave with Wainwright. Very first things we did was have a good meal. Fancied a good homely tea so had bread, butter, jam and scones. We were so hungry that we finished one tea off and then another straight away.

Alec Robertson March 6th 1916

Breaking open the battery stores, each man of the brigade was issued with new khaki drill tropical uniforms, and reunited with his rifle. With the intent of providing exercise and restoring soldierly manner, the now smartly turned out brigade undertook a series of route marches around the city of Durban and its environs. The beach adjacent to Durban provided the brigade with a suitable place to take a rest break and Captain Floyd, deeming it safe, permitted the men from his battery to go swimming before the resuming the march. On the morning of departure and with the intention of encouraging South Africans to recruit, a parade was organised at the request of the Mayor and Corporation of Durban. It did not meet with much enthusiasm from the troops:

> We are paraded on our respective parade decks at 6.30am, then marched ashore to a parade ground near the quayside. We are dressed in new khaki drill uniform, slacks, puttees, tunics, belts, bandoliers, rifles, etc. We march away at 9.15am. After standing about two hours and three quarters under a sun that was already very hot, while we were very thirsty. We march along the harbour side, which looked very pretty with its avenue of palm trees, etc. We arrive at the park, where we are formed up, and wait for another hour or so. This is typical of Army routine for any ceremonial parades. Waiting about for an hour or so here, an hour or so somewhere else, but more consideration should be given, especially under a burning sun. We are marched to tables, where the ladies of Durban supply us with ale and cakes. Ale! It was truly the nectar of the gods this morning. I had two glasses and could have drunk more, but I had not the nerve of Oliver Twist to ask for more.
>
> Joseph Dan Fewster, March 7th 1916

Charlie wrote:

> We right dressed, left dressed, stood at ease and stood at attention and fooled about properly for four hours on end, until we were just about at our wits end. However, I suppose to an outsider we appeared to be having the time of our life, particularly when it came to refreshments – beer, cakes

and stone ginger (iced) at the expense of the burghesses of Durban. There are some jolly fine looking girls there I can tell you. One fellow got his leg broken and had to stay in hospital there. He was generally envied by the men.

Charlie Rimington, March 13th 1916

Standing in the sun for many hours, some men succumbed to the heat and dehydration, several collapsed. Once the parade was dispersed, the brigade marched back towards their ship. As they passed along West Street, one of Durban's main thoroughfares, the Durbanites showered the men with flowers, fruits, and cigarettes, encouraging the troops, and sharing their patriotic fervour.

Mar. 8th – Left Durban at 8 o/c PM thousands of people on the quayside cheered us as the ship moved away from the quay, other ships in harbour blew their sirens & railway engines on shore did their best to blow Hip Hip Hooray.

Jack Drake

'There are some jolly fine looking girls there I can tell you' – West Street, Durban (author)

Following the excitement of Durban, the routines of shipboard life were decidedly stale. Enforced idleness can become dispiriting, especially to those who had enjoyed active lives in their peacetime occupations. It is said that the devil finds work for idle hands; this adage proved true for some of the Hull men who found themselves a new pastime, stoking the ship's boilers. This, compared to the monotony of their normal day, was refreshing despite the hard labour involved, and raised their spirits considerably.

> My drawers and trousers were black. I had been down the stoke hole with four other fellows for the sport of the thing and we did a four hour shift coming out of it like darkies.
>
> Charlie Rimington, 13th March 1916

The *Huntsgreen*, its passengers settled once more to the shipboard routine, continued its voyage along the seaboard of South Africa. For six days they steamed northwards, along the humid river deltas and fevered coasts of Portuguese and German East Africa, passing Zanzibar on their port side, before closing with the British shore near Mombasa on the 14th March 1916.

Chapter 5

Operations in East Africa 1914–1918

AT the outbreak of war, and throughout 1915, the German colonial forces of Doctor Schnee, the governor of German East Africa, commanded by General Paul Emil von Lettow-Vorbeck, raided the Uganda railway and border areas in southern British East Africa (Kenya) and occupied the small border town of Taveta in British territory. Von Lettow-Vorbeck had arrived in German East Africa in 1914 having served during the Boxer Rebellion of 1900 in China and as a commander in German South West Africa during the Herero revolt of 1904. Originally trained as an artillery officer, he now commanded his force, a mixture of trained European and native askari soldiers, becoming adept at living and fighting in this demanding landscape. Making use of local supplies and with a ready resource of manpower, von Lettow, using small mobile patrols, damaged bridges the permanent way and on occasion attacked trains on the Uganda railway. His methods proved effective in disrupting the flow of trade from the lakes region whilst his main force enjoyed well defended positions in the rocky outcrops, swamps, low bush and rivers that protected his flanks in the border area between Lake Chala and Lake Jipe. Highly mobile with artillery and machine gun support and with significant numbers of riflemen, the force of around 4,000 troops in this area posed a real threat to the British East Africa colony.

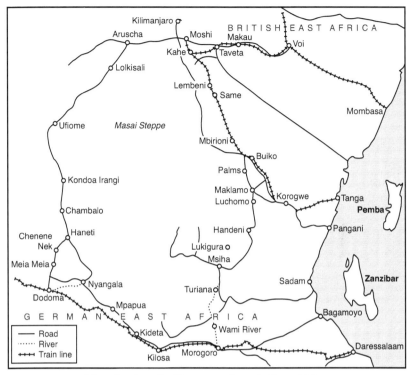

Map showing the German colony in East Africa

Opposing von Lettow during the initial stages of the war were the native 3rd Kings African Rifles and contingents of the East African volunteer units of mounted riflemen, infantry and machine gunners formed from colonial settlers of European origin. Insufficient in number or arms, the volunteers were reduced to a defensive role spread thinly along the border area and railway, posing little threat to German ambitions. Von Lettow's forces deployed across the colony's 600-mile frontier were estimated to consist of 16,000 men of whom 2,000 were white. They were organised into companies of between 150 and 200 men, excluding their officers, and equipped with sixty artillery pieces and eighty machine guns with two machine guns per company. Each company was commanded by a German officer and a complement of German non-commissioned officers.

In November 1914, Major General Arthur Aitkin arrived in Mombasa, his flotilla of troops having departed from Bangalore in India some days earlier. Aitkin's force, formed in part from the 27th Bangalore Brigade and the 2nd Battalion Loyal North Lancashire Regiment, made an amphibious landing at Tanga in German East Africa on the 3rd of November 1914 and suffered a resounding defeat at the hands of the German and askari troops opposing them. The action was characterised by several farcical incidents, but mainly the apparent incompetence on the part of the British commanders, despite the troops showing exceptional bravery in their actions. Following the withdrawal of the troops from Tanga, the majority of those who survived were returned to Mombasa, some repatriated to India. The Loyal North Lancashire Regiment remained in British East Africa and joined the defence force there.

The 25th Battalion Royal Fusiliers (Legion of Frontiersmen) embarked from Plymouth in April 1915 and landed at Mombasa in the first week of May 1915, and were deployed defensively along the Mombasa to Voi section of the Ugandan Railway. These two British units, after several local actions, eventually formed the nucleus for two British infantry divisions under Lieutenant General Michael Tighe and were brought up to strength at the end of 1915 by the addition of South African, Rhodesian, Indian and further African contingents. Notable of the East African campaign is the heterogeneous nature of its forces, there eventually being a multitude of nationalities, religions and cultures which made the East African force unique in this respect.

It can be said, with hindsight, that prior to the landing of these British troop details at Mombasa, von Lettow could have advanced with little resistance into British East Africa and potentially taken control of the coast and captured the harbours there, a feasible objective for his force at this juncture. Such a bold manoeuvre would have prevented the future landing on this coast, of any significant force by the British. Instead of the action suggested, and that feared by London, von Lettow, whose supply line would have been sorely stretched, contented himself with continued raids on the British railway and establishing a strong defensive line. Employing great skill in the use of the natural barriers available von Lettow maximised his position, in anticipating a British reaction. Reinforcements for a planned offensive campaign were to be mobilised from Britain, whilst the two divisions recently formed from the existing units in the country commenced operations in the border and Kilimanjaro districts in January 1916.

The course of action taken by von Lettow is seen by some historians to have been a careful strategy to draw allied forces into the theatre of war without extending his own logistical and military needs. Whether this was his initial plan is unknown but he did succeed in achieving this objective. Britain and her allies committed a total force in excess of 350,000 mainly colonial troops to this theatre of war throughout the campaign. Arguably some of these troops could have been more usefully employed in Europe and possibly contributed to bringing the war to its conclusion earlier than was the case. At the peak of the operation more than 110,000 men were pitted against 8–16,000 native ranks; von Lettow's adversary, Smuts, during his offensive campaign, never confidently established the number under von Lettow's command. Von Lettow who was never defeated in battle had the privilege of writing an account of his campaign after the war and summarised his initial strategy briefly in his book *My Reminiscences of East Africa: The Campaign for German East Africa in World War One* (London: Hurst and Blacken, 1920). How much of von Lettow's memoir can be considered hindsight is debatable, however he says:

> My view was that we would best protect our colony by threatening the enemy in his own territory. We could very effectively tackle him at a sensitive point, the Uganda Railway.

The command given by Doctor Schnee, the governor, to von Lettow was restricted to defending the German colony and maintaining compliance with agreements between the two colonies and the tenets of the Congo Act of 1885 with respect to the neutrality of British and German East African colonies in time of war. Von Lettow, in defiance of Schnee, purposefully instigating a confrontation with the British, with the intent of their being forced to take action against him. In so doing, and disobeying Schnee's orders, von Lettow placed the German colony at risk; it is considered that he may have underestimated the will of Britain to protect its African interests. His subsequent mobile tactics as the German colony was invaded and progressively captured by the British remained not so much a planned strategy but his only honourable option. Von Lettow effectively ensured the loss of the colony.

The 38th Howitzer Brigade, assembled from the 1st Hull Heavy Battery, formed part of the reinforcements sent from Britain to bolster the existing force in East Africa. The battery's arrival in Mombasa anticipated the campaign under preparation by Lieutenant General Jan Christian Smuts that had the intent to clear the German East Africa border of enemy forces and to defeat the enemy force in this theatre of war.

Much has been written concerning the skills of von Lettow, his character and his execution of this campaign. He has grown in the public perception through a variety of media. Whilst von Lettow's force was never defeated, as such, he was forced to continuously fall back before the advancing British forces, outnumbered, outgunned and out provisioned, eventually losing the colony with considerable loss of men. At his eventual surrender to the British at Abercorn, in what is now Zambia, in 1918, his force consisted of little more than 1,100 troops and just over 100 officers. The success of his strategy resulted from the fact that he had no alternative that he could employ, other than a continuous rear-guard action. Unfortunately, Smuts' strategy was to rely very much on textbook outflanking movements which, given the nature of the terrain and consequent difficulties of timing and communication, lost their effect and were to some extent predictable to von Lettow. Smuts' effort must however be commended and his skills appreciated in this difficult campaign. Both leaders had great admiration for each other and the campaign was very much one of personal and professional rivalry. Smuts had met with von Lettow briefly in the pre-war years whilst von Lettow was recovering from an injury in South Africa. In later years, Smuts would assist von Lettow during the stark post-Nazi period that Germany experienced following the Second World War and ensured he received food, and in later years, a South African pension.

Chapter 6

A Foreign Land

Mar. 14th – Entered Kilindini Harbour, Troops commanded to disembark. My regiment disembarked and went into rest camp; ladies at the Docks gave us lemonade, tobacco & cigarettes.

Jack Drake

Kilindini Harbour, Mombasa, British East Africa (McBain)

IN the first of several despatches to the *Hull Times* newspaper, Sergeant Sydney Wainwright, formerly a farm foreman, describes the arrival of the Hull Heavy Battery at Mombasa camp in British East Africa:

When we entered camp we were halted under a tree and given "Stand easy" and we proceeded to dump our kit, when to our amazement and alarm we found that the ground was literally covered with black and red ants, and upon looking round we discovered that wherever we moved the same conditions prevailed, so we entered our tents, and ere the first night was over we found that we had tent mates, not only ants but lizards, chameleons, centipedes and multipedes. These we managed with, but when we found that there were full sized tarantulas about we made a close inspection each evening before turning in.

Two days after the battery's arrival in Mombasa, the guns, ammunition and stores were brought ashore which allowed a routine of gun, rifle drill and musketry to be commenced. Rifle practice took place at the existing Mombasa butts. One howitzer was brought into the camp for daily drill purposes. Until this time, the battery had not had an opportunity to fire live ammunition in practice, but due to Captain Floyd's assiduous attention to training, the battery maintained a high level of competence in their gun drill.

N.C.O.s of the 11th Hull Heavy Battery R.G.A., Mombasa March 1916
L-r: Bland, Robertson, Hastie (A.S.C.), Wainwright (seated) Downs and Fewster (Hopkin)

We arrived here in the wet season, a matter of which we soon become fully alive to – rain, rain, rain, absolute downpour, making watercourses for itself as it rushed in torrential streams through the camp. Tents washed down, and those that remained standing were covered over the floor with water to a height of six to eight inches, parts of kit floating about and the men gathered around the pole in their bare feet, powerless to do anything except watch the wonderful downpour. Finally it ceased, and the most willing fatigue that ever worked soon dug huge trenches around the tents, so that by the time the next deluge came we should be able to cope with it and not have our rest disturbed.

Sydney Wainwright, March 1916

A combination of the climate, and camp conditions soon resulted in illness being experienced by the battery, this, in spite of the greatly improved diet compared with that previously enjoyed aboard the troopship H.M.T. *Huntsgreen.* Freshly killed oxen were readily available but, with no refrigeration, required cooking immediately to avoid the meat putrefying. This provided a tough but edible meal that required much chewing. Canned vegetables, rather than fresh, were the normal issue. All the foods consumed by the army had to be imported: the scale of supply requirements and the logistics involved were considerable.

> All cooking is done in the open air under a tree but meat doesn't go down very well in this hot climate.... we sleep in tents when it looks like rain, but ordinarily we stick four sticks up in the sandy soil and fix our mosquito curtains over them.

Charlie Rimington, March 18th 1916

Mombasa Camp. Standing: Fred Hunter, Harrison Roydhouse, Charles Clarkson, Robert Hornby, Arthur Frost. Sitting: Cyril Stamper, Henry Roper, Charles Jebson. Mombasa, March 1916 (Hull History Centre)

Whilst the battery was at Mombasa, the spring rains commenced. The Hull men, not natural campers, failed to loosen the guy ropes of their tents when it rained. In some instances, as the guy ropes became taut when wet, their tent pegs became loose allowing the tents to collapse upon them as they slept. Another unfortunate group, having such strong and long tent pegs, despaired when, under the terrific tension induced by the guy ropes shrinking, the central support pole of their tent snapped.

Flooded camp during the rains of March 1916 (author)

The severity of the rains, during the early spring of 1916, was such that many of the bridges and road infrastructure that Smuts had already established, was washed away. Before further military action could be undertaken, it would be necessary for all of the infrastructures to be rebuilt, requiring great effort of manpower, significant expense and, more importantly, time.

The difficulties of maintaining good sanitation in the camp, exacerbated by an inadequate supply of clean water to meet

Mombasa Camp
Standing: Jim Magee, Alfred White, Percy Shanks.
Sitting: John Yates, Alfred Traynor.
Mombasa, March 1916 (Hull History Centre)

the requirements for the large number of troops in camp, brought disease. Lieutenants Harrison and Mackenzie became early casualties to dysentery which required their admittance to hospital. Death in the camp started to become a common event:

> Fever and dysentery are attacking the troops. When anyone dies the body is not kept long here. I have seen a man on the 8.30am parade and attended the funeral at 3.00pm.
>
> Joseph Dan Fewster, April 9th 1916

Jack, in what would become the first of his many encounters with numerous tropical diseases, was similarly afflicted:

> April 25th – Good Friday, still at Kilindini, I went down with dysentery, admitted into Mombasa Hospital discharged after 3 days treatment.

The deteriorating situation was a matter of deep concern to Captain Floyd:

> During this time the health of the Battery gave cause for anxiety – severe cases of dysentery and a few fever cases occurred – the average number in hospital at one moment was about 15% – 2 officers, 1WO and 28 NCOs and men were admitted during this period (April). Everything possible was done to combat this rate of sickness – serious illness was undoubtedly avoided by advising men to report sick at the first sign of sickness rather than trying to fight it for a day or so.

Other than the demands of daily drill and camp fatigues, the men were afforded some light relief; within easy walking distance of the camp there was a beach graced with white sand. It was here that the men could relax, swimming in the coolness of the blue waters of the Indian Ocean. The unrelenting sun, which had caused some men from the battery to suffer severe sunstroke, one man in particular being debilitated for three weeks with his back a raw blister from shoulders to waist, made it necessary for orders to be issued to the effect that this activity be limited to the hours before seven o'clock in the morning and after five o'clock in the evening. The numerous shops of Mombasa, run predominantly by local Portuguese and Indian families, provided an opportunity for the men to spend their money, soon learning how easily they could be "fleeced" when bartering for trinkets.

> The Yorkshire spirit of the "boys" soon showed itself in the fact that before the first day was over they had mastered the native coinage, and were able to barter in a most useful manner, although it was disconcerting at first to have given in change a hundred coins like "washers" with a hole through the centre, the whole only worth one shilling and fourpence, but gradually annas, pice, cents and rupees became as familiar as our own coinage at home, and the native village became a happy hunting ground for the "boys".
>
> Sydney Wainright, March 1916

A view of Mombasa (McBain)

The motorised transport for the brigade, which had been embarked aboard the S.S. *Anselma de Larrinaga* at Avonmouth some weeks early, arrived at Kilindini, the port for Mombasa. Its arrival brought the weeks of acclimatising, extensive gunnery and signal training to a conclusion. The brigade was ready to join Smut's main force that was being concentrated at the forward base camp, established by Smuts, at Mbuyuni near the border between British and German East Africa. A branch line of the Uganda Railway had been planned between Voi and Taveta. It was constructed by the army that by April 1916 had progressed from Maktau and reached its terminus at Mbuyuni camp. Taveta, the border town some miles forward of Mbuyuni, was occupied by the German forces of von Lettow. A former German position in British East Africa, Mbuyuni had been captured by the British during July 1915, which enabled the railway and a parallel water pipeline to be advanced to Mbuyuni from Maktau, the new railway's previous terminus. Today, Mbuyuni is the western gateway to the Tsavo West National Park, when approaching from the Taveta or Lake Jipe roads, Maktau forming the eastern gateway along the same route. The Tsavo National Park is noted for its large mane-less lions, which the author J. H Patterson, in his near contemporary work *The Man-Eaters of Tsavo*, described during the construction of the Uganda Railway some seventeen years previously.

> May 3rd – Left Kilindini for Mbuyuni reached Voi same night.
>
> Jack Drake

Sydney Wainwright wrote:

> Camp was struck at 6:15 a.m. and all our baggage carried to the train in a downpour of rain, the men trudging across with equipment, absolutely soaked through, and the heat so intense that they looked like walking steam packets, the steam coming off their wet clothes; but in spite of the discomfort everybody was cheerful because they were on the move.

At Kilindini, guns, limbers, stores, ammunition, and men were entrained for the journey along the Uganda railway, across the semi-arid Taru plain, to Voi. The journey was relatively straightforward.

> At 2 p.m. the carriages arrived. We looked in consternation at our travelling accommodation. The coaches were like cattle trucks, with iron bars across; some of the doors

were off altogether, and pieces of wood placed across the opening; other doors were forced open and a native joiner planed pieces off to make them close again. No windows in any carriages, wooden shutters taking their places. Inside of the coaches were seats with backs to them, arranged so that you could step over out of one compartment into another, and so we were packed into our places, and made ourselves as comfortable as possible for our 100 mile journey on the Uganda Railway, the railway company who have first, second, third and intermediate class passengers. We travelled third class, and have no desire to test the intermediate class.

Sydney Wainright, May 1916

Charlie Rimington was also aboard the train for the journey and describes further:

Eight in a compartment and knees touching, you may have an idea what it was like! Four of us slept on the floor and under the seats and the other four did the best they could on the seats. The four on the floor had the best spot.

Charlie Rimington, May 3rd 1916

Mazaras railway station on the Ugandan Railway between Mombasa and Voi (McBain)

Upon their arriving at Voi, the railway branch line that continued through to Mbuyuni was not utilised by the gun sections of the battery. Contemporary accounts tell that this branch line, being new and hastily constructed, was laid upon bare ground, without embankment. It was prone to frequent derailments which were made worse during periods of rain. The terrain it traversed turned quite swamp-like in the rainy season.

> The sleepers sink in the boggy soil under the weight of the train & Indian & Native troops are stretched along the line packing the rails with huge plantain & palm leaves before we can go over it in the train.
>
> Fred Jackson

The locomotive and carriages had, on previous occasions, sunk axle-deep into the soft ground following derailment; it is evident that the weight of the brigades' guns and ammunition would exceed the capacity of this line and accounts for the subsequent overland march of the brigade gun sections. The staff of the headquarters, depot section and those of the observation party, who were more lightly equipped, were able to continue their onward journey by train. Travelling in questionable comfort, through many unscheduled halts, the men were accompanied by swarms of mosquitoes that plagued them as the evenings advance brought darkness to the carriages. The train and its occupants arrived at Mbuyuni at eleven o'clock in the evening; they spent the remainder of the night on the train. The branch line was not permanently engineered until the mid-nineteen-twenties: after a period of disuse following the war, it has since become redundant.

> May 4th – Set off remainder of journey from Voi to Mbuyuni by road, all the guns towed by motor lorries, men, equipment, ammunition in the lorries. At night on first days trek we halted on the roadside pitched tents and had a meal of bully beef & biscuits the night was very cold & we had only one blanket but we had plenty more nights after without tent.
>
> Jack Drake

Jack, keen for adventure, wrote more than was his habit, but it was Sydney Wainwright who provided the better insight:

Eight guns, four four wheel drive motor lorries, one Ford car, and 15 Napier lorries were detrained and packed ready for our trek across the veldt, the guns fastened behind the lorries, the men and kits in the lorries and at 2:30 we started along the road upon our first experience of road traffic in the East. We went gaily along for the first five miles until we came to Voi bridge, which had been built by our engineers. It is a wire suspension bridge and we lightened our load, as the bridge would not stand a great strain. It was an anxious time until the heavy lorries were safely over. Then we breathed freely again, and off we went through the real African bush. We kept on until 6 p.m. and as it was getting dark we pitched camp for the night on the lonely veldt, with only our own company to cheer us up. That night was a lively one for those on guard. You could hear the call of the jackal, the hyena, and the roar of the lion in the distance, and these noises kept the sentries on the move all night, but dawn arrived without a visit from any of these friends from the jungle.

The biscuits referred to by Jack, and to which the battery would become very accustomed, were, amongst others, those of the Hardman Biscuit Company from Australia. Commonly referred to by their troops in Mesopotamia as 'dog biscuits' and, apparently, fitting of their manufacturer's name, they provided a 'hard tack 'style of sustenance that had good storage qualities. Similarly of Australian origin was much of the corned beef produced by the Queensland processors that was supplied to East Africa at various times. Australia had suffered a severe drought for many years; by 1915 the drought was causing a shortage of meat for their domestic market. At the outbreak of war Lieutenant Colonel Sir Thomas Robinson, GBE, KCMG, who had experience of the industries as a director of a meat works and a shipping company, was appointed agent general, in London, for Queensland and became the director of meat supply for the allied armies. Consequently, as the drought eased, large quantities of Australian produced meats reached the allied armies including those in East Africa.

Following breakfast, the battery left their overnight camp, between Voi and Maktau, and continued their journey along the 35-five mile stretch of road recently constructed by the Faridkot Sappers and Miners, provided by the Indian Princely Ruler of the independent Faridkot State, and paid for by him. At times the lorries attained a speed of 8 miles per hour, which pleased Captain Floyd. Later that day, just past Maktau, where no new road had yet been established, difficulties were met with the lorries sinking in the loose cotton soils. Four lorries of the column got stuck and required the use of manropes and all hands to extricate the vehicles, although the majority of the brigade were able to continue to the camp at Mbuyuni unhindered. The 158th (Hull) Heavy Battery, established from the ranks of the Hull Heavy Battery whilst at Denham, had been left at Mombasa and would rejoin the brigade some two days later after the train had retraced its journey to Kilindini and then for it to return.

> May 5th Reached Mbuyuni, saw the Mountain of which is said to be one of the wonders of the world being only about 2 deg south of the equator & has a perpetual covering of snow. Kilimanjaro.
>
> Jack Drake

It is evident that Jack's original diary entry had the word Kilimanjaro added a little later than the main body. Undoubtedly, some troops would be unsure of the name and spelling of this spectacular mountain until they were better informed.

A photograph of Kilimanjaro taken by John McBain. June 1916 (McBain)

Mbuyuni was the forward base camp for the planned invasion of German East Africa and had contingents from a multitude of units from the British Empire and its allies.

> This is a great camp … and we find it filled with Indians, Boers, South Africans, and a few English ASC (Supplies). I see the Bengal Lancers for the first time, and one need wish to see no finer men, nor cleverer horsemen than these chaps. There are also two or three Indian Mountain Batteries, with several battalions of Punjabis, Gurkhas, etc., and we have a couple of batteries of South African Field Artillery, parties of Boer Mounted Infantry forming a nucleus of General Britts' Flying Column. Indian ammunition columns are here with ox transport, the oxen skins scoured with fantastic designs, while at the other side of the camp is a big aerodrome. So you see, we have some variety in the camp.
>
> Joseph Dan Fewster, May 5th 1916

The new camp, located on the plains, some 3,000 feet above sea level brought some relief to the troops. Although the days were very hot and dry, the humidity of the coast had dissolved and the nights and evenings were caressed with cool breezes that made sleep more restful. Dysentery to some extent abated but was replaced with an increase in malaria cases, as mosquitoes were prevalent. Rations could be supplemented with wild game.

> We left three NCOs and one Gunner in hospital at Mombasa, and we no sooner got here than two more gunners went into hospital, one with enteric and the other with malaria.
>
> Charlie Rimington, May 13th 1916

The unfortunate Gunner left behind in Mombasa was George Ablett. George, a farm labourer from Hedon, had enlisted in late December 1914 and, like Jack, had originally been posted to the battery as a driver. Now that the battery was motorised, the drivers had been retrained as signalers. He would rejoin his comrades at Mbuyuni after his spell in hospital.

At Mbuyuni, breakfasts were often made up of beef and tea, and on occasion enhanced by a bacon ration. The heat of the tropics made lunch a lighter affair and generally, for simplicity, was jam and biscuits. Evening meals of canned beef stew accompanied by biscuits or bread ensured adequate nourishment if not a particularly appetising choice of meal for the tropical climate.

> Usually we get bread, but being on our own, and in a rather isolated spot we are using biscuits of the dog variety. They are jolly good too, but require soaking, as dentists do not abound in this country.
>
> Charlie Rimington, 13th May 1916

Arthur Beagle's father was a Hull printer and his mother was from Keyingham in East Yorkshire: he was working in South Africa when war was declared. He enlisted in the 1st Mounted Brigade, South African Horse in Pretoria, before being transferred to the 2nd Mounted Train South African Horse as a wheeler on a mule convoy. Sailing on the H.M.T. *St. Egbert* he had landed at Kilindini on May 9th and had arrived at Mbuyuni on the 15th.

> Arrived M'bununi, the big base camp where all kinds of troops were gathered. On the first day I walked over to the Camp of the 38th Howitzer Brigade, which was formerly on Hedon racecourse. As nearly all the men were from Hull and only out from home three months I was very pleased to have a chat with them. Here I met the Roydhouses from Keyingham.
>
> Arthur Beagle, May 15th 1916

Tom Roydhouse and Harrison his younger brother had both enlisted in Hull. Tom had originally enlisted into the Royal Field Artillery as a shoeing smith on the 12th September 1914 but had been transferred to the Hull Heavy Battery where his skills could be better utilised. Tom who until 1918 retained his RFA regimental number would be awarded the Distinguished Conduct Medal for his future service as a gun layer.

> 91038 Gnr./ S. Smith T. Roydhouse RFA (Keyingham and Hull). For conspicuous gallantry and devotion to duty. In

gun laying and as a gun member he has shown a fine example of endurance.

London Gazette, 3rd October 1918

Tom Roydhouse DCM photographed at Keyingham War Memorial in 1977 (Stancliffe/ Roydhouse)	*The grave of Gunner 290221 Harrison Roydhouse Westoutre British Cemetery, Belgium (author)*

Harrison, after suffering prolonged illness in East Africa, was repatriated to England in early 1917. After a period of hospitalisation and recovery he was posted overseas to the North Riding Heavy Battery R.G.A.. During the German spring offensive of 1918 the battery was in position near Mount Kemmel in Flanders. In what has since been designated the Second Battle of Kemmel, on the 26th April 1918, Harrison was killed. Harrison is buried at Westoutre British Cemetery, Flanders.

The already large camp at Mbuyuni, and the increasing number of troops coming there, had put a strain on the water supply. Until this time water had been shipped from springs in the Bura Hills, some 37 miles away, in water bowsers pulled by oxen, more recently by rail tankers. With the area now cleared of German forces and the establishment of the forward base camp the new water supply pipeline, which ran parallel to the railway, could be commissioned. This was a welcome relief to the battery and other units who had managed on very little water for some time.

> We have plenty of water now – 2 gals per man for all purposes, including cooking – but until this morning we have been fortunate if we have got a quarter of a mugful to wash and shave in. We get plenty of tea at meal times. The method of working was this: – First we shaved; then we lathered our face and neck well, and rubbed down on the towel; then we lathered our knees well and rubbed them with the towel and looked spick and span for parade barring our mucky hands.
>
> Charlie Rimington, 13th May 1916

The apparent excess of water now enjoyed by the battery would, however, prove to be a temporary situation. As the South African mounted units concentrated at Mbuyuni, along with their horses and remounts, the supply proved inadequate. With Smuts' campaign already underway, the Hull Battery would soon be ready to join operations in the field.

Disposition of the Observation and signalling party of the 11th Hull Heavy Battery whilst undertaking live firing practice at Mbuyuni during May 1916 (Chandler/Dixon)

Despite their long period of training and frequent gun drill the battery had not, at this time, had the opportunity to fire live ammunition. It was whilst at Mbuyuni that the battery enjoyed its first real practice. Out in the bush, near the camp, several target observation posts and trenches had been established to offer targets for the artillery units assembled at Mbuyuni to practice upon. Each section of the battery was required to fire on each target. To develop their skill, the positions of the battery officer and that of the forward observation officer were alternated with each series of shoots. The battery signals sections were kept active in laying cables and establishing field telephones. Having successfully destroyed the mock trenches, dugouts and gun emplacements with their efforts the battery considered that they were now becoming 'old hands'.

Chapter 7

General Smut's Campaign

LIEUTENANT General Jan Christian Smuts took command of the East African campaign on the 12th February 1916, landing at Mombasa, from South Africa, on the 19th. General Sir Hubert Smith-Dorrien, the hero of the battle of Mons, was appointed to the command on December 12th 1915 but became ill whilst travelling to take over the command, subsequently contracting pneumonia in Cape Town during January 1916. The concerns regarding his health compelled him to return to England. During this interlude, the allied force of two divisions, effectively commanded by Brigadier General Michael Tighe, captured Longido in German territory on the 21st January and Serengeti Camp, four milles north-west of Mbuyuni, on the 24th January. The section of the branch railway line from Voi as far as Maktau was completed during his tenure and proved invaluable to future operations, after it had been extended to Mbuyuni.

Smuts had initially been approached by the War Office with an offer to this command in October 1915. On that occasion he had turned down the opportunity as he was, at that time, involved in the election campaign in South Africa, which ultimately saw his friend, Louis Botha returned to political power. With the election settled, Smuts felt confident in accepting the position when it was once more offered. The appointment gave him a welcome relief from the political scene, and the election process, that had become personalised and aggressive. Smuts, the secretary of state for defence in the government of the Union of South Africa, had been instrumental in bringing the South African to the assistance of Britain. A lawyer by profession, and his former role as a Boer commander during the South Africa's earlier conflict with Britain had brought his attributes to prominence. His efforts for reconciliation and the strengthening of ties with his former enemy had created in him the qualities of statesman and military commander. Prone to impatience and imbued with endless energy, Sir Douglas Haig, the British Commander in Chief by this time, viewed Smuts favourably. Haig had met with Smuts during the settlement negotiations of the Boer war some years previously.

Upon his arrival in East Africa, Smuts assumed command of the two existing divisions, the 1st (East African) Division and the 2nd (South African) Division. The proposed campaign, planned previously by army commander Brigade General Michael Tighe was outlined to Smuts who readily gave his approval. Having become satisfied of its feasibility, and mindful of the impending rainy season, Smuts cabled London on the 23rd February 1916 informing them of his readiness to occupy the Kilimanjaro region. Smuts received an affirmative response from the War Office on the 25th.

Tighe's 2nd Division, under the command of Major General Wilfred Malleson, and including Lieutenant General van Deventer's mounted brigade, had advanced along the proposed railway route from Voi prior to Smuts' arrival. The German forces were strongly entrenched on the British East African border, beyond the Lumi River, in the swampland and bush between the natural features of Lake Chala and Lake Jipe. German forces occupied Taveta, the main town, lying to the fore of the intended line of advance, and astride the road route into German East Africa.

Brigadier General James M. Stewart's 1st Division, that had captured Serengeti Camp in January, moved southwards from Longido on the north-west border and into the German colony. The division endeavoured a flanking movement to the west of Kilimanjaro, intending to bring the British force to threaten the enemy positions to the rear of Taveta and, in so doing, prevent the German withdrawal. In conjunction with Stewart's manoeuvre, the 2nd Division, leaving Mbuyuni on the 7th March, forced the enemy withdrawal from Salaita Hill, following a brief action, before crossing the Lumi River north of Taveta. Salaita Hill had been the scene of severe fighting during February, when an ill-informed attack by Mallenson's troops had failed to dislodge the German forces entrenched there.

British guns in action during the fight for Salaita Hill (author)

This advance by the 2nd Division succeeded in displacing the German forces from Taveta and the positions that they had occupied for over one and a half years. The retreating German force fell back to the Latema–Reata ridge, or Nek, a natural constriction and defensive position that had the potential of blocking the route from Taveta into German territory. Following a fierce infantry and artillery action at the Latema–Reita position, Deventer's mounted brigade outflanked the German force and succeeded in occupying the town of Moshi on the 13th March. In capturing Moshi, the German railhead was secured by the allies. This success enabled the continuation of the railway branch line from Mbuyuni in British East Africa to Moshi, and its interconnection to the German railway system that terminated there. General Stewart's 1st Division, who had trekked south from Longido in the north west, skirting Mount Meru and Kilimanjaro, in the hope of securing the enemy line of retreat, joined Deventer at Moshi having not succeeded in preventing the enemy withdrawal. The German force escaped the intended trap that would have dealt with von Lettow's main force at an early stage. In consequence the enemy force withdrew relatively unhindered.

Von Lettow withdrew his force to the settlement of Kahe, south of Moshi, near to the Ruwu River. Deploying his troops skilfully, he closed the strategic gap between the North Pare Mountains and the Pangani River, preventing the further advance by the allies. Smuts' combined forces, of the 1st and 2nd Divisions, advanced and attacked Kahe from the north. Several days of intense fighting followed before Kahe was finally taken by the infantry. Concurrent with Smuts' attack, Deventer's mounted brigade had outflanked the left of the German line, capturing Kahe Hill and railway station, rendering the German position untenable and causing them to withdraw. Deventer, however, did not follow through with this success, failing to prevent von Lettow and his force from escaping once more. The advance by Smuts, between the 7th and 19th March 1916, resulted in the German forces withdrawing south-eastwards towards the village of Lembeni, a station on the Usumbara Railway that parallels the Pare Mountains and Pangani River. At this point, with the possible intent of splitting Smuts' force, von Lettow ordered a number of German detachments towards Ufiome and Kondoa Irangi to the south-west, across the arid waste of the Massia Steppe.

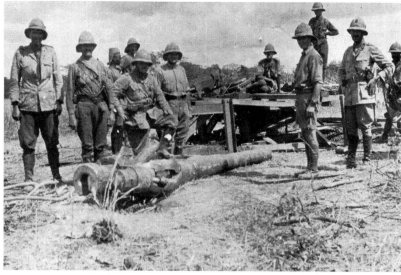

Enemy Gun destroyed to prevent its capture by the British at Kahe (author)

The capture of Arusha by Deventer completed the operations in the Kilimanjaro district; the impending rainy season prevented further operations. Smuts, satisfied with the progress made, contenting himself in securing dry positions for his main force whilst forming a defensive picket line along the banks of the Ruwu River near Kahe. Deventer established his mounted brigade at Arusha, in the German boma, where the climate and absence of tsetse fly was better suited to his animals.

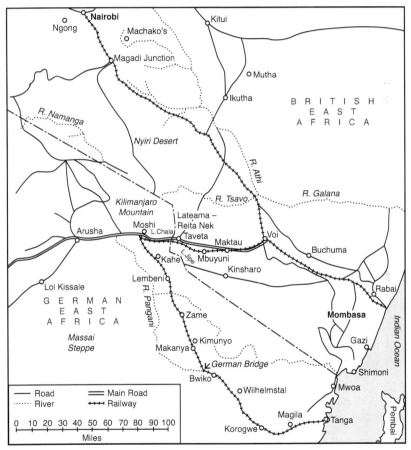

Map showing area of operations near Kilimanjaro

At this juncture, General Smuts reorganised his divisions. He disbanded the structure that had existed upon his taking command, and formed three new divisions, supplemented by new units that had recently arrived at Mbuyuni, The army and divisional commanders

Tighe, Stewart, and Mallenson were replaced at this time. Smuts wrote:

> The question of reorganisation of the East African forces, which I deemed necessary not only for the vigorous prosecution of the coming campaign, but also to secure the smooth and harmonious working of a most heterogeneous army, drawn from almost all continents and speaking a babel of languages. I decided to abolish the two divisions formed by my predecessor and to organise my forces into three divisions, two of which were to consist of the contingents from the Union of South Africa, and the third was to include the Indian, and other British forces. The Union Divisions were again so organised that each should eventually contain a mounted and an infantry brigade, so as to secure the necessary mobility to enable us to cope more expeditiously with the enemy Askari army of fleet footed Africans.

After considering several options for his renewed offensive, one of which included an amphibious landing at Dar es Salaam, Smuts decided that the newly formed 1st and 3rd divisions were to advance along the Pangani River valley, and in so doing, clear the Pare Mountains of the enemy forces. By taking the Tanga district and its coastal port, and securing the Usumbara Railway, an important line of communication would be available to his force before he could contemplate advancing southwards towards the Central Railway that linked Dar es Salaam to the lakes region. Deventer's 2nd Division was to advance from Arusha towards Ufiome and Kondoa Irangi, where reports had confirmed a build-up of enemy forces. Kondoa was strategically placed on the southward route to the Central Railway and Dodoma, and its capture was necessary in order that this important line of communication could be won. The success of this plan would additionally secure the right flank of Smuts' intended front, and, as proved the case, divert part of von Lettow's force away from Smuts' main advance. Additional forces, commanded by Lieutenant General Northey, would advance into the German colony from Northern Rhodesia (Zambia) in the south-west, additionally, the Belgians would move eastwards from the

Congo border, intending to secure the west of the German colony and the Central Railway around Tabora.

Smuts, anticipating the onset of the rainy season and hoping to secure an advantageous position prior to their commencing, ordered Deventer's mounted column of three regiments of the South African Horse to move from Arusha to Kondoa. Deventer began his advance on April 3rd across the Massai Steppe, a normally arid region of semi desert. His rapid advance exhausted his horses and troops, they ran short of water in the rocky scrubland, and outpaced his supply column; enemy rear guards and patrols resulted in numerous skirmishes. Some 35 miles south of Arusha lay the high granite outcrop at Lolkisali, with springs that provided the only water supply in the area. A brief but desperate fight ensued on the 5th and 6th April. Lolkisali was captured and was the only occasion throughout the East African campaign that the Germans surrendered under a white flag. The Germans had not realised the attacker's plight, Deventer's horses and men having gone without water for three days and being close to exhaustion.

Artillery shells bursting during the fight at Lolkisali (author)

Following the success at Lolkisali, the rainy season commenced. It rained incessantly, swelling previously dry stream courses to raging torrents; mile upon mile of bush became inundated and turned the light cotton soils into muddy slurry. Tracks, such as existed, were washed away along with any bridges that had been constructed by Smuts' army. What had been waterless desert now became near impassable swamp tiring both man and beast, taking its toll on the motorised and wheeled transport drawn by draught animals. With such a rapid advance, Deventer lost all communication with his supplies. Smuts summed up the situation:

> By the middle of April the rainy season had set in with the greatest of violence in the whole area from Taveta to Kondoa Irangi. The numerous rivers came down in flood and swept away almost all our laboriously built bridges, the roads became impassable mud tracks, and all transport became a physical impossibility. The rains fell steadily day after day, sometimes as much as four inches in one day, and the low lying parts of the country assumed the appearance of lakes.

The Germans, having divided their force some weeks earlier, had meanwhile, prepared their fortifications at Kondoa in readiness for Deventer's arrival. The mission station at Ufiome (Gallepo) was taken after several running battles with German patrols; Kondoa was evacuated by the Germans and occupied by Deventer on the 19th April. In his 200-mile advance to Kondoa, Deventer had lost hundreds of animals from horse sickness and his troops, few of whom remained fit, were worn out after ceaselessly marching and fighting. The majority of his transport animals were lost to disease.

The boma at Kondoa Irangi, burnt by the Germans during their evacuation
(author)

Having lost his transport capability and without having established a line of supply, Deventer was effectively isolated at Kondoa, in a precarious position. The horses that remained were dying, his men were now victims to dysentery, malaria and the loss of animals to transport supplies, which made starvation a possibility. His men were in no position to fight. Deventer called for reinforcements from Mbuyuni, but whilst the rains continued, Smuts could render little assistance.

The Germans, on their withdrawal from the town of Kondoa, barred Deventer's further progress by establishing a defensive line of trenches and strong points in the range of hills to the south and east of the town that commanded the heights overlooking Deventer's position and the route to Handeni and Dodoma. To counter the German position, Deventer established and maintained a thinly held defensive line on the opposing high ground, defending Kondoa, whilst he awaited the reinforcements he desperately needed. The superior observation the enemy enjoyed soon became apparent: with a clear view of Kondoa and the roads approaching the town, the German artillery was brought into action. It was not until the abatement of the rains in May that Smuts could mobilise reinforcements to Deventer.

The 2nd South African Field Artillery in position at Kondoa Irangi (author)

The 38th BL 5-inch Howitzer Brigade R.G.A., which had arrived at Mbuyuni on the 5th May, became part of the divisional reorganisation instigated by Smuts. Initially administered by No 1 Artillery Group under the command of Brigadier General Crowe, the brigade was dismantled and the batteries renamed. The 158th (Hull) Heavy Battery R.G.A. became the 14th Howitzer Battery R.G.A., retaining four howitzers; the 11th (Hull) Heavy Battery was split into two, two-gun batteries: the 11th and 13th Howitzer Batteries R.G.A.. The 11th was assigned to Deventer's 2nd Division, whilst the 13th would be attached as Army Troops to the 3rd Division, the command of the recently arrived Brigadier General Coen J. Brits. The 14th was assigned as Army Troops to the 1st Division but remained in reserve under Smuts' direct command. Jack's unit, 11th Howitzer Battery, comprising the left subsections of the 11th Hull Heavy Battery, were assigned to the reinforcements destined for Deventer and would subsequently endure the unremitting work of traversing the still swollen rivers and swamps that the recent rains had ensured.

> We were all encamped on a wide plain at the foot of Kilimanjaro and its healthy breezes and cool nights were a delicious change after the overpowering heat of Mombassa. We were able to go out and shoot waterbuck or wildebeest and thus add to our larder a little venison to relieve the army ration of bully beef. We remained at Mbuyuni for twelve days and then the brigade was split up, the 11th Battery being divided into two batteries, the right battery under the command of Captain Floyd and the left battery under command of Lieutenant Nannini... I was in the left section.
>
> Sydney Wainright, May 1916

Amongst other artillery units at Mbuyuni during this period was the 3rd Heavy Battery, now renamed, whilst in country, as the 10th Heavy Battery, which was manned by personnel from the Royal Navy. This battery was armed with the guns from the sunken H.M.S. *Pegasus* which upon their reclamation had been fitted with improvised gun carriages and limbers manufactured in Nairobi railway workshops. The Germans also, had reclaimed similarly sized naval guns from the cruiser SMS *Konigsberg* after it was trapped and subsequently sunk by the Royal Navy in the Rufigi Delta.

Captain Floyd, as the commanding officer, was not impressed with the reorganisation of the 11th (Hull) Heavy Battery and voiced his concerns:

The division of the signallers and observation party illustrated in Jim Dixon's pocketbook. To the left is the combined party for the 11th Hull Heavy Battery, to the right is the 11th Howitzer Battery subsection (Chandler/Dixon)

Battery is divided into two section with personnel made up from Brigade HQ, Ammunition Column and Depot Section. This division leaves each section, though on paper a self-contained unit, badly off as regards section HQ, observation party e.g. a section has a BSM or BQMS with the new arrangement, with the same amount of administration work to be done as for a Battery; also a Battery's establishment for observation party consists of 22 men; a section with exactly the same amount of personnel required for the same work is left with 11 men.

Basil Edward Floyd, May 1916

Captain Floyd's concerns were proved correct; the division of the available manpower combined with the high casualty rates experienced through disease, soon made it difficult to maintain an effective unit.

Heard we are to move off tomorrow, right section one way and left section another. I was in left section and we made all preparations for moving off next day.

Jim Dixon, 16th May 1916

Chapter 8

The 11th Howitzer Battery R.G.A.

May 17th – Left Mbuyuni with the Right [sic] Section of the battery remainder of the battery left behind; passed Salaita Hill where there had been a stiff fight a few weeks previous. At night we camped at Himo River, next day we loaded up with shells & left all our spare kit behind. We trekked day after day over rough stony roads, bogs, rivers, and mountains, passed through the town of Moshi only recently captured from the Germans. 17 days from leaving Himo River we reached Kondoa Irangi, tired, hungry & dirty, 200 miles from our Base and as far from a British railway. Joined Van DeVenters Column at Kondoa Irangi.

Jack Drake

FOLLOWING the division of the two battery sections, Jack's unit now comprised two 5-inch calibre howitzers, two FWD lorries, seven Napier cars and six Douglas motorcycles, the signalling equipment and 372 rounds of 50-pound shells. Temporary 2nd Lieutenant Anthony James Nannini and Temporary 2nd Lieutenant Harry Tayler, from Withernsea, were assigned to the battery; Nannini acted as the battery commander.

The reorganisation had left the battery subsection with insufficient resources, so, in the absence of other officers, Battery Sergeant Major Samuel Doyle acted as the section officer whilst

Sergeant Harry Downs and Sydney Wainwright took command of one subsection each. The battery establishment was completed by forty-five gunners and an attachment of drivers from the Army Service Corps, making a total of seventy-nine men. The battery arrived at the Himo River on the 17th May.

Salaita Hill, British East Africa, photographed in March 1916 (D'Olier)

Leaving their surplus kit at Himo Bridge depot, the battery joined with the artillery column of Captain Orde-Brown that was to trek southwards to join Deventer at Kondoa. Captain Granville St. John Orde-Browne R.A. was the commander of the 10th Heavy Battery; a unit manned by Royal Navy personnel and armed with the naval guns recovered from the wreck of H.M.S. *Pegasus*. It was equipped with motorised transport of Packard manufacture with REO trucks employed by the battery ammunition column. Captain Orde-Brown had been the Assistant District Commissioner in British East Africa in 1914 and, with the outbreak of war, had volunteered his services for the campaign in East Africa.

> Two naval guns & 2 howitzers, also ammunition section with motor lorry transport move off (from Himo River) 10am & await our arrival at first halt as we have to escort them to Kondoa. We leave early tomorrow.
>
> Fred Jackson, 19th May 1916

Due to the very steep embankments and the loss of the bridges that followed the rains, great difficulty was experienced in crossing the numerous rivers. The rains of the previous month had left the normally dry rivers in flood. The road from Himo River that passed through Moshi and continued west to Arusha was in a poor state of repair, the lorries became bogged down in the soft ground very easily. The Napier cars, used for transporting personnel and equipment, broke numerous steering rods under such difficult driving conditions; this became a regular cause for breakdowns. Jackson continued:

> Experience our first transport difficulty at the Wuri Wuri River (Weary Willie); the water is about 4ft deep & cars & wagons are pulled through by hundreds of Swahili Natives & up a very steep bank the other side. Infantry are taken across in cages suspended from aerial wires. Trek until 10pm then halt for the night at Sanja River.
>
> Fred Jackson, 20th May 1916

Bombardier Jim Dixon, of the signal section, accompanied the battery on his motorcycle:

> Had to ford river (waist deep) drag the guns and lorries across assisted by about 200 natives. I took my motor bike across on a wire with a kind of tray suspended there from. Not enough room for bike front wheel hanging over the edge. I sat in the saddle and hung on to the rope above my head and hoped for the best.
>
> Jim Dixon, 20th May 1916

Native labourers assisted the battery across the fast flowing stream of the, as yet, un-bridged Wuri Wuri River. To the west of Moshi, some 30 miles distant, are the Sanja marshes that form from the drainage from the slopes of Kilimanjaro. Upon the battery reaching the marshes they have further difficulties. One of their lorries, its driver losing control, careered off the road before sinking deep into the swamp. Only after expending great effort and incurring loss of time was the lorry able to be pulled free. Tow ropes coupled to the remaining vehicles of the battery and assistance provided by an American manufactured Sandusky tractor enabled the lorry to be released. With all the battery vehicles chained together, the tractor towed the 11th Howitzer Battery for the remainder of the 7-mile passage across the marsh.

The following day, moving out from their overnight camp, the battery reached the flooded Ssabuk River. To prevent their damage from immersion, whilst the lorries were towed across the stream, it was necessary for the magnetos to be removed from the lorries until the battery reached the dry ground of the opposite bank in safety.

> Coming up country in motor lorries is tremendously hard work. One day we make good running on hard sandy roads and the next we may be lucky to do 6 miles in 7 or 8 hours owing to drifts or bad roads in which the lorries sometimes sink up to their axles and have to be dug out. The drifts and streams are the worst. We have to lower the lorries and guns into the stream – they all have high banks – and then take the drag ropes across and pull them up again for they can't do it on their own power.
>
> Charlie Rimington

On the 23rd Fred Jackson wrote again:

> Now in very interesting country, large thorn bush & long grass & simply teem with large game & wild animals of every description …We camp at Alanga–Langkop-Bridge tonight. OC Post here is Capt Bagshaw… He warns us not to bathe in the river as it is full of crocodiles, the trees on the banks are swarming with monkey …This will be a very awkward drift to cross as water is 4'-6' deep & current swift. We have to take off all magnetos from cars & lorries & get pulled through by natives…The two naval guns with us are named Peggy III & Peggy IV they are off the HMS *Pegasus* that was sunk at Zanzibar by the Konigsberg.

The SMS *Konigsberg* was a German light cruiser which had taken up station at Dar es Salaam on 6th June 1914. Following a short career as a commerce raider, and after sinking H.M.S. *Pegasus* in Zanzibar on 20th September as the British ship took aboard coal, the *Konigsberg* sought refuge in the mosquito-infested, humid delta of the Rufiji River. With no fuel available, the *Konigsberg* was cornered with little chance of escape to the open ocean. Despite the precarious position of the *Konigsberg*, it took the Royal Navy eight months to find and sink the ship. The German crew put that time to good use; by the time the ship was finally destroyed by the Royal Navy, the crew had removed the cruiser's ten guns. These were subsequently fitted with field carriages made in the railway workshops of Dar es Salaam. These large-calibre weapons then accompanied von Lettow's land forces, seeing action at Kahe, and one such weapon was positioned at Kondoa firing at the remnant of Deventer's force isolated there. Upon learning of the recovery and subsequent use of the *Konigsberg*'s guns, the Admiralty in London admitted that it was a 'priceless acquisition' on the part of von Lettow.

A gun from the Konigsberg photographed by Lieutenant E. W. D'Olier following its abandonment by the Germans (D'Olier)

Lieutenant Nannini, commanding the 11th Howitzer Battery, expressed their difficulties as they continued upon their trek:

> At bridges of unknown strength, rivers with steep approaches, the guns had to be unlimbered from the towing lorry. In these cases it was necessary to remove the short

motor towing attachment and insert the poles owing to the extreme difficulty and danger in controlling the limbers when man handling.

Leaving the Moshi to Arusha road, Orde-Brown's column headed south-west across the Massia Steppe to reach Lolkisali, an area traversed by Deventer a few weeks' before and where he had met success in its capture following the German surrender.

> We branch off the Moschi-Aruscha main road here & get on the Lolkissale-Road which is just a beaten track through long grass & open country except for scattered bush. See lots of big game here & grass is 5ft high. There are thousands of Native Porters carrying forward supplies, they each carry 50Lb loads & supply dumps are established at intervals & supplies are thus sent forward on the relay system... Again we have to dismantle all motor transport to cross river owing to depth of water. We then push on another 12 miles & rest until 3 pm we then trek right through the night, pass one camp of Indian troops, & outspan 1 am about 3 miles from Lolkissale.

Fred Jackson, 24th May 1916

Native porters transporting supplies to Kondoa Irangi (author)

There were frequent halts to allow other sections of the column to catch up with the motorised battery. The infantry, many of whom travelled on foot, were faster and were able to overtake the cumbersome train. Not all of the units in the convoy had the benefit of motorised vehicles and proceeded at varying speeds with the ox carts and horse-drawn supply trains to the rear. During one such halt caused by the 10th Heavy Battery and ammunition column taking the wrong route, Sergeant Harry Downs, Jack's battery section sergeant, was detailed to take a dispatch motorcycle to the rear to locate and deliver a message to the missing section of the column. During this journey his BSA mount burst into flames becoming a total wreck. The machine was later salvaged for spare parts. Harry Downs later recalled:

> One night I had to take a dispatch and set off on a motor cycle. I had gone only a mile when the bike burst into flames. I decided to press on and walked the next 11 mile through the jungle at midnight.

Harry Downs demonstrated some courage in undertaking his moonlit walk considering that Fred Jackson tells quite vividly the apparent risks the journey entailed:

> There are many lions around here & we have to light huge fires to keep them from coming in the camp after our horses & we are told that the further we move inland now, the more will be our trouble with lions & other wild animals; so this is cheery news.
>
> Fred Jackson, 25th May 1916

After camping overnight at Lolkisale, the column crossed towards the Tarangiri River, halting at a waterhole, the midway point, to camp overnight. One of Jack's enduring memories was of the foul water at this waterhole that the battery used during their march to Kondoa. Trooper Francis Lister of the 4th South African Horse had made an overnight stop at the same waterhole on the 16th May, nearly two weeks earlier. Lister was riding from Arusha as part of the force despatched to reinforce Deventer at Kondoa and described his stay there:

> Left at 6AM proceeding to the front, a 200 mile march. Self in charge of 12 men. "What an adventure"! Slept at

water hole. Water green & full of dead animals but never the less was well appreciated. Lions visited us and dozens of hyenas. One of my men shot one from his bed, a huge brute.

Fred Jackson made further comment regarding the quality of water enjoyed by the column at this waterhole.

Have to water all the animals with buckets from the water holes, this is a slow job and the holes have dead horses, mules and oxen in them. Our first horse dies here from snake poison and four more suffering from horse sickness.

Fred Jackson, 27th May 1916

Today, the Tarangiri River forms the main feature at the centre of a large and popular national park of similar name. It is noted for its large elephant herds and numerous baobab trees.

Continuing their journey south-west from Tarangire River the column reached Ufiome (Gallepo) mission settlement. Deventer had cleared the mission of enemy forces during his advance to Kondoa.

With the disbandment of the ammunition column at Mbuyuni, Gunner Charlie Rimington was now part of the battery signal section. He contracted dysentery, following the battery's stay at the waterhole, and was left at Ufiome mission which had been established as a field hospital and vehicle repair workshop. Charlie was sent back via Lolkisali field hospital to Moshi and the convalescence camp there but, to compound his problems, he contracted malaria.

Twelve miles from the mission, on the route south, the long ascent of 1,500 feet to the summit of the Pienaar Heights tested the strength of the men as they hauled their howitzers and lorries up the incline. After a very tiring day in the sweltering heat, and having experienced great difficulty, they reached the high wooded plateau of the summit before establishing camp at Salanga a few miles further towards Kondoa. At this point Lieutenant Nannini, the officer commanding the battery, travelled ahead by car to Kondoa in order to reconnoitre the enemy positions. The road up the Pienaar

Heights, the escarpment of the volcanic highlands, still forms part of the main road from Arusha to Kondoa. It was originally established by the engineers of Smuts' army, and avoided the flatter but fly-infested route across the Massia Steppe that had previously cost Deventer many horses.

> This is a lovely place and is approached from the plains below by 7 miles of steep winding road with hairpin bends through the mountains that are covered with dense bush and jungle and on the slopes and plains below are extensive lands planted with mealies, kaffir corn, pumpkin, bananas etc. some of the crops stand from 6 to 9 feet high.
>
> Fred Jackson, 29th May 1916

In the early part of the century East Africa was still a very wild environment. Urban development was negligible and the sparse population of the hinterland was pastoral and lived in small tribal villages or near the church missions established there. Wild life abounded unhindered by the pressures of human development, there were no game parks, the animals ranged freely. The descriptions of grasses 5 feet high recall a different environment to that seen today where drought and the cattle herds of the Massai have denuded the pristine environment. In the high forests of the Irangi Hills the animals found natural refuge and predators found an easy living. The camp at Salanga with its transport animals proved irresistible to the resident lions:

> I get up at 5:30 am and find that lions did pay us a visit, the sentries state there were several about and I am inclined to think this correct as they killed three oxen and one horse which we later find dragged a long way down the mountain slopes towards the water.
>
> Fred Jackson, 30th May 1916

The battery spent much of the remaining journey to Kondoa travelling high above the clouds of mist that rose from the plain below, cloaking the hillsides, infiltrating the timbered ravines, and dampening all with heavy dew.

We heard the guns firing at Kondoa this morning and should
get there tomorrow but we are now going slowly as so many
of the animals are sick and we may not arrive until Saturday.

Fred Jackson, 1st July 1916

Descending from the heights near Kondoa their route took them
by way of a seasonal but at this time dry watercourse that in times of
rain would drain the foothills of the Irangi Hills into the Mkondoa
River at Kondoa. The main road route to the town was visible to
the enemy and offered little cover; the dry creek bed afforded the
battery some concealment. The unconsolidated sand, friable soil
structures of weathered and eroded tuffs, remnant from ancient
volcanoes, realised the limitations of their lorries which quickly
floundered. Mule wagons from Kondoa were arranged to lighten
their loads and allow for some progress to be made but this met with
little success. With the aid of an additional forty-eight bullocks, also
acquired from Kondoa, the lorries were pulled from the sand and
towed singly in half-mile relays before proceeding to within 4 miles
of the town where a little cover was gained near some thorn scrub.

Had a very hard morning on a motorbike pushing through
hilly, sandy country, came off once. Expect to reach our
destination (Kondoa Irangi) tonight under cover of darkness.
Halted for dinner at 1 o'clock proceeded at 3. From here we
had to have two teams of oxen (14 to a team) to assist us. At
one place it required the other "FWD", 60 men, 28 oxen and
16 mules to pull the last four wheel drive out of a hole where
it had dug itself in.

Jim Dixon, 1st June 1916

Due to the proximity of the German forces the column and
battery did not proceed to the town until nightfall. Given the
rising clouds of dust created by the passage of the column it was a
precaution that had merit: the road was also within observation of
the German artillery batteries, who to date had had considerable
success in preventing supplies and men passing this route. After
further troubles with the sand, broken steering arms on the Napier
cars and other mechanical failures, the column, the remaining five
lorries and two guns of the 11th Battery reached Kondoa at 5.30 in

the morning on the 3rd June 1916 having travelled 295 miles across the Massai Steppe, swamps and mountain wilderness in seventeen days. Everybody slept.

Troops enter Kondoa Irangi across the Makondoa River (author)

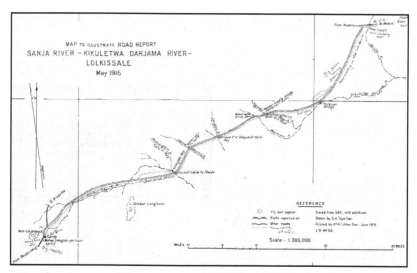

Map showing part of the route traversed by the 11th Howitzer Battery on the route to Kondoa Irangi in May 1916
(Lewisham Local History and Archive Centre)

Chapter 9

The Battle of Black Rock

June 3rd – 7o/c PM Mules took our guns & shells & our waterproof sheets & blankets only 25 LB of kit per man, we had 12 mile to go through sand up to the boot tops in full marching order, before we reached our position it was 11 o'clock at night, when we had got our guns into action, the Germans sent 3 shells over us to welcome us.

Jack Drake

EVENTER'S force, that had left Arusha some weeks previously, had met with stiff resistance from von Lettow's askaris at Kondoa. He had been attacked in some force and had narrowly avoided being overwhelmed, except for the tenacity and marksmanship of his troops, who had held their position in the face of repeated bayonet charges. The Germans had been repelled but the damage to the already weakened South Africans forced Deventer to call for reinforcements, which, when mobilised from Mbuyuni, included Jack's unit, the 11th Howitzer Battery R.G.A., Orde-Brown's 10th Heavy Battery, and two regiments of South African infantry from Brigadier General Beves' 2nd South African Brigade. These fresh troops would bolster the troops of Brigadier General Berrenge's 3rd South African Infantry Brigade already at Kondoa. The reinforcements found, upon their arrival, the German forces entrenched some distance south and east of Kondoa in strategically important and threatening positions high in the Irangi ridge. The situation required the immediate deployment of the artillery to bring heavier firepower onto the cleverly established German fortifications and to prevent the continued outflanking movements by von Lettow on Deventer's left flank.

Shrapnel shells fired by the 2nd South African Field Artillery explode over enemy positions at Kondoa Irangi (author)

Jack's battery, the 11th Howitzer Battery of two guns, went into position immediately alongside the 12th Howitzer Battery South African Garrison Artillery on what had become known as 'Battery Hill'. The 10th Battery manned by the Royal Navy positioned further back, given their greater range, on North Hill. The allocation of the half battery of the 11th Hull to Deventer's force became apparent at this time; the 12th Howitzer Battery South African Garrison Artillery, originally the 4th South African Howitzer Battery from the Cape, had suffered a premature detonation in the barrel of one of its guns some days previously, destroying this weapon:

> Again occupied Howitzer position, Fired 41 Rds. Shell exploded in bore of gun Reg. No 157-blowing gun, gun carriage and limber to pieces.
>
> F. W. Boyce, 14th May 1916

The half section of the Hull battery would make good this loss and from this date until early 1917 the battery would be tactically aligned to the 12th South African Howitzer Battery.

At the time of Jack's arrival at Kondoa, von Lettow's troops had succeeded in gaining possession of another hill in the arc surrounding Kondoa. The hill, known as 'Black Rock', threatened the left flank of Deventer's position, and due to its strategic importance became, amongst others, one of the targets for Jack's battery section. In order to prevent Deventer's position being turned and his tenuous lines of communication coming under threat, the extension of the German line around Deventer's position had to be prevented.

> Two guns of 11th Hull heavy battery arrived and were placed under command of Capt C. De C Hamilton took up position using the mules of 12th Battery to do so.
>
> F. W. Boyes, 3rd June 1916

Abandoning the lorries, now deemed to be too noisy when in close proximity to the enemy, the battery moved to a position 5 miles east of Kondoa and 2,000 yards from the enemy positions. Jack, who formerly enlisted into the battery as a driver, was amongst those charged with coaxing the mules onward towards the positions on Battery Hill. To prevent inopportune braying, the mules, loaned from the South African battery, had had their vocal chords severed to prevent alerting the enemy; their hoofs muffled for similar reasons. Despite these precautions the German forces were soon attracted to their activities as the battery clattered and creaked its passage through rock-strewn thorn scrub of the bush. The Germans responded by firing a number of shells in their vicinity as Jack and others note.

A battery subsection prepares to load a howitzer in German East Africa (South African National Museum of Military History)

Private C. S. Thompson, whose unit, the 7th South African Infantry, was entrenched on Battery Hill, was waiting to be transported to Kondoa hospital at the same time that the 11th Howitzer Battery occupied its position.

> A young chap from the artillery came and talked to us for quite a long time ... Was woken by 2 shells from the Germans bursting 500 yards off. There must have been some spies about as that is the first time I have known the Germans fire at night and they certainly fired at our men.
>
> C. S. Thompson, 3rd June 1916

Thompson, suffering an accidental self-inflicted burn to his leg from his spilling cooking fat, had been placed on an ox cart for evacuation to hospital. He related further:

> The wagons started back after midnight. It was very smooth going in the thick sand but we had no sooner started than we heard the far-off, long-range gun go off. I wondered where the shells were meant for but they never came near us.
>
> C. S. Thompson, 4th June 1916

For Jim Dixon, a former solicitor, it was a different story. Jim was charged with getting the signal section and stores to the battery position.

> Slept in till 11am. Went to the river for a wash. Moved out to our position at 8pm; arrived there 2 am next day. On the way out I was with the last bullock cart owing to one of our oxen nearly pegging out, we were left behind and had to push on our lonesome. While going along the Germans shelled the road about 500 yards in front of us and owing to the unhappy condition of one of the bullocks we outspanned same and decided to leave the cart. On second thoughts however, we went back and brought the wagon along, finally arriving at the battery position about 2am. Got through on the telephone to O.P. and turned in.
>
> Jim Dixon, 3rd June 1916

*Bombardier Jim Dixon
(Chandler/Dixon)*

Captain Fred Jackson, who along with Jack, had arrived with Orde–Brown's column in Kondoa that same day also had a close encounter with the shelling from the German guns:

> We all turn in around 10pm but the Hun starts shelling at Midnight so we get up and take cover, also again at 2am.
>
> Fred Jackson, 3rd June 1916

Along with the other recently positioned batteries, and the increase in firepower now available to Deventer, the 11th Howitzer Battery first went into action at 4.30 on the morning of the 4th June 1916, firing fifteen rounds at enemy redoubts and observation posts until dusk.

> Nothing doing all the morning, as we were not to open fire until the Germans did so. Nothing happened until the afternoon when, as we were commencing to bake our bread, the Germans opened fire. We at once went into action firing our first shot at 4:40. We carried on until nearly dusk and then packed up for the day after a very exciting and interesting afternoon.
>
> Jim Dixon, 4th June 1916

The following day "all our guns are pounding away at enemy positions", the bombardment continued with a further nineteen rounds, forty-nine rounds expended on the 7th June where Jackson notes, again, there was "Heavy bombardment and fighting going on". From the battery forward observation post Jim Dixon witnessed the day's events:

> Had dinner, shortly after, went into action again. Our field battery, 4-inch guns and ourselves. The Germans opened the ball and we replied. Great row on watching the German

shells burst on the ridge behind us where the 4-inch battery was. Just before tea, action again.

Jim Dixon, 5th June 1916

Thompson, who was now in hospital at Kondoa, could hear the activity in the nearby hills.

Just before dinner we could hear a heavy artillery duel going on, the far-off German guns joining in. It was kept up well into the afternoon.

C. S. Thompson, 5th June 1916

The following day was quiet; the recent news of the Battle of Jutland occupied the conversations of the battery out in the hills near Kondoa.

During the afternoon two aeroplanes arrived. They could be heard a long while before coming into sight. No guns fired during the day but we could hear a Maxim going…Awakened by our big guns firing on the enemy… Our big guns kept on firing most of the day and the aeroplanes went out scouting. Could hear a machine gun going every now and then.

C. S. Thompson, 6th June 1916

The aeroplanes that Thompson heard were those of the No. 7 (Naval) Squadron, which had been formed in April 1916 from the mainland detachments of the Naval Station at Zanzibar and commanded by Squadron Commander Nanson. The journey by the squadron to join Deventer is described by H. A. Jones in the official history *War in the Air*, published in 1935:

On taking over, Squadron Commander Nanson at once made arrangements to send petrol and spares to Kondoa Irangi. Flight Sub-Lieutenant Gallehawk set out for Kondoa with 4 mechanics and 1,000 porters. The party paused at Lol Kissale for four days to make the beginnings of an aerodrome and then pushed on to Kondoa where, after a hazardous journey during which three porters were eaten by lions, they arrived on 28 May 1916. Flight Sub-Lieutenant Gallehawk directed his men in cutting and burning of mealie fields until a passable aerodrome resulted.

Two Voisin aircraft piloted by Lieutenants Moore and Dawson flew from Mbuyuni on 30th May 1916 en route to the new airstrip at Kondoa. Poor maps caused the pilots to become lost which resulted in their landing on the Massai Steppe and their walking to Ufiome. The two Voisins which were undamaged were flown into Kondoa on 6th June 1916 at two o'clock in the afternoon as Thompson had noted.

A Voisin aircraft of No. 7 Squadron, RNAS, at Kondoa Irangi June 1916
(author)

With the improvement in observation afforded by this newly arrived aircraft, there developed a prolonged artillery duel between the Germans, the 11th Howitzer Battery and the other artillery units now positioned at Kondoa. The infantry was continually involved in skirmishes with the German askari troops and patrols, many becoming victim to enemy machine gunners and persistent sniper fire. On the 7th June, Jim Dixon wrote from the battery observation post:

> We had been told that if we heard a big row during the night it would be our infantry attacking. Went into action before and after breakfast. Fired 36 rounds on this occasion. In

action again in the afternoon, knocked off just before tea time after firing 49 rounds during the day. Our last round knocked out a machine gun.

Jim Dixon, 7th June 1916

The actions of the battery during early June are notable. With the infantry having little opportunity or advantage to dislodge the enemy by frontal attack the battle became reliant on the artillery:

At 11am Battery ranged on target with 40 lb shell. After 6th round enemy put 13 successive rounds into 200 yd radius of our guns. We replied with 2 rounds of 50lb shell and the enemy sent 3 more into us. We put 2 more rounds up and received no reply. No men were injured but only thanks to the excellent cover. Foresight of No 1 Gun bent by fragment.

Anthony Nannini, 8th June 1916

Photograph of a BL 5 inch howitzer in position at Kondoa Irangi, taken by Lt. Boyes of the 12th. Howitzer Battery.

Following the close encounter experienced, one gun was moved to a new position, some 800 yards east of the second gun, the same night. It was evident the German observers had accurately located the battery position. There were concerns about enemy spies, both in Kondoa and at the battery. Given the presence of both German immigrant and displaced Boer amongst the population these concerns were well founded.

> In action before breakfast, on and off all day. Germans shelled us both in the morning and afternoon, rotten game. Lt. Nannini complained that he had been nearly bitten by a very large black snake still at large – much to the annoyance and discomfort of the O.P. staff.
>
> Jim Dixon, 14th June 1916

Lieutenant Nannini failed to mention his encounter with the snake and recorded dutifully the day's action.

> Enemy twice fired on Battery positions, 33 rounds dropped in neighbourhood of guns, we replied with 24 rounds.
>
> Anthony Nannini, 14th June 1916

By this stage in the campaign, with limited prospect of re-supply, some calibres of German ammunition were manufactured locally; these consisted of a machined casing filled with black powder. It is presumed that some of the ammunition fired by the Germans during these artillery duels was of such provenance, for had this it been of normal manufacture, it would seem likely that the German counter-fire would have resulted in significant damage to the battery.

> A few days after I left Battery Hill the Germans shelled the top but no one was hurt... Saw an aeroplane out scouting and dropping smoke bombs over the enemy position. When the aeroplane descended the Germans put 2 shells into the aerodrome... Not much shelling during the morning... In early June two British naval guns and a crew from HMS *Pegasus*, several other guns and two aircraft arrived at Kondoa. The aircraft provided aerial observation for the

guns and also bombed the German position… Aeroplane went out and was fired at but it managed to drop some bombs. Our artillery started bombarding the enemy and later on the far-off, long-range gun of the Germans replied.

C. S. Thompson, 8th June 1916

Soldiers' graves in Kondoa Irangi Cemetery, 1916 (author)

Despite the severity and proximity of the shell fall, casualties are not apparent. Arduous physical conditions, but poor rations and the onset of disease took their toll on the men of the battery. Gunner William Yeaman died of fever on the 9th June. A sale of his effects, some days later, saw his half-pound of tobacco fetching the exorbitant sum of £3-6/8d (£3.34). Gunner Yeaman was originally buried in the cemetery established at Kondoa, he is now buried in Dar es Salaam War Cemetery.

Gunner Nicholas Williams contracted relapsing fever, a disease borne by ticks. He was evacuated from Kondoa for return to England. Gunner Williams, following treatment, recovered and remained on service in East Africa; he was mentioned in despatches for his service by General Deventer in his submission to the War Office published in the *London Gazette* of 6th August 1918.

With the improvement in the supply situation, the increase in artillery, and the greater number of troops now at Deventer's disposal von Lettow's position at Kondoa became more critical. The situation had already motivated him to join his force to direct operations personally and in so doing he hoped to prevent Deventer

The grave of Gunner William Yeaman in Dar es Salaam War Cemetery
(Fecitt)

progressing his advance to the south. At this stage in the campaign von Lettow had the advantage of the Central Railway, which, as it ran from the east to the west, he was able to use for transferring his troops from one side of his front to the other with comparative ease, providing greater force at the decisive point. It was during this period von Lettow was wounded by British artillery:

> He shelled us at long range with heavy guns of about 4 to 5 inches calibre. His observation and fire control were worthy of all respect; anyhow on June 13th his shell fell with great accuracy on our Headquarters Camp. I stopped my work, which I had commenced under cover of a grass roof, and took cover a little to one side behind a slab of rock. No sooner had the orderly officer Lt. Boell also reached the spot, than a shell burst close above us, wounded Lt. Boell in the thigh, and myself and a few other Europeans slightly. Otherwise the fire of the enemy's artillery did us hardly any material

damage, but it was a nuisance all the same to have his shell pitching into our camp every now and then.

Paul Emil von Lettow, My Reminiscences of East Africa

Sergeant Harry Downs (crouching) with B Subsection in action near Battery Hill at Kondoa Irangi (Pullen)

The 11th Howitzer Battery and its South African counterpart the 12th Howitzer Battery (formerly 4th South African (Cape) Heavy Battery) and the naval guns of the 10th Battery maintained their action against the German artillery, observation posts and redoubt positions using a mixture of shrapnel and high explosive charges. Equally active were the German gunners firing on the battery positions, the infantry entrenchments and working parties.

> Germans did a little in the morning. We went into action in the afternoon. Feel a bit off colour today. The BSM (Doyle) had a narrow escape yesterday. A piece of shell tearing through a paper he was reading. In action till 5pm.
>
> Jim Dixon, 16th June 1916

An additional threat to Deventer was the regular bombarding of Kondoa town and the military camps located there. The church at Kondoa, an improvised hospital, had been hit by shellfire in late May necessitating the hospital being moved to a tented facility outside of the town. The livestock and horse transport compounds provided

Kondoa church damaged by enemy shellfire whilst used as a military hospital (author)

favoured targets given the reliance of the army on these animals for both food and transport.

Francis Lister who, having survived drinking from the polluted water hole near Lolkisali, had arrived at Kondoa two weeks before the arrival of Orde-Brown's column. He had until recently been in the trench positions facing the enemy on the hills outside of town. Returning to Kondoa on the 18th June he had a close encounter with fire from the German guns targeting the town:

> The devil is shelling our horses. The horses stampeding like hell, all men chasing them. About 8 killed & 20 wounded. It strikes me we are all in for a bad time. 3 guns on us. Nobody hurt. Marvellous escape.
>
> Francis Lister, 18th June 1916

The 20th and 21st June saw continued activity by the combined artillery, with sixty-two rounds fired by the 11th Battery.

> Morning quiet but afternoon very lively. We did some jolly good shooting – our last shot blew up a German gun pit. The Germans shelled us – the shells whistling just over our heads and bursting in the valley below our ridge.
>
> Jim Dixon, 21st June 1916

General Deventer took the opportunity to visit the battery whilst inspecting his defensive line on the 23rd June.

> Late on in the afternoon overheard on the telephone that the enemy were retiring rapidly from the position in front of us and that the infantry (ours) are going to attack at daybreak. Quite exciting.
>
> Jim Dixon, 24th June 1916

At five o'clock in the morning on the 25th June the 2nd South African Division infantry attacked the enemy-held ridges, supported by the artillery.

> Our infantry attacked at daybreak and we were in action for about 1½ hours. After breakfast the attack continued. In action for the greater part of the morning but no enemy artillery against us. About 12 noon we captured "The Rock". Lt Nannini went over the captured position and returned with various trophies. The position was smashed up, not a single trench that we hadn't blown up, very good shooting this morning.
>
> Jim Dixon, 25th June 1916

Just after midday the enemy retired from its long-held positions in the hills around Kondoa. The following day the battery withdrew from their position and thus ended the battle known to Jack as Black Rock. Sergeant Harry Downs was awarded the Distinguished Conduct Medal for this action and Battery Sergeant Major Samuel Doyle was Mentioned in Despatches.

> June 25th – Germans retreated towards Dodoma, we left our position & went for a much wanted rest in Kondoa Irangi.
>
> Jack Drake

Thompson confirms the end of the action at Kondoa:

> Heard rumours that the Germans had retired. Our big guns fired a good deal during the morning but got no reply

A German gun position at Kondoa (author)

German trenches at Kondoa (author)

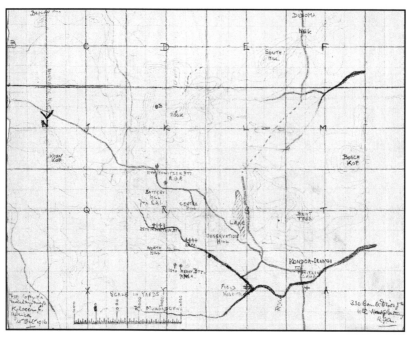

"Copied map of our position at Kondoa. Watched our pet baboon (Horace) dissect and salute a rat". Jim, 15th October, Kilosa (Chandler/ Dixon)

Sergeant Harry Downs (Pullen)

from the enemy… Heard the Germans had started to retire 4 days ago and that we had captured their observation post. The artillery kept on firing all through the day.

C. S. Thompson, 25th June 1916

The action and subsequent withdrawal of the enemy from Kondoa was an important event in the campaign. Smut's with his 1st and 3rd Divisions had commenced his Pangani offensive (the left of his planned advance) on the 23rd May, and by 24th June had reached the Lukigura River on the road south to the Central Railway. Both Smuts and Deventer were at a similar distance from the Central Railway and it seems likely that von Lettow, his force split, decided to concentrate on Smuts where he could have greater impact than on Deventer's mounted columns who could, as before, outflank his position. Von Lettow could not maintain both positions with his limited force and thus optimised his engagements to gain the most effect at what to him seemed the decisive point in Smuts' front. For some weeks the 1st and 3rd Divisions had been halted at Msiha through lack of supplies and von Lettow's robust rear-guard action.

Their onward progress could be hampered in the easily defended coastal plain and more importantly the bulk of the impassable Nguru Mountains that lay before and to the right of Smuts' force. By moving his main force to this front von Lettow could delay or halt the advance with the hope that Deventer could not continue to the railway without his own left flank becoming exposed.

> July 20th – Left Kondoa Irangi after several engagements with the enemy, reached Dodoma on the German Central railway 350 miles from Mbuyuni. Aug 5th.
>
> Jack Drake

Thompson, who was to remain at Kondoa for several more weeks, had the opportunity to visit von Lettow's now abandoned positions:

> As soon as the parade was over I started for 'Black Rock', a German position. I arrived after 1 1/2 hours brisk walk and had a good look around. Saw the observation post and the splendid lookout it held, also the well-dug trenches. Pieces of our shells were lying all over the place and there were many big holes, which they had made. Saw the first howitzer shell that was fired and didn't burst.
>
> C. S. Thompson, 31st July 1916

After a period of rest and re-supply from Mbuyuni, the battery followed Deventer south for the march on Dodoma and the Central Railway. Eight lorries, four motorcycles, three officers (including one from the A.S.C.) and forty-four ranks along with the attached drivers of the Army Service Corps completed the battery disposition. Battery stores were established at Barei on the Dodoma road with Gunners Wilby, Raleigh and Towers remaining there to form a depot guard.

> It was like coming home, to see the three faces I knew, when I landed here. Lt Nannini came up this way on Wed night, had a look at the stores to see they were all right, and went on to the battery in the morning. He has been in hospital with malaria and weighs stones less than when I saw him last.
> Charlie Rimington, 11th August 1916

So wrote Charlie Rimington on his arrival at Barei. Having recovered from his illness, Charlie had walked over 200 miles from the convalescence camp at Mbuyuni in order to rejoin the battery. He had not seen any men from the battery since becoming ill at Ufiome en route to Kondoa in May. Upon leaving Mbuyuni, Charlie had joined with a number of Afrikaners who were also rejoining Deventer after periods of illness. Together they had crossed the Massia Steppe, sleeping out each night on the trail, cooking on an open fire. Charlie and Alfred Tower had been allocated to the same tent whilst training at Hedon, his pleasure at seeing him again in this barren outpost is understandable following the rigours of his trek.

Deventer's force, that advanced south from Kondoa, was split into three main columns. The South African Horse taking the western, right flank, towards Kilamatindi, a second column destined for Kikomba and his main force of infantry heading directly south for Dodoma. A smaller mounted force, split off from the main column, headed eastwards across the mountains towards Njangalo. Deventer's strategy was to capture a significant length of the railway in one advance. This he achieved with all three columns arriving in close succession and successfully capturing their objectives. The advance was characterised by continual skirmishes with the small pockets of the enemy, the Germans hoping to eventually join with von Lettow's main force that, by this time, had begun to retire towards Morogoro on the Central Railway.

On the 26th July 1916, the 11th Howitzer Battery having travelled from Kondoa via Barei and Aneti, following Deventer's main column, arrived at Chenene Nek (Tchenene), a rocky ridge straddling the road south to Dodoma and forming a natural defensive position. More importantly, Chenene was one of only two water holes in this area. Upon their arrival the Germans had just been displaced from their positions following an assault by the infantry which was supported by the machine guns of the 4th Light Armoured Motor Battery. The infantry pursued the enemy and once more engaged with them the following day at Meia Meia. This was the location of the second important waterhole, some 15 miles south of Chenene Nek and 40 miles north of Dodoma. The 11th Howitzer Battery was called into action, but not required to fire and was frustrated by the lack of identifiable targets.

> Moved off (from Chenene) at 7:30 am, half an hour after the infantry. Had to halt about half an hour after leaving to give the infantry a little start. Had two armoured cars as escort. Had coffee at 10am then moved on with the infantry very cautiously. Nothing happened until about 4pm when we came into contact with the enemy. We took up position and laid out nearly 3 miles of wire. There was a sharp action with the infantry and armoured cars, which included a charge by the enemy on donkeys and mules of which we captured 9 white prisoners. The enemy fled and we packed up as we were not required.
>
> Jim Dixon, 27th July 1916

Historian Holger Doebold describes the action at Chenene and Meia Meia from the German perspective:

> After protecting a mountain pass during a couple of days, the 9th SK was ordered to a settlement nearby, called "Meia-Meia" to rejoin "Abteilung Linke".When reaching Meia-Meia, they spotted a line of askaris in the high grass and approached them to a distance of about 40 meters. Suddenly they realized that they stood in front of English askaris. The English opened fire and the men of the 9th SK dispersed, trying desperately to reach cover. On the right flank the survivors assembled and tried to break through the enemy lines. Those who managed to break through the askari line galloped straight into a unit of 150 mounted South African scouts. Only a few survivors escaped capture and managed

to return to the German lines. The 9th mounted SK had ceased to exist after this death ride. The few survivors joined the 8th SK.

The German forces were driven out of their positions and retired towards the Central Railway. The prisoners, which the battery assisted in capturing, were sent to Kondoa where they were soon usefully employed:

> While having our dinner we saw some German prisoners coming in on the transport. There were about 10 whites and 8 askaris. The Germans looked fat and well but a bit pale. Great excitement in camp, especially amongst our native porters. They were captured near Dodoma. Funny sight watching them breaking in bullocks for our transport.
>
> C. S. Thompson, 2nd August

The battle at Kondoa, and subsequent action at Chenene and Meia Meia, would be the last major involvement of the right section of the Hull Battery during the phase of the campaign north of the Central Railway.

> Moved off at 6am to within 12 miles of Dodoma which fell this morning, camped for the night at 6pm.
>
> Jim Dixon, 29th July 1916

After the reformation of the original Hull Heavy Battery, in early 1917, the left section would rejoin its former right section and recombine with the 158th Heavy Battery for operations to the south of the Rufigi River.

> Stuck here through lack of juice.
>
> Jim Dixon, 30th July 1916

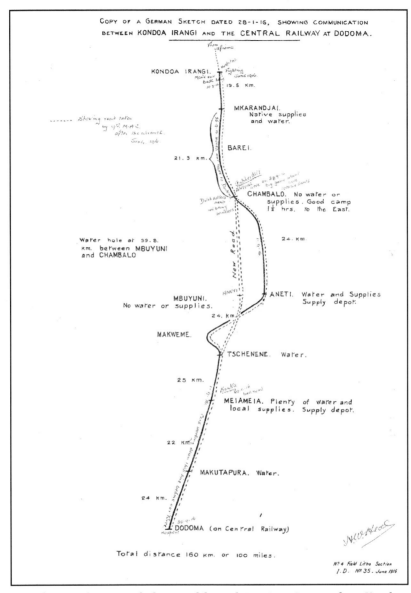

Map showing the route of advance of the 11th Howitzer Battery from Kondoa to Dodoma in July 1916 (Lewisham Local History and Archive Centre)

Chapter 10

The Capture of the Central Railway

THE 2nd Division captured the town of Dodoma on the 29th July 1916 and, in combination with the force despatched to Kilamatindi, gained a foothold along a significant stretch of the Central Railway. Deventer having secured the town and cleared the area to the immediate south of the railway of any remaining enemy forces, concentrated his troops at Nyangalo where the division awaited resupply. Before the advance eastwards along the railway towards Morogoro, and a possible juncture with Smuts' 1st and 3rd Divisions, it was necessary for the division to be resupplied. The mounted column that had been despatched westwards, towards Kilamatindi, achieved its objective. This force continued towards Iringa to assist General Northey, his advance into the German colony from Nyasaland had been halted by strong German resistance. The 11th Howitzer Battery, marched the remaining 12 miles southwards, reached Dodoma on the 6th of August.

> Arrived at Dodoma during the morning. Saw the railway and water tanks blown up by the Germans… Went into the town had a jolly good feed, steak and chips etc. (one rupee, 25 cents), went back had ration of bully and bread and returned to the eating house with Dewey and Tweddell for a second go. Out of steak and chips so had the leavings of the soup, bits of meat etc.
>
> Jim Dixon, 6th August 1916

Dodoma railway station from a contemporary postcard (McBain)

The 11th Howitzer Battery and the 10th Heavy Battery had been delayed in their advance to Dodoma from Kondoa due to a shortage of petrol for their motorised transport. Their departure from Dodoma to join the main body of the 2nd Division, concentrated around Njangalo was further delayed as the shortage continued; Deventer's priority was in maintaining the horses of his mounted troops.

> Aug. 8th – Reached Njangalo 50 miles east of Dodoma, 8 miles north of the German railway.
>
> Jack Drake

Leaving Njangalo along the narrow passage through the mountains afforded by the Mkondokwa River valley, the battery and the 2nd Division renewed the advance on the 10th August. With the mounted troops in the vanguard, the motorised and animal drawn transport followed, heading eastwards in an extended column formation, along the single-track road that soon became congested.

> Move on until 5pm over 17 miles. Germans in front. Surrounded by transport wagons, much chaos; could not get out of block until night. Moved about 8pm. 2 miles to camp. Firing all night.
>
> Anthony Nannini, 10th August 1916.

The 12th Howitzer Battery of the South African artillery, to which the 11th Howitzer Battery was tactically attached, had sent its remaining gun forward with Deventer's infantry. As the battery was drawn by mules the South African battery did not suffer the delays caused by the lack of fuel the motorised 11th Howitzer Battery were currently experiencing. Being in part manned by men from the 11th Howitzer Battery it neared Chunya (Tschunjo) in the afternoon of the 10th. The retreating German force had occupied the hills around Chunya, effectively halting the 2nd Division's advance, whilst once again preventing access to the only waterholes available in the area. The infantry supported in part by the 12th Howitzer Battery, who fired three rounds, attacked the enemy whilst the mounted troops simultaneously outflanked his positions.

> Left Njangalo our halting place at daybreak. Had our breakfast at 9am (coffee only) and encountered a snake. Had our next meal jam and coffee at 3 pm. Saw Van DeVenter as he passed us once more in his car. About 5pm the infantry ran into the enemy in some force. We were ordered to stand by but did not come into action. We watched the action from a distance of about two miles. Saw two small German guns (10 pounders supposed) firing from the hillside also our field artillery replying. Firing continued until 3am. Camped about 9pm, turned in 10:15. Very exciting afternoon. Found piece of German shell.
>
> Jim Dixon, 10th August 1916

After fighting that lasted throughout the night the Germans withdrew leaving the road to Mpwawpa clear.

> Occupied Tschunjo, no water for animals though they marched 12 miles to obtain same. 5pm marched for Mpwawpa arrived Kissakwe River 2am; animals had been 60 hours without water.
>
> F. W. Boyce, 11th August 1916

The vanguard of the 2nd Division, with continued skirmishes with the isolated detachments of Germans, reached Mpwawpa, exhausted by their rapid advance, on the 12th August. The remnants of the division, including the 11th Howitzer Battery, who were once more awaiting petrol supplies, followed shortly afterwards.

14th – Reached Mpwapwa.

Jack Drake

The remainder of the 11th Howitzer Battery and the 10th Battery would arrive at Mpwapwa by the 18th August but not before repairs had been affected to their lorries, the damage caused by the appalling road conditions that had also prevented the armoured cars of the No. 4 Light Armoured Motor Battery from joining the fight at Tschunjo.

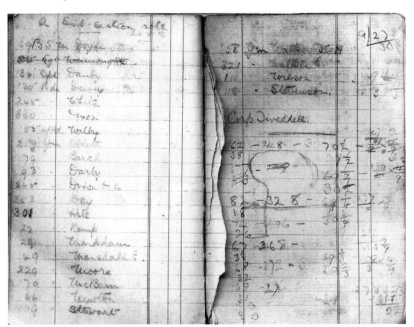

Personnel of A Subsection on the 26th August 1916, Mpwapua Chandler/ Dixon)

On the 14th, after being resupplied, the mounted columns of the South African Horse left Mpwapwa in pursuit of the enemy now retreating eastwards along the railway in the river valley. Highly mobile, the mounted troops raced ahead of the division: the lighter guns of the South African Field Artillery and the Indian Mountain batteries supported them. Particularly hard fighting was met with in the narrows of the valley just west of Kideta. The 12th South African Howitzer Battery eventually reached the forward positions and came into action. The battery fired thirty rounds in an effort to quell the German artillery battery that was ranging against Deventer's troops; two of the rounds fired detonated within 10 yards of the enemy gun. With support now offered by the infantry, who had joined with the mounted units, the German forces abandoned their positions and Kideta fell on the 15th August. Twenty-one rounds were fired by the 12th Howitzer Battery on the 20th at Ssagara where further resistance was met, closely followed on the 22nd by the capture of the town of Kilossa.

29th – Left (Mpwapwa)
30th – Reached Kideta station

Jack Drake

Kideta station on the Central Railway east of Dodoma (McBain)

Alongside the gains made by the 2nd Division, a combined force detached from Smuts' 1st and 3rd Divisions, who had recently driven the German forces from the coastal plain and Nguru Mountains, marched on Morogoro to the east of Kilossa. The town fell to the allied forces on the 26th August and Smuts' mounted troops made contact with those of Deventer's that had advanced from the west.

Moved off 7am. Passed through several fine fertile valleys. Saw vultures waiting on the ground near a horse for the latter to die. Arrived at Kilossa 3.30pm.

Jim Dixon, 1st September 1916

Deventer, in his despatch to the War Office, describes the actions of his division during the advance along the Central Railway:

The railway from Kideta to Kilossa for a distance of twenty five miles follows a narrow defile cut through the Usugara Mountains by the Mkondokwa River; every yard of advance was stubbornly resisted by the enemy. Of the more important engagements those on the 19th at Msagara and on the 21st before Kilossa should be mentioned. In all the actions of this advance the fighting consisted of the enemy receiving our advance guard with one or several ambushes, then falling back on a well prepared position, and retiring from that on to further well selected ambush places and positions, All the time our less advanced troops were subjected to vigorous shelling by means of long range naval guns.

At Kilossa, with the Central Railway now effectively in the hands of Smuts' forces, the 11th Howitzer Battery became part of the force reserve; and, as a unit, would not take direct part in further operations in this area.

Sept. 1st – Kilossa, German railway in possession of the British forces, camped on rubber plantation, built huts out of straw or grass, had several visits from lions & had unpleasant encounter with a puff adder.

Jack Drake

In later years Jack elaborated on this event.

We had made some grass huts and a snake had got in through the wall of the hut at the head of my bed. I frightened it off but by that time the whole camp was awake. A Sgt.-Maj. Doyle came out and shot the snake, which I think was a puff adder, with his rifle. We also had some bullocks, which we used to keep in a stockade. One-night lions got in. We had to keep fires burning all night to keep them away. When the lions got in the Sgt.-Major went out with his gun and later came back and said he had fired at random.

Jack and his encounter with the snake had obviously caused a bit of a commotion in the camp.

In the middle of the night one of our coves woke up and discovered a six-foot snake on his chest. The snake required 5 shots to dispatch it. Had boiled eggs for tea – fine.

Jim Dixon, 30th Oct 1916

With Smuts' initial objectives of the campaign achieved, and with remaining operations executed by the mounted troops and infantry, the battery was stood down from operations and remained in camp at Kilossa throughout October.

Gunner John McBain (McBain)

A picture of a battery despatch motorcycle and pet monkey, Katdora, Ruaha District, December 1916 (McBain)

In an effort by the allies to bolster the Tsar's war effort on the eastern front, a large number of 4.5- and 5-inch howitzers had been sent to Russia, reducing the number of weapons available in

England for training purposes. In consequence, one howitzer from the battery was despatched to Dar es Salaam for return by ship to England. Similarly, three more howitzers from the 38th Brigade were repatriated; one from the 13th Howitzer Battery (former left section 11th (Hull) Heavy Battery) and one from each section of the 14th Howitzer Battery (formerly 158th (Hull) Heavy Battery). The guns returned from the 38th Brigade to England would help fulfil this need.

On the 13th November, at Kilossa, a medical parade was called. Of those men that remained with the battery, and those already in hospital, thirty-one of the remaining men were declared medically unfit for further service in East Africa. Those selected were entrained to Dar es Salaam for onward sailing to South Africa to receive hospital treatment there; some were repatriated directly to England. Jack remained at Kilossa.

> We do no parades now except loading parade at 6pm (5 rounds in the rifle magazine) and we do no work at all. There are only 21 of us left now – all ranks – of the 80 men and 5 officers. The rest of them are either at Dar es Salaam or being sent there, whacked by fever or blackwater. I was lucky to get that 400 miles constitutional before joining the battery. The camp is awfully desolate now, two or three living in bandas, grass huts, which accommodate 8 men.
>
> Charlie Rimington, 18th November 1916

On the 5th November the 11th Howitzer Battery, at Kilossa, was amalgamated with the 12th Howitzer Battery from South Africa. It had been tactically linked to the 12th Battery since its arrival at Kondoa in June. By December the 12th Battery was reduced through illness to two non-commissioned officers and two men. With only two howitzers remaining between the two batteries the amalgamation seemed logical.

> Nov. 25th – Left Kilosa for Dodoma. 150 miles by road.
>
> Jack Drake

Charlie Rimington, following his long trek from Mbuyuni, had eventually rejoined the battery at Kilossa. On the 13th September the remnant of the battery retraced their route back to Dodoma from Kilossa.

> The old game! Shovels, dragropes and jacks to get the cars over bad places. We are quite a pleasant little party with just enough natives with us to pull the cars out when we stick and we have a ripping fellow for an officer. It is grand to be sleeping under the stars again and to need an overcoat as well as a blanket at night. We have come a good height since leaving Killossa and it is appreciably cooler.
>
> Charlie Rimington, 28th November 1916

Sickness still affected those who remained with the battery. Upon the battery moving to Dodoma, as at Kilindini, George Ablett was left behind at Kilossa hospital suffering from malaria. On this occasion he would not rejoin the battery but was sent to Dar es Salaam and then onward to Cape Town for treatment.

> Dec. 1st – Reached Dodoma camped in the bush rigged up shelters with tarpaulins, rainy season commenced.
>
> Jack Drake

A programme of drill, gun maintenance and retraining in telephony and signalling occupied their first weeks at Dodoma. Being relatively inactive with respect to military operations the battery signallers were employed in helping to establish the telegraph system along the Central Railway that had recently been captured. Jack related that, in order to prevent giraffes becoming entangled, the telegraph wires had to be erected upon poles of sufficient height.

During their retreat from the Central Railway, the Germans had taken every opportunity to deny its future use by Smuts' army. The many bridges so skilfully constructed by the Germans during peacetime were destroyed with explosives; the engines and rolling stock were driven into the ravines below. Smuts had a major task before him to restore the railway to his beneficial use.

> They put an explosive charge into the cylinders of all their big engines and left us to get new cylinders cast in Scotland. They blew out the grease boxes of the trucks; but their

A motorcycle being carried across the Ruaha River. From Kilossa despatch riders maintained communication with General Northey's force advancing from the south-west (McBain)

performance, on the whole, was amateurish. For they blew up, with dynamite, the masonry of many bridges and contented themselves that the girders lay in the river below. But this was child's play to our Sappers and Miners. With hand jacks they lifted the girders and piled up sleepers, one by one beneath, until the girder was lifted to rail level again. Now any engineer can tell you that the only way to destroy a bridge is to cut the girder.

Robert Dolbey

Engineers demolish the remains of the destroyed bridge near Kahe (author)

Much of the rehabilitation work on the railway and bridges was carried out by the resourceful engineering companies of the Indian Army. The engines and rolling stock required other skills. Some fifteen years previously Bombardier Frank Ledran had served his apprenticeship in Hull as a boilermaker and had pursued this occupation until the outbreak of hostilities and his enlisting into the army. With the obvious need for such skills, Frank was posted away from the battery to the East African Railway Corps, to assist in the restoration of the steam locomotives. Despite the efforts of the enemy the railway, with the aid of converted road vehicles, was operational to some degree within months of its capture. The first steam train arrived at Kilossa on 9th December 1916. Frank Ledran was mentioned in despatches for his work on the railways, this was posted in the *London Gazette* of 6th August 1918.

A REO truck converted to run on the Central Railway after the destruction of locomotives by the retreating German forces. Kilossa, October 1916 (McBain)

With the onset of the rainy season came the increase in malaria and soon hospital admissions became regular features in the lives of the static troops.

Dec. 11th – First attack of Malaria fever admitted to Hospital.

Jack Drake

A true indication of the state of the battery can be gleaned from the following extract from Charlie's letters, noting Jack and a comrade being admitted to hospital:

> We have only 13 NCO's and men left and two gunners went to hospital this morning. We are expecting reinforcements up from Dar Es Salaam shortly to make a <u>one</u>! gun battery of what remains of us and the 12th Howitzers. They were originally a two gun battery but they have only two NCO's, two men and three officers left.
>
> Charlie Rimington, 11th December 1916

At Dodoma, the battery prepared for Christmas. For Jack it was spent in hospital, but for the remaining men they enjoyed a festive time and enjoyed what would seem to have been a sumptuous feast given the circumstances.

> Meat pies and coffee for breakfast. They had lovely short crusts and the meat was finely minced. I had to call a halt when I got ¾ of one down. Simply couldn't eat any more as I would have liked to do so… For lunch roast chicken, biscuits and cheese, roast beef and beans. For dinner we are having another chicken, plum pudding (the real article sent out by a comfort fund) and a ton of fruit and three eggs on toast. The chickens are our own as well as some of the other items… There are some more Xmas comforts which came in this morning, just a year and two days late, as they are marked for 1915!…The officers gave so much money to be deducted off the articles we had ordered from Dar es Salaam and it just ran round to R3.20.
>
> Charlie Rimington, 25th December 1916

At Dodoma, with many different army units stationed there, and few other forms of entertainment available, sporting competitions were organised between the different groups. Gymkhanas, football matches, cricket and, the old army favourite, tug of war were all popular and became regular features of their stay there. A variety of card games filled the long hours of the day, the men became practiced players, especially of euchre. On one occasion when the battery's spirits were at low ebb, Jack suggested that they play cricket,

Christmas cards made from bark and brown paper by Charlie during his time at Kilossa (Rimington)

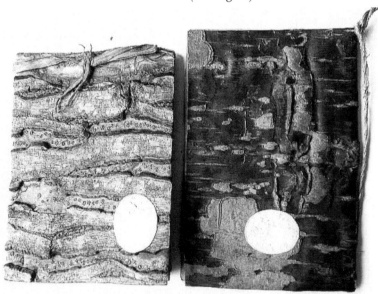

to which they readily agreed. Not being a sportsman himself and as sufficient players had volunteered, Jack went for a walk to explore a nhulla near to the camp. After a little while he rested to smoke his pipe, but his reverie was soon interrupted, first by the smell and then by the arrival of a lion near to where he sat. Jack, watched by the lion and knowing that running would be futile, slowly retraced his route back towards the camp where upon his arrival the cricket match was still underway. Ultimately, the morale of the battery, not unlike other soldiers, relied very much on creature comforts and the supply of food:

> Three of us have beds made of branches, raised about 18 inches from the floor, in a tent which reckons to hold 8, so we have plenty of room, but we have arranged the lads so they occupy nearly the whole of the tent. The idea is so they cannot put anyone else in with us without a lot of trouble and to make them put another tent up if more men come… We also have a big tarpaulin made into a tent for a cookhouse dining room, about 120 yards away. We have a Mohammedan called Ali who cooks for us, washes our clothes etc. We have to cook our own bacon for breakfast, as it would defile him. I have rigged up a field telephone in the tent and one in the cookhouse so when meals are ready, he just calls us up on the telephone and if it is about 12 or 5 o'clock we know he is telling us that the meal is ready, and if we hear the word "chaii" we know he has just made tea. At other times we have to listen closely to be able to catch the drift of 75% of what he says. I think he credits us with an extensive knowledge of Swahili.
>
> Charlie Rimington, 25th December 1916

Their lack of mobility and removal from normal army discipline allowed for a pastoral existence to develop within the camp. Livestock was acquired and a stray dog was adopted and, being a Dachshund, it was unsurprisingly given the name of Fritz.

> The hens are laying splendidly now, and are a source of income. We swap them for some fancy thing or other if we do not feel on egg form.
>
> Charlie Rimington, 31st January 1917

Excepting for the regular attacks of malaria that the men from the battery suffered, life at Dodoma was not altogether uncomfortable,

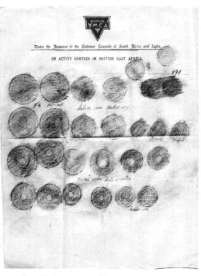

Bombardier Charlie Rimington (Rimington)

Charlie's coin collection. With the withdrawal of General von Lettow's forces from most of the territory the German coinage became worthless (Rimington)

but it became monotonous. Jack returned to the camp from hospital in the first days of the New Year. Further south, the 13th Howitzer Battery spent its Christmas in less comfortable straits on the rain soaked front line on the north bank of the Mgeta River near Duthumi.

In this sketch by Charlie, Ali prepares a meal whilst the signallers play cards and smoke pipes in their banda. Dodoma, December 1916 (Rimington)

Chapter 11

The 13th Howitzer Battery R.G.A.

IN contrast to the 11th Howitzer Battery, that had left Mbuyuni to meet the enemy occupying entrenched positions at Kondoa; the 13th Howitzer Battery became engaged in a long and frustrating pursuit of von Lettow's forces, who used every conceivable tactic and opportunity to strike at his enemy. General Smuts' Pangani offensive had commenced on the 23rd of May but the renamed left section of the 11th Hull Heavy Battery, commanded by Captain Floyd and 2nd Lieutenant Walter Maslin, did not leave Mbuyuni until the second week of June. The battery was attached to General Smuts' 3rd Division that was commanded by the recently arrived South African, Brigadier General C. J. Brits.

Two of the battery's FWD lorries towed the howitzers, Captain Floyd noting, with some despair, that the lorries 'have to be started down hills'. The battery section and its ammunition column, escorted by the 7th South African Horse, set out for Makanja, on the Pangani River, through the Ngulu gap between the north and south Pare Mountains.

> We left M'buyuni at 8.00am. and set off in a south-easterly direction, leaving Moshi on our right and skirting the shores of Lake Jipe on our left. After about 20 miles, we came to a plain which we have to cross. It is nothing but sand. There is not a tree, shrub, or blade of grass to be seen. It is easy to

believe that this plain is a swamp for nine months of the year. A more desolate place I have never seen up to now. After a good deal of hauling, we reach the further side where our OC decides to outspan for the night. Our first job is to search for water. After our tins are filled, we sit down for our meal of bully beef and biscuits. These biscuits are 'Hardman's', and I can truthfully say that they are most appropriately named.

Joseph Dan Fewster, 17th June 1916

The ammunition column, assembled to accompany the battery, comprised nine carts and eighteen oxen, under the charge of one non-commissioned officer and seven men from the 134th Cornwall Battery R.G.A.. To manage the oxen, six Indian and three Cape boy drivers joined the section from Himo River camp. Sixty rounds of ammunition for each of the two guns and sufficient supplies to cater for the battery for fourteen days were loaded aboard the transport; surplus kit was sent back to Maktau along the road to Voi. Five Napier cars, four of which were used by the ammunition column, provided additional transport. Within a short time of travelling on the rough terrain, problems developed with the steering rods on the cars, and two of which were rendered unserviceable.

> We are away this morning and strike some very difficult roads. Some parts, having a gradient of 1 in 4, make it extremely hard for us. We have to unhook the guns, pull up the FWD lorries, then go back and haul up the guns. The same treatment for the Napier cars, which carry our ammunition, stores, etc. In the evening we reach Makanga where we outspan by the roadside, near to a river.

Joseph Dan Fewster, 19th June 1916

Leaving Makanja, the battery met with few incidents as it followed the Pangani River south-easterly along the road recently upgraded by the Pioneer companies of the Indian Army. Smuts' 1st Division had advanced along this route several weeks earlier, it had met with hard fighting and many ambushes by the Germans who had used the impasse caused by the rainy season to establish carefully prepared positions. Roads and tracks, such that existed, had been mined with improvised charges, and any bridges had been destroyed, all of which had to be rebuilt by Smuts before wheeled traffic could advance. The steep slopes of the Pare and Usumbara mountains, that parallel the left bank of the river to the north east, provided ideal refuge for German snipers and concealed machine gun positions which could overlook the ground across which Smuts must advance. It was not uncommon for the Germans to fell trees across the roads or create other impediments in order to delay the progress of Smuts' troops. The likelihood of the Germans having planted a booby trap at such locations consumed valuable time. An additional reason for caution was the German snipers and possibly machine guns that added further risk to such situations.

> The retreat of the Germans is very rapid. We are advancing at anything from 12 to 20 miles per day but we never get a 'slap' at them, except running rear-guard actions, in which artillery is not required.
>
> Joseph Dan Fewster, 25th June 1916.

The battery made good progress where the roads had been newly constructed by the army; Floyd describing them as 'good' or 'excellent'. The steep approaches near to the Pare Mountains resulted in the battery spending several days manhandling the trucks uphill, with the reverse situation on the downward journey, the difficulty compounded by the heavy loads on board. The battery travelled some days to the rear of the mounted and infantry units which precluded their involvement in the arduous task of cutting new roads through the bush. This task, which was generally undertaken by units from the Indian Army, quickly found casualties from exhaustion and disease. The pace of Smuts' advance was considerable despite the continual skirmishes and set fights with the Germans. Smuts' troops had advanced through semi virgin bush and had rapidly covered over 200 miles in a few weeks. This success, without the development of the necessary infrastructure to support such a large army, prevented the delivery of essential rations and supplies. Mombasa, hundreds of miles to the rear, remained the only seaport available to the allies; the logistical arrangements were incapable of maintaining the army beyond the established road and rail systems.

At a corner where the Pangani swirls in towards the railway, we found another surprise: a fine trestle bridge, unfinished, which the Germans had recently been building: why, it was difficult to imagine, unless they had thought it would open a shorter way to the Mombo trolley line, that very effective piece of war-engineering of which we had heard so much but knew so little. Still, it was a beautiful bridge, the white planks shining in the sun, and above and below two reaches of smooth, swift water. By the time that it reaches 'German Bridge,' the Pangani is a fine stream.

Francis Brett Young

After passing the German Bridge that crossed the Pangani near the narrow passage between river and the steep sides of the Pare Mountains, the battery reach Buiko that had recently been captured by the 1st Division.

The location of the German Bridge on the Pangani River (author)

We were told that it was difficulties of supply which kept us so long in Buiko; but I doubt if even such a thruster as Smuts could have got more out of the men who thankfully rested there, or the beasts, who now began to die in great numbers. At first we made a pyre on which they were consumed; but our sweepers were lazy with their fuel, and the heaps of charred flesh became, in the end, so noisome, that we had the carcasses dragged into the bush, a mile or more from the camp, to be dealt with by the hyenas and the vultures. All day long we could see little clouds of these obscene birds hanging in the sky. It seemed as though half the eagles of Africa had descended on us, and, in the dead of night, we heard the lions, who had stolen down from the hills.

Francis Brett Young

At Buiko the battery turned south towards Luchomo where they established camp.

We are staying here until our supplies catch up to us. Our rations are not good so far as quantity and variety goes. Our drink is coffee or water and our food is biscuits, bully beef (eight men to a 12oz. tin), with a cup of mealy meal and an occasional ration of fresh meat, which is so hard and tough that one cannot eat it. No sugar, tea, milk, butter, bread or bacon.

Joseph Dan Fewster, 27th June 1916

Due to the difficulties in resupply Smut's whole force was reduced to surviving on one quarter of the normal rations, if and when they could be brought forwards by the motor transport and ox carts. The poor roads and increasing incidence of malaria badly affected the transport arrangements, compounded by a shortage of drivers and many broken vehicles. Under these circumstances it would take time to accumulate sufficient supplies to continue the advance.

We leave Luchomo this morning and arrive at M'bagui, a distance of 22 miles. For some time now, one half of the battery has marched one day, while the other half has ridden.

Today, I have had the dismounted party. Now today's march has been a particularly trying one. The whole column has moved along the same path. This consisted of field batteries with mules, batteries with oxen, our battery with mechanical transport, thousands of Boer mounted infantry and I believe we were the only white troops 'padding the hoof'. The thermometer registered 105 degrees in the shade before we left at 8.00am. What it would be at noon, I do not know. We had full equipment with 50 rounds of ammunition, two days rations, iron rations and one pint of water.

Joseph Dan Fewster, 5th July 1916

By July the 6th the battery had reached the town of Handeni which had recently been captured by the 1st Division.

Found Handeni situated in the best country we had passed through. Lots of rubber

Alec Robertson, July 6th 1916

The old German boma at Handeni (author)

Handeni, was one the district German administrative and military outposts and the terminus of the narrow gauge railway which ran south from Mombo, a village on the Usumbara Railway. Whilst Smuts awaited the spring rains to abate, the Germans had established two light railway lines using materials recovered from the sisal plantations in the area. Used in conjunction, these two lines enabled von Lettow to rapidly move his men between the Pangani front and the actions against Deventer at Kondoa, by their connection with the Central Railway. Von Lettow's forces, in their retreat, had destroyed this track, and in so doing denied Smuts any benefit from its future use without him rebuilding the line completely, which he did.

> Left Handeni about noon and had gone about a mile when the FWD leading overturned down a bank at the side of the road. About 7 men in the lorry. Sergt. Fewster hurt a little. Had the lorry righted in less than two hours. Arrived Mjimbiwi.
>
> Alec Robertson, July 7th 1916

Passing through Kangata and south towards the towering Nguru Mountains the battery halted at Lukiguri River and made camp. The supply situation had not improved, causing Smuts to call a halt once more and allow both the railway and the trolley line from Mombo to be restored to use. The pace of Smut's advance not only made supply a problem but it had severely tired his troops. The 13th Howitzer Battery, having marched with little respite, was not immune to its effect. Lukiguri Bridge had been captured by General Sheppard's troops following a fierce battle, which involving the first use of Lord Willoughby's armoured cars and a bayonet charge by the 25th Battalion Royal Fusiliers; on this rare occasion the Germans were defeated. Some eight miles in advance of the Lukiguri, where adequate water supplies were available, Smuts concentrated his troops at the village of Msiha in what would become known as Shell Camp. General Sheppard's infantry brigade, part of the 1st Division that joined the camp at Msiha included the 200 remaining troops of the 25th Battalion Royal Fusiliers and the remnant machine gun sections of the 2nd Battalion Loyal North Lancashire

Regiment; the mounted infantry company had been disbanded at Lukigura following the action there. The main body of the latter unit, following severe casualties from disease, had left German East Africa in May 1916 for recuperation in South Africa.

Shell Camp was so named following the apparent ease with which the Germans could target it with its artillery. The German guns, concealed in the overbearing Nguru Mountains, were a frustration. The range and elevation limitations of Smuts' own artillery made it impossible to retaliate effectively. The choice of Msiha by Smuts proved to be very costly in casualties from both disease and enemy action.

> Still at Lukiguri. Heard German shelling next camp in the evening. Saw flashes and reckoned distance 13 to 14 miles. Our A.S.C MT were in that camp and had some narrow escapes.
>
> Alec Robertson, July 10th 1916

The Nguru Mountains viewed from Kanga (author)

The battery remained in Lukiguri camp until 5th August 1916, where, during this rest period, they were joined by the Cornwall battery. The Territorial Force 134th (Cornwall) Heavy Battery R.G.A. had left Charlton Park whilst the Hull battery underwent training there. They had embarked for East Africa on 26th December 1915, and arrived in Mombasa on 1st February 1916. It was armed with four, 5.4 inch, breech-loading howitzers that had been supplied from India; for which service the weapon had been specifically designed. In earlier operations the Cornwall battery was in action during the Kilimanjaro offensive, most notably at Salaita Hill and at Lateama Nek. It had more recently followed the advance along the Pangani with Smuts' 1st Division.

General Brits mounted brigade, part of the 3rd Division, advanced from Lukiguri into the Nguru Mountains.

> The order to advance has come at last. We have to join up with Britz's column in a flanking movement around Shell Camp. Everybody is excited and delighted thinking our chance for action has really come at last. We left our camp at 12:30 pm and proceeded to Likiguri Bridge camp where we joined the column. A lot of the 1st Div. were with the 3rd Div. We took up our place and started, but had not gone far when the difficulties started. The road was terribly rough. In fact it was nothing but a mere track cleared by the pioneers through the forest and bush, up and down terrific hills and dry river beds etc. Numerous tree stumps stuck up all along the track making it very bad for the motor lorries. By sunset we were still a long way from the place where we were to camp.
>
> After dark set in travelling became even more difficult and was in fact well nigh impossible. We were not allowed to use any lights as the Germans would have seen them from the surrounding hills. But we still pushed on and were still at it at midnight and several miles to go. Eventually we arrived in camp just after 3 am of the 6th having worked hard on the drag ropes for 13 solid hours, just pulling one lorry up a hill and then back for the next one and so on time and time again, until all the men were dead beat. We had nothing to eat or drink (except the water in our water – bottles and that did not last long) from 11 am until we stopped at 3 am, 16

hours. As soon as we arrived we received orders that we had to move on at 6:30am in the morning.

Alec Robertson, August 6th 1916

Several more hard days followed with little headway being made before it was recognised that for the wheeled transport of the 3rd Division the route was impassable. The 13th Howitzer Battery and other wheeled units returned to Lukiguri Bridge to await further orders. When the general advance resumed, the battery joined the main column that followed the road south from Lukiguri, passing through Kanga and was the main route towards Morogoro on the Central Railway.

Upon reaching a branch of the Wami River at Turiana, it was found that the Germans had destroyed the bridge that traversed the fast flowing stream. Having made a camp there, the battery assisted in the construction of a new crossing that, upon completion several days later, allowed their progress to be resumed.

We have been travelling all night (from Turiani) but have made very little progress owing to the road being so congested. The infantry, of course, did not wait for the bridge but waded across at a ford. This leaves the road full up with vehicular traffic... About noon, we get orders to travel ahead with all speed, as a battle is taking place some 15 miles ahead of us. Everybody has to stand to one side while we get through. The road is pretty good, so we soon make headway.

Joseph Dan Fewster, 17th August 1916

Had breakfast and set off again. Got on alot better in the day-light. We heard there was heavy fighting ahead on the banks of the Wami River.

Alec Robertson, August 17th 1916

Sheppard's infantry had been engaged with the enemy for fifty hours before the 13th Howitzer Battery arrived at the Wami River. The Germans and their native askari troops had prepared strong positions in the reed beds and dense bush of the opposing bank. Upon arrival, the battery was ordered into action and soon opened fire with six rounds at a range of 2,500 yards. The askari native troops, who made up the German companies, experiencing their first encounter with heavy artillery fire, fled from their positions in panic. The attack by Sheppard's infantry proved successful and was greatly assisted by the barrage provided by the battery, which, according to intelligence reports, caused 'confusion and panic' amongst the enemy.

> 11:00 Got orders to push on as fast as possible which of course we are only too glad to do. After noon we were able to cover the ground in good style. The last few miles before reaching the firing line we did in record time and were cheered all along by various units we passed. When about 1½ miles from the river we came into action, about 3:0 pm. Only fired 6 shots but did good work and put the wind up the blacks. Everyone was of the opinion that we shifted the enemy as no shots were fired from the opposite bank after our third round and the infantry on our side could hear the blacks of the Germans yelling. They don't like Liddite and didn't expect it.
>
> Alec Robertson, August 17th 1916

Dan Fewster, section sergeant of the 13th Howitzer Battery describes the battery's involvement in this affair of the 17th August 1916.

> We now have abundant evidence of recent fighting, because dead askaris (native soldiers) are laid all the way along the roadside. It is not a pleasing sight to see dead bodies a day or two after death in this climate. The stench is something that will cling for days. At 2.45pm. we halt and prepare for action. Apparently this is interesting work to some ASC men who draw around to look on, but two of them stop a couple of bullets, so the others take cover pretty smartly under some cars near at hand. We are now 'ready for action' so go further ahead to take up our position. It is rather 'warm' here, for bullets are flying all around from machine guns. There is a South African field battery somewhere on our left which has come by another route, and what with artillery, machine gun and rifle fire, the din is pretty heavy. Our chaps are in high glee, because now we are going to give them a bit of

The present bridge at Turiana (author)

'hot stuff' to hold. We take up our position in the midst of some elephant grass. This grass grows to a height of 10 or 12 feet. We are also camouflaged with grass tucked into our sun helmets. We are very short handed so some of our A.S.C. drivers volunteer to run out our wire to the battery commander's post and to the Forward Observing Officer, a very creditable offer, which is gladly accepted. At last we 'open out' and give the enemy his first taste of Lyddite. A startling thing happens. After the first round, there is no reply from the enemy position. After six rounds we get 'cease firing'. The range has been very short. Our elevation was only between 12 and 13 degrees or about 800 yards range. We stand by until dark, when we limber up and pull onto the roadside. It is midnight by the time we find our telephone wire and reel it in. We have a meal of the usual bully and biscuits and turn in under our guns.

Joseph Dan Fewster, 17th August 1916

Took up positions as orderd but enemy had evacuated the river during the night and were in hasty retreat towards Morogoro. Went into camp in village of Dakawa.

Alec Robertson, August 17th 1916

Thus the battle of Wami River ended, the German forces withdrawing. Smuts now clear of the confined corridor alongside the Nguru Mountains and the coast marched across the flat plains towards Morogoro. The prospect of Smut's now making contact with those of Deventer's 2nd Division, approaching from the west along the Central Railway, was now realised when a combined force from both divisions captured Kilossa on the 26th August 1916.

Whilst von Lettow retired southwards towards Morogoro, the Royal Navy landed troops at Bagamayo, who joined with detachments from Smuts' forces, before capturing Dar es Salaam. This important seaport was found to be generally undefended, the Germans surrendered readily to the allied forces. The Royal Navy had played a significant part in achieving this surrender, given their capability for shelling the town should resistance have become apparent. The Germans had, however, made an orderly withdrawal under cover of a number of diversionary ploys. The Navy though, in forcing a decision, had succeeded in destroying the town's brewery by shellfire, making them very unpopular with the occupying army.

Left camp 7 am followed by Cornwall Battery. Halted at 8:15 am and parked on side of road. Had to fight big bush fire. Cornwalls nearly lost a lorry. Saw two rhionoceros that had just been shot. Tried to get a toe but had to leave it on account of the fire. Went on again about 1 pm. Camped 6 pm.

Alec Robertson, August 24th 1916

Despite Smuts' expectation that von Lettow would put up a fierce last stand at Morogoro, von Lettow did not; his forces, as on almost every previous occasion, drifted in dribs and drabs southwards into the densely forested Uluguru Mountains and eventually reached the Mgeta River, closely pursued by the South African mounted troops.

> We have a day's rest. Yesterday the enemy evacuated Morogoro and our troops took possession.
>
> Joseph Dan Fewster, 28th August 1916

> Enter Morogoro which we thought a well laid out town for GEA. Parts very pretty at foot of big range of mountains. German women still in the town. First white women we have seen since June.
>
> Alec Robertson, August 29th 1916

Thus, with the capture of Morogoro, both the right and left subsections of the old 11th (Hull) Heavy Battery R.G.A. had reached the Central Railway within a few days of each other. The right remained in camp at Kilossa, the left subsection went into camp at Morogoro.

Chapter 12

Battery Operations on the Mgeta and Rufigi Rivers

T HE German force that had fought Deventer at Kilossa had, along with those displaced by Smuts' at Morogoro, escaped to the south into the Uluguru Mountains to the south. Despite the capture of a large number of the von Lettow's troops, they remained an effective fighting force and still numbered roughly one hundred Europeans and over 7,000 askari troops. The Germans, at this time, retained four of the original ten Konigsberg guns, sixteen smaller field guns and seventy-three machine guns.

It is perhaps telling of Smut's confidence, that from August he had made requests to von Lettow to surrender, thinking that in capturing the major part of the German colony von Lettow would consider his position untenable. Von Lettow's response to this proposal was contradictory to Smuts' expectation, von Lettow saying of Smuts that… he had 'reached the end of his resources'. This comment by von Lettow was somewhat optimistic, considering that von Lettow himself had minimal resources upon which to draw, but that Smuts, due to his success to date, was fully supported by Britain. Smuts, however, had to make greater effort than did von Lettow, with respect to material supply and logistics, to achieve his objective.

Smuts' impatience had driven his forces hard in his pursuit of von Lettow, commencing his offensive operation at the height of the rainy season in the spring of 1916, when malaria and other disease abounded; he had outpaced his supply capability which had badly affected his own force, whilst the enemy suffered little impediment. The loss of transport animals and manpower was unsustainable for continuing operations into the fevered swamps of the Mgeta and Rufigi river systems, where von Lettow's force had now established itself.

Paying little regard to the condition of his troops, and by using the few mounted troops that remained, Smuts continued the pursuit through the Uluguru Mountains, skirmishing with rear guards of von Lettow's troops, eventually reaching the Mgeta River, a tributary of the Rufigi. Upon reaching the river, the German forces were found to have formed a defensive line along the southern bank; Smuts established his own line opposing them.

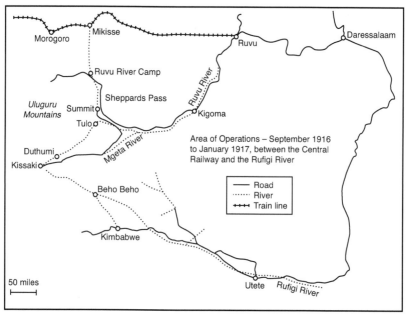

Map showing operations on the Mgeta and Rufigi Rivers

Following its capture, Dar es Salaam was rapidly brought into service as the main supply port which, by use of the Central Railway, reduced the line of communication by hundreds of miles. In addition, many European and South African troops were in the process of being repatriated due to illness. Their replacements were from the colonies of Nigeria, the Gold Coast and additional battalions of the Kings African Rifle that had undergone a massive expansion of numbers, in preparation for this occurrence. The effects of the climate, disease and the logistical problems had culminated in a decision by Smuts, encouraged by Louis Botha his friend, to replace European troops with native troops. Some army units that comprised European troops were disbanded at this time, notably Brigadier General Brits' 3rd South African Division.

General Brits says farewell to his troops at Morogoro (author)

The 13th Howitzer Battery, previously attached to General Brits' 3rd Division, was now mobilised to support Brigadier General Sheppard's 2nd Infantry Brigade, part of the 1st Division, who along with the combined remnants of the South African mounted units had advanced towards the Mgeta River through the Uluguru Mountains. Leaving Morogoro on the 6th September 1916, the battery half section made good progress and reached the Ruvu River, a northern tributary of the Mgeta.

> Sept 6th. Leave Morogoro to join up with the 1st Div. which is now well South of the railway. First portion of the road very bad and a solid tyre of the FWD was torn right off and also a spring broken. Later road very good, best so far in all our travels. Numerous bends and very easy gradients. We learn afterwards that the Germans intended it for a railway...
> Reached Ruvu River after passing through most beautiful scenery. Dense forest where ferns grow such as I have never seen before.
> Alec Robertson, September 7th 1916

The Uluguru Mountains had no road system that could be used by Smut's army. To this effect the engineering companies of the Indian army were engaged blasting a new road, Sheppard's Pass,

The crossing and camp at Ruvu River on the route south from Morogoro to the Mgeta River (IWM Q15586)

into the face of the mountain side some miles ahead of Ruvu Camp. Until the completion of this road it was impossible for wheeled traffic to advance to the Mgeta.

> Camp on a bend in the river. Surrounded by hig hills on every side, forming quite a basin with a sandy bottom which is only ½ mile wide and 1 mile long. The only opening in the hills around is where the river flows in and out. Here we are told we will have to stay for some time waiting for the road to blasted clear of huge rocks with which the Germans blocked the road when they retired. In some places they have blasted great boulders from the hill side and these as they came down carried everything before them and a large slice of the road. The Germans are reported to be making for the Ruffigi some 100 miles from here.
>
> Alec Robertson, September 8th 1916

Whilst the road was still under construction, the battery remained at the river crossing for several weeks awaiting its completion. Ruvu River became a crucial supply dump on the line of communication between the Central Railway and the Mgeta. Around this time Smuts received a shipment of Ford Model T pick up cars which, when combined with the new road that was being built, enabled relays of supplies to be made from Ruvu to Summit camp, and southwards through Tulo, to the front line between Duthumi and Kissaki on the Mgeta River.

The autumn rainy season started whilst the battery was in camp at the Ruvu River crossing. With the river rising rapidly to within inches of the bridge deck, all roads already established rapidly turned to slop and were closed to wheeled traffic to prevent their complete destruction.

> We are still on the banks of the Ruvu River. The rains are still with us and the river, which was a swiftly flowing river before the rains, is now a raging torrent. The bridge was in danger of being carried away, but we saved it by dumping hundreds of tons of stone round the piers of the bridge, thus somewhat breaking the strength of the current. We are now living in a very frugal manner. We have been on quarter

rations since the 13th of this month. Our full rations since we left M'buyuni have been 8ozs. mealie meal (crushed Indian corn), 4ozs. flour (when we could get it), 4ozs. of bully beef and a quarter of an ounce of coffee, also 4ozs. biscuits. No milk, no sugar, unless we 'found' a bag which was intended for somewhere else.

Joseph Dan Fewster, 27th September 1916

The continuing wet weather, poor rations, and the static disposition of the troops on the Ruvu and Mgeta Rivers saw the rapid increase in malaria and enteric fever. Many army units were decimated throughout this period; the 25th Battalion Royal Fusiliers were amongst some of the worst affected which resulted in their being withdrawn from field service and being sent to South Africa for recuperation.

Taken bad with bad attack of malaria. Had rough time for four days.

Alec Robertson, September 26th 1916

We are not having so much rain now but the roads are bad. I shall be very glad when we get away from here. The health of the battery has been bad and we have been unable to get any medical attention. If a chap went down with malaria or dysentery, he stayed there till nature picked him up. We haven't a grain of quinine, aspirin or phenacetin in the stores…some of the chaps have been delirious for days together, but we have not had a death since we have been here.

Joseph Dan Fewster, 6th October 1916

Eventually the rains diminished and the engineers completed the road over the mountains. The battery can at last move forwards over Sheppard's Pass.

The rains have stopped and now we are getting a few Ford cars through. Today we get the news that one of our guns has to go forward. The FWD lorries are still unable to get through. I expect it will be some time before the blasting is far enough advanced to allow the lorries to get through…

My gun is the one selected to go through. Our OC gives me permission to pick my own detachment while he picked the signallers and telephonists. This has brightened things up a lot here. Our chaps were getting very glum. Now they are holding an impromptu concert. All are happy, some because they are going, others because they hope to be following shortly. This is the spirit which has possessed our chaps right through. All past hardships are forgotten when there is any likelihood of having a go at Fritz.

Joseph Dan Fewster, 10th October 1916

The half section of the battery set out from the Ruvu River camp for the Mgeta on the 11th October. The gun hauled by mules driven by Cape boys and the ammunition carts hauled by oxen, the party reaches Buku Buku the same night.

Shortly after leaving Buka-Buka, we arrive at 'Shepherd's Pass'. This pass is named after General Shepherd and is really a fine piece of work which that general had done during the last three or four weeks. When first entering the pass, you see the plains covered with bush and jungle thousands of feet below you. The surprising part is that one has no idea that one is at such an altitude, until this view suddenly opens out before one. I can imagine that before this pass was cut, it was just like walking to the edge of a cliff, thousands of feet high and no means of getting down. But Shepherd cut a road out of the cliff side. It is very steep and about five miles long. Of course it winds about considerably, but this distance gives one an idea of the great height of the 'cliff'. When we went down, we had both brakes on the gun wheels, but the speed was such that it kept us on the trot all the time until we reached the bottom. When I say it took us an hour and a quarter, I think I am within bounds when I estimate the distance at five miles. It was a rather nerve-testing journey, because, if you are travelling a short distance with the brakes 'easy' and suddenly had occasion to apply them 'hard', if you applied them too hard in your excitement, in all probability the gun would skid over the side, taking mules and drivers with it. Or if not applied hard enough, and the gun got away, the result would be similar. The road was about eight to twelve feet wide, so there was not too much room to swerve about in. Anyway I heaved a sigh of relief when I got the gun down to the bottom 'all correct'.

Joseph Dan Fewster, 12th October 1916

The party arrived at the village of Tulo after midday, and remained in camp there overnight, reaching the Mgeta River following day.

The pass engineered by Brigade General Sheppard through the Uluguru Mountains in the autumn of 1916 to enable the advance to the Mgeta (IWM Q 15634)

We find the 'line' here only very lightly held, no one being permanently in the trenches. Our front extends from Duthumi to a town named Kissaki, 16 miles away, both places being in our hands. There are not many troops here, and the 'line' itself is held by patrols of the various units, which mount for 24 hours duty.

Joseph Dan Fewster, 14th October 1916

Battery took up position and registered a target. Fired at night 7 pm - 12 midnight, 12 rounds all told.

Alec Robertson, October 15th 1916

186

Moved on to Dakawa (No. 2) about 9 miles. Took up position and gave them 10 rounds in the afternoon and 5 at 7 pm. Got lost in bush at night

Alec Robertson, October 16th 1916

The village of Duthumi on the Mgeta River. General Smuts' headquarters
(IWM Q 15640)

On the Mgeta, offensive action by both sides was minimal, patrols would occasionally clash, continued sniping and machine gun fire was a reminder that the enemy were still there. Each day the battery took their howitzer from their camp to their gun position, each night returning it to camp. As opportunity allowed, the battery were called upon to fire upon any enemy concentrations that were sighted along with machine gun outposts and stores.

Gun taken out again. Pulled by about 40 boys this time as we can't get mules. Looking very funny. Fancy, battery started out with new, up to date, motor lorries, then mules and now natives. Some drop. Lt. Guildord at O.P. Gave Huns 10 shots. Returned to camp about 10:30 am.

Alec Robertson, November 16th 1916

Von Lettow had been careful to ensure he reached an area where his food supplies could be maintained throughout the wet season. Crops of maize that he had had the foresight to plant previously, were available nearby and livestock could be driven from southern districts of the colony. The riverine areas also provided abundant supplies of hippopotamus meat, the fat of which was relished by his troops. Smuts, who relied completely on the importation of his supplies, did not enjoy this advantage. The heavy rains and consequent transport difficulties made his supply situation, once more, tenuous.

> During the day General Shepherd came up. He would have a few shots at one target, and then a few at another. At last he finds a machine gun emplacement. He points it out to our OC "Give them a round there, Floyd", he said. The OC in about two seconds, sends down to the gun the necessary angle, elevation, etc. I am getting rather excited. In a very short time, the message comes, "No. 1 ready, sir". I have my glasses glued to my eyes. I want the boys to do their best now. Immediately the answer goes back, "Fire, No. 1." A few seconds pass by. I forget to breathe when up goes the whole lot. Fragments of timber and bodies go up with a cloud of lyddite fumes. I could have cheered. I turned my head and looked at the general. He was spotting through a telescope. He closed up the glass, stood upon his feet and said, "Damn it Floyd, you could hit a half-crown at 6,000 yards." What the OC felt, I don't know. I felt as if I was up in the skies. The old battery had upheld its reputation once more.
>
> Joseph Dan Fewster, 19th November 1916

General Brits' 3rd Division was disbanded during this period and, in most part, repatriated to South Africa. Smuts concentrated his efforts on re-supplying his existing forces and establishing the infrastructure necessary for the next stages of the campaign.

> Gave Hun 22 rounds. Saw some men run out of trench near where one shell fell.
>
> Alec Robertson, November 19th 1916

On the Mgeta, the rains ensured a period of stalemate between von Lettow and Smuts' troops; neither side was in a position to move. It was during this period that the battery became involved in pioneering work, in the field of map making.

Throughout the campaign, operations in German East Africa had been severely hampered by the lack of accurate maps. The speed of the advance compounded the problem making it difficult to create representative maps for timely use by the forward troops. Making maps was not a quick process and required a dedicated staff to carry out this work. To facilitate this necessity No. 6 Section (B, Army Printing Section), Royal Engineers, landed at Kilindini in May 1916, their initial efforts restricted to the immediate and local needs of Smut's advancing columns. As the campaign developed and large tracts of the colony came under Allied control, mapping could be better organised and provide more detail, standardised to a common grid with British East Africa.

In the front line on the Mgeta, where the 13th Howitzer Battery was now positioned, enemy patrols, dense swamp forest and the lack of roads made access difficult. To overcome these impediments the services of the Royal Flying Corps were employed in what must be seen as an innovative application of aircraft in developing mapping techniques. Using a camera mounted upon an aircraft, the observer was able to photograph the terrain below which, when the images were developed, could be pieced together to form a pictorial representation of the areas over which they had flown. Lieutenant Leo Walmsley, a Yorkshireman, who would be awarded the Military Cross for his service in East Africa, became involved in developing this method of map making. Leo had already established himself as an author before he enlisted into the army in 1914. He was soon transferred to the Royal Flying Corps and arriving in Mombasa in December 1915.

Leo was with the 26th (South African) Squadron, Royal Flying Corps, flying as an observer in the squadron's BE2c aircraft over the enemy-held territory. As this technique was evolving from the collective experience of those involved, it became apparent that over large swathes of country that had few distinguishing features and where navigation was somewhat empirical, some other method of fixing the image positions would be necessary.

A BE2 of 26 Squadron RFC seen at Kimbabwe in January 1917.
Leo Walmsley flew with this squadron during the map reconnaissance of the
areas across the Mgeta River (D'Olier)

On photographing an entirely unmapped district it occurred to me that a modification of a method we used for range finding might be employed, requiring the assistance of a ground party to determine the range and azimuth of smoke bombs or very lights dropped over objects photographed. Employing the method in conjunction with a range finding party of the Hull Heavy Battery (RGA), I was able to make a map of the German positions in the flat swampy valley of the Mgeta River of satisfactory accuracy.

Leo Walmsley, 1919

Following a serious flying accident whilst in East Africa, Leo was repatriated to England, where his injuries could be treated more effectively in a hospital there. Upon his recovery, he returned to his native Yorkshire and his writing career.

The advantage Smuts now gained by the close contact with the Royal Navy following the capture of Dar es Salaam had allowed, since September 1916, for the establishment of new bridgeheads at the southern coastal ports of Kilwa and Lindi. Throughout the standoff with von Lettow on the Mgeta River, and despite the rains, Smuts prepared for a new offensive. From the coastal bridgeheads, operations were in hand to secure the coast and for detachments to advance inland. Part of the 1st Division, including the former 158th Heavy Battery, now known as the 14th Howitzer Battery, had been landed there with the intent of cutting off von Lettow's retreat southwards from the Mgeta and Rufigi areas and to deny him access to the coastal region where the prospect of his re-supply by sea was probable. By late October Smuts' force had pushed inland from Kilwa, north-west towards the Rufigi and the settlement of Kibata. To secure his retirement to the south, von Lettow had directed his force at Kibata to engage the allied force assembled there. A fierce and prolonged battle ensued with the allies suffering numerous casualties. The lack of suitable roads had made it impossible for the artillery to be deployed at Kibata which had left the allied infantry at the mercy of the German artillery and without the means to retaliate. The German force eventually retired from Kibata before moving into the Matandu River valley, from where it could directly threaten Kilwa.

To the north, with the resupply of the army complete, and the troops either replaced or rested, Smuts' renewed the offensive by crossing the Mgete River on the 1st January 1917.

> We man the gun three hours before dawn. The attack commences in earnest just as day is breaking. The rattle of rifle and machine gun fire is very heavy till mid-day. The artillery is also busy, so we have a noisy forenoon. During the afternoon the firing becomes fainter and we were out of action, but still standing by. The heat of today has been terrific, and by nightfall we are pretty well done up.
>
> Joseph Dan Fewster, 1st January 1917

Faced by superior forces von Lettow withdrew southwards towards the Rufigi River. On the 4th January, at the village of Beho Beho, the German forces struck hard against their attackers and caused many casualties before their position became untenable.

> Our losses seem to have been fairly heavy, but I expect the enemy will have suffered still more. Perhaps the most notable amongst our killed was Captain F.C. Selous of the 25th Fusiliers. This man had a world-wide reputation as a big game hunter and explorer in Africa. His loss is keenly felt

by all ranks of the Fusiliers. He was brave even to the point of rashness, and I am told he refused to take cover, with the result that he was mown down by machine gun fire.

Joseph Dan Fewster, 7th January 1917

With the success of the offensive, and the rapid advance, the fighting was now beyond the range of the 13th Howitzer Battery. With von Lettow now having crossed the Rufigi River, the battery moved forward to Kimbabwe, a settlement on its north bank.

We found our old friend, the enemy, holding the south bank of the river, while we come into action on the north bank. The river here is about 700 yards wide, so there is not a great distance between us. We are in position behind a bank. Jerry searches for us with his artillery but does not meet with any success. There has been heavy fighting all day. We again receive praise from General Sheppard.

Joseph Dan Fewster, 10th January 1917

The climate and location did not improve the situation for the battery personnel. The spring rains started early and would prove to be the worst rains for nine years. The line of communication, so vital in getting supplies to the forward areas, almost collapsed; the roads became impassable and the land was flooded over hundreds of square miles. If it were not for the use of thousands of native porters, wading waist deep through the floods, the troops could not have been fed; starvation was a real possibility and consumed much of Smuts' attention.

Our section officer is again in hospital. I believe this is the most deadly place we have yet struck. We are having some 'light' rains. After half an hour's rain our gun stands in water up to its axle. The heat during the day absolutely burns one up, while at night one swelters in it. Mosquitoes, tsetse fly and all other crawling insects are here by the million. At night the yelping and howling of wild beasts keep us awake half the night through. We are having a bad time with fever. While we have been here, we have received six men as reinforcements, but our total strength has fallen to 15 NCOs and men, all told. Out of this number, we have found men to connect up all the batteries here with the observation post. We also keep the telephone communications in repair. There are six men to work the gun. This includes the men's cook, the OC's cook and the OC's servant. We are quite ready for a rest when we can snatch one.

Joseph Dan Fewster, 13th January 1917

With von Lettow increasingly concerned with the allied forces concentrating and operating inland from Kilwa to his rear, he withdrew the remainder of his force from the Rufigi River and moved towards the Matandu River valley, inland from Kilwa. The 13th Howitzer Battery, unable to advance across the Rufigi River because of the absence of roads, became redundant.

> We have now driven the Huns from their hold on the river bank and they are out of our range.

Joseph Dan Fewster, 18th January 1917

The men of the battery returned to the Imperial Detail camp at Morogoro. There they were soon joined by the remnants of the 11th Howitzer Battery who were returning there from Dodoma.

Crossing the Rufigi River at Kimbabwe following Smuts' successful offensive of January 1917 (D'Olier)

We are back in Morogoro again having come back for a rest. We are quite well off in this camp; there is a YMCA and one or two other places of interest. It is about time we got into a decent place, the first thing we did when we got here was to make a raid on the YMCA so that we could have a good feed, we had almost forgotten what it was like.

Arthur Cowbourne, 1st March 1917

The remaining howitzer and gun stores of the 13th Howitzer Battery was left at the Rufigi position as a precaution against von Lettow re-crossing the Rufigi River. One non-commissioned officer and a guard detachment of two gunners remained with the gun. The position was not relieved until April 17th 1917, the howitzer eventually being withdrawn in July 1917.

Situation map, originally printed in the Yorkshire Post of 29th January 1917 showing the German force in the area of the Matandu valley area south of the Rufigi River (Rimington)

Chapter 13

The 14th Howitzer Battery R.G.A.

T HE former 158th Heavy Battery, part of the 38th Howitzer Brigade, had been left at Mbuyuni in reserve for Smuts' 1st Division. We now turn our focus to their hitherto limited, but now important, movements.

The grave of Gunner 61 Arthur Bilsdon, Voi Cemetery, Kenya (Fecitt)

I have received photo of my husband's grave, Gnr. A Bilsdon 61 RGA, and wish to thank you and the officer that so kindly had it taken, very much for it. The children and I look on it as our lost hope.

Mrs. Honor Bilsdon, 20th February 1917

Throughout Smut's offensive through the Pare and Usumbara mountains during June and July 1916 the battery, now renamed the 14th Howitzer Battery whilst in the country, remained at Mbuyuni on the border between British and German East Africa. On the 1st August 1916, in the absence of half of his brigade, Major P. N. G. Reade, the 38th Brigade commanding officer, assumed command of the 158th Heavy Battery as senior rank to Lieutenant Frank Harrison. It was not until Smuts' 1st Division captured the Tanga district that the battery, now reduced from four to two guns owing to half of their armament being returned to England, entrained for Korogwe. They arrived on the 4th August, and there going into camp. Korogwe had been established as a major supply depot by Smuts for his first 1st and 3rd Divisions. Korogwe was serviced by road and conveniently positioned on the Tanga (Usambara) railway from Moshi that was now connected, by the new branch line, through Voi to Mombasa by the Uganda Railway.

Training continued throughout August whilst at Korogwe, the battery leaving by rail for Tanga on the 27th. Major Reade, Lieutenant F. Harrison, 2nd Lieutenant E. C. Mackenzie, 2nd Lieutenant Boyes and 2nd Lieutenant Farley accompany the battery. The following day they commenced embarkation upon the troopship, S.S. *Montrose*, sailing from Tanga for Zanzibar on the last day of August 1916.

In the east a force of some 2,000 rifles under Brigadier-General J. A. Hannyngton, C.M.G., D.S.O., had been conveyed by sea from Dar-es-Salam and concentrated at Kilwa, and formed the nucleus of the First Division, which, after some reorganisation and transfer of units, was assembled later at the same place, and was intended to take part in a great encircling move south of the Rufiji.

Jan Smuts, Oct 1916

Thus, on the 11th September 1916, the 14th Howitzer Battery was transferred from Zanzibar to Kilwa, where they would support operations against von Lettow's forces during his withdrawal from the Mgeta and Rufigi Rivers to the north-west of Kilwa. Throughout the autumn of that year the battery was little troubled by hostile action, continuing battery training, whilst further reinforcements were concentrated at Kilwa. Major Reade left the command due to illness and was repatriated to England. Lieutenant Farley, who first enlisted into the Royal Artillery in 1893, and had commanded the brigade ammunition column until its disbandment, was transferred to South Africa in October, suffering from dysentery. In January 1917 he was repatriated to England.

The grave of Bombardier 141 Arthur
Ryder
Dar es Salaam War Cemetery,
Tanzania (Fecitt)

On January 1st 1917, Smuts commenced his offensive, south-wards, across the Mgeta River. Anticipating the German force retreating, and with the intention of encircling the enemy, the 14th Howitzer Battery moved out from Kilwa to take up positions westward of the port at Chemera (Tchemera), attached to No. 1 Column of General Hannygton's 1st Division.

No. 1 Column commanded by General Orr comprised:

33rd Punjabi Regiment
Gold Coast Regiment
2/ 2nd Kings African Rifles
22nd Mountain Battery R.G.A.

Soon after the commencement of Smuts' offensive, the spring rains started, the worst in living memory, preventing further offensive action. Smuts at this time would briefly cede command of the forces in East Africa to General Hoskins, before appointing General van Deventer. General Hoskins and Deventer used the impasse caused by the rainy season to muster reinforcements and supplies for future offensive operations.

In April 1917, the remnant of the 14th Howitzer Battery R.G.A., whilst still at Chemera, was absorbed back into the reformed 11th (Hull) Heavy Battery R.G.A., their original unit; the 158th (Hull) Heavy Battery R.G.A., ceased to exist.

The 14th Howitzer Battery parade at Kilwa, January 1917 (D'Olier)

Chapter 14

The Reformation of the 11th (Hull) Heavy Battery R.G.A.

SMUTS' expectation that the enemy forces would be brought to battle and defeated by his superior force, or, that having lost the most valuable part of the colony, including the Central Railway and the seaports, von Lettow would surrender, remained unrealised. Unfortunately for Smuts, von Lettow had little compulsion to surrender and, as a result, the campaign and its objectives became confused. The high incidence of disease affecting the troops occupying the camps along the Central Railway had compelled Smuts to consider repatriation of those units that were unfit for further service, and the disbandment of the remnant of his 3rd Division. To this end, in October and November, all European troops were medically examined which resulted in a large proportion leaving East Africa for the hospitals in South Africa. Inevitably some units became unsustainable simply because their manpower was no longer sufficient for them to be effective. As was the case with the 11th Howitzer Battery, informal amalgamations and loaning of equipment and personnel became common, whole divisions were reorganised until an effective fighting force was rebuilt.

General Smuts relinquished his command on January 20th 1917, and was succeeded briefly by Lieutenant General A. R. Hoskins. In the following May Major General J. L. van Deventer was appointed to the command upon Hoskins being posted to a command in Mesopotamia.

Following Smuts' offensive, and in order to continue the campaign, Hoskins had a formidable task in rebuilding the force and conducted difficult negotiations with the War Office in order to be resupplied with the necessary equipment and consumables that Smuts, who had expected the German surrender, had failed to procure. At this juncture the batteries and sections of the original 38th Howitzer Brigade R.G.A. were dispersed at different locations throughout German East Africa. Effective command as a distinct fighting unit had been lost. Captain Floyd, now the commanding officer of the 38th Brigade R.G.A. in the absence of Major Reade, and commanding the 13th Howitzer Battery R.G.A., recognising this situation. Floyd took steps to re-establish the original structure of the battery directly with Brigade General Sheppard of the 1st East African Brigade. Floyd wrote in early February 1917 as follows:

> Sir,
>
> I have the honour to request that at an early date steps may be taken to bring together the scattered portions of the Batteries of the 38th Brigade RGA, and to bring together the Brigade itself whenever the contingencies of the campaign permit.
>
> In order to make clear my request it is necessary to trace the history of the Brigade since its arrival in this country. The Brigade landed from England in March 1916 and consisted of: -
>
> 38 Bde. RGA Headquarters
> 11th Hull Heavy Battery RGA (Capt B.E. Floyd)
> 158th Heavy Battery RGA (Major P.A.G. Reade)
> 38th Brigade Ammunition Column.
> And a Depot section of reinforcements.
>
> In the absence of Lt. Col. H.M. Slater owing to sickness, Major Reade was promoted Temp. Lieut. Colonel whilst commanding the Brigade.
>
> In May 1916 the following changes were ordered to be made "whilst in this country":

(a) 11th Hull Heavy Battery was divided into two
  1. 13th Howitzer Battery (to 3RD. Then 1ST. Division – now Kimbabwe)
  2. 11th Howitzer Battery (to 2nd. Division – now Dodoma)
(b) 158th Heavy Battery was renamed 14th Howitzer Battery (now operating from Kilwa?)
(c) Brigade Ammunition Column temporarily in abeyance.
(d Brigade HQ (now DSM) continues to exist though with no tactical and little or no administrative control over the batteries of the Brigade.

In November 1916, 2 guns of the 14th Howitzer Battery, 1 of the 11th Howitzer Battery and 1 of the 13th Howitzer Battery were sent to England.About this time the 11th Howitzer battery was attached to and temporarily incorporated in the 12th Howitzer Battery (from S. Africa).

In January 1917, Lt. Col. Reade went to England and control of the Brigade devolved upon myself.

It might be seen therefore that the Brigade is scattered all over the country, and I would ask that the War Office constitution of the Brigade (as it landed) may be borne in mind when the exigencies of the campaign allow of the Brigade being brought together as a Brigade.

As regards the actual Battery's themselves, I submit that the call for bringing together of the scattered parts of each Battery under the control of the Battery commanders is a matter of more urgency. Firstly, the portions of the Batteries have been renumbered and renamed, and I respectfully submit that this is unnecessary and can only lead to disintegration, lessening of esprit de corps, and the loss of a Battery's identity of which it is proud. Secondly, the fact that the administrative control over the internal affairs of a separated portion of a Battery by its Battery commander is reduced to a nominal one cannot be but bad in principle. To take a simple example, I command the 11th Hull Heavy Battery and I am with and control tactically and administratively one half of it (13th Howitzer Battery) whilst the other half (11th Howitzer Battery) is, though necessarily tactically out of my control, it is incorporated in another Battery under another commander. It is possible, and in some cases has happened, that promotions, changes in establishment etc. can be made in half of my unit without any reference to myself, its commanding officer. I contest that this is absolutely unsatisfactory and that a Battery commander is entitled to the control, administratively of any part of his unit even though it is tactically lent away.

The case of a section of a Battery or a Battery of a Brigade being lent away in France has to my personal knowledge no parallel. When this is done, the numbers are not changed, the Battery or Brigade commander controls administratively the lent section or Battery and the section or Battery shall keep its identity as part of its War Office Battery or Brigade.

I am very anxious to press this point as I feel that the bringing together of the scattered portions of the battery under the control of their Battery commander and the resumption of their proper titles is in the best interest of the service and will prevent these units losing their identity as units which has always been considered of such importance in the keeping of Esprit de Corps.

Captain Floyd's request was approved by General Sheppard who, recognising that the situation was problematic, gave Floyd his wholehearted support to consolidating the scattered parts of the brigade into one unit. All the remaining subsections and their personnel were brought together under the original battery name, the 11th (Hull) Heavy Battery R.G.A.. All previous battery titles were discarded and the nucleus of the original unit restored, the 158th Heavy Battery being re-amalgamated into the 11th (Hull) Heavy Battery once more. The importance of this consolidation would not be fully apparent until the battery, renamed and rearmed went to France in July, 1918, and the esprit de corps that Captain Floyd was keen to maintain would show its value during the formation of the 545th Siege Battery R.G.A. and its subsequent actions.

In order to carry out the amalgamation of the battery, Floyd had to gain the approval of the War Office in London. Approval was received in April 1917, with the authorised war establishment as follows:

8 British Officers
1 Battery Sergeant Major

1 Battery Quartermaster Sergeant
4 Sergeants
4 Corporals
8 Bombardiers
66 Gunners (inc. 6 Acting Bombardiers)
16 Horses
                                          Frank Harrison

Battery headquarters was moved to Morogoro. Each of the four subsections, each of one gun, was temporarily redesignated as the 11th (Hull) Heavy Battery, numbered one to four. Each subsection was tactically independent but administratively under the command of the Officer Commanding, 11th (Hull) Heavy Battery R.G.A., Captain Basil E. Floyd R.G.A.. One howitzer from subsection number four was lent to the 134th Cornwall Heavy Battery, who were operating from the coastal port of Lindi. At the end of April 1917 the officers were assigned as follows:

No. 1 and No. 2 Subsections – Morogoro
Capt. B. E. Floyd RGA
Temp. Lt. F. Harrison RGA
Temp. 2nd Lt. W. Adams RGA (SR)
No. 3 Subsection – Kilwa
Temp. Lt. A. J. Nannini RGA.
Temp. 2nd Lt. E. C. Mackenzie RGA
                          WO 95 Battery War Diary

Jack and the remnant of the 11th Howitzer Battery personnel, who had spent the autumn and winter at Dodoma, in keeping with Floyd's consolidation, moved to Morogoro in April. Here they joined with remnants of the right section of the Battery (formerly the 13th Howitzer Battery), who had returned to Morogoro from Kimbabwe, on the Rufigi River in January. Lieutenant Nannini relieved Lieutenant Frank Harrison of the command of number three subsection at Kilwa. Harrison returning to Morogoro took command of number two subsection. This combined establishment at Morogoro would form a base depot supplying drafts to the two remaining guns of the former 14th Howitzer Battery (158th Heavy Battery) who had been operating from the southern port of

Kilwa since the previous September. By the end of April 1917 the reformation of the Hull battery was complete, but persistent illness experienced by the men, ensured that the battery never attained the number of personnel authorised under its war establishment.

Chapter 15

The Renumbering of Territorial Units

T HE men of the Hull Heavy Battery, formed as a New Army unit by the East Yorkshire Territorial Association, were, upon enlisting, allocated a regimental or service number consistent with the practice of the Territorial Force and outlined in the Army Council Instruction cited below.

> The NCOs and men of the Territorial Force will be numbered by units, and each man when posted or transferred to a unit will receive a number in that unit. The series of numbers will run from 1 to 9,999; when the latter number is reached a fresh series will be commenced.
>
> In all documents relating to a man his regimental number will precede his name. This number will not be changed so long as he remains in the unit. If he is transferred, deserts, is discharged or dies, the number will not be given to any other man.
> Army Council Instruction, WO 293 National Archives

For the Hull Battery, the number series started at number 1 on the 11th September 1914 for the first man to enlist. The last man to join, Maurice Boyd, was allocated his number 336 on the 2nd October 1915.

With the rapid increase in the size of the British army at the outbreak of war and the subsequent increase in the Territorial element of it, the numbering system described became problematic as many men from different units, but the same Corps i.e. Royal Garrison Artillery, had the same regimental number. To the army, for administration, each man was a number, his number preceding his name in all administrative matters.

It was recognised that in order to remove this anomaly, and the possibility of duplication, in the management of pay, pensions and innumerable other clerical necessities, a new number system should be devised specifically for the Territorial Force. Thus, on the 1st of January 1917, each territorial unit was issued a new six digit series of numbers that did not duplicate within the Corps. Those artillery units, like the Hull Heavy Battery, that had been raised locally were similarly included in this renumbering exercise, with unique number blocks allocated to each unit. For the Hull Heavy Battery, senior by establishment to all other new army batteries, the number series commenced at 290000.

Chapter 16

Battery Operations at Morogoro

April 11th – Left Dodoma by rail for Morogoro

Jack Drake

WHILST at Kilossa and Dodoma under the command of the 12th South African Howitzer Battery, life for the men of the 11th Howitzer Battery had become relaxed. Daily parades, signalling and gun drill left plenty of time for leisure. The reformation of the 11th (Hull) Heavy Battery, instigated by

The Imperial Detail and Convalescence Camp at Morogoro in 1917
(IWM Q 15460)

207

Captain Floyd, and the resulting move to Morogoro changed these arrangements considerably. The immediate consequence being that the remaining chickens belonging to the battery section at Dodoma were despatched and eaten; Fritz, the dachshund, would travel to Morogoro with them. Their arrival at Morogoro would recombine the remaining personnel of the 11th and 13th Howitzer sections of the old Hull Heavy Battery.

> This is a decent town of big houses and is the biggest town we have struck since leaving Mombasa. The white quarter we should call a village at home, but the native and Indian quarter which is separated from the white quarter by a stream is very big. Fruit and vegetables are plentiful and the meat tastes decent owing to the good pasture I suppose. There's a range of mountains at the back of the town – in fact the town is built on the slopes and in consequence the clouds bank up against them and we get a superabundance of rain and mud everywhere.
>
> Charlie Rimington, 22nd April 1917

At Morogoro, a large tented camp, the men had to undertake parade drill and fatigues again. The living arrangements were, however, still of a less formal nature, but army discipline was gradually restored.

All our time – barring 9:30 to 4pm is parading – and we needed it! We had got into very slack ways.

Charlie Rimington, 28th April 1917

The shortage of writing paper made the troops resourceful. This shows the reverse of one of Charlie's letters posted to home (Rimington)

Improvisation, and a sharp eye for opportunities, equipped the battery with the necessities.

My bed consists of the bonnet of a Ford motorcar stretched out, and propped up on stakes, to protect me from white ants. It is not bad, but it is rather bumpy at the hinges, and needs careful packing with trousers, tunics, socks etc to make it comfortable.

Charlie Rimington, 28th April 1917

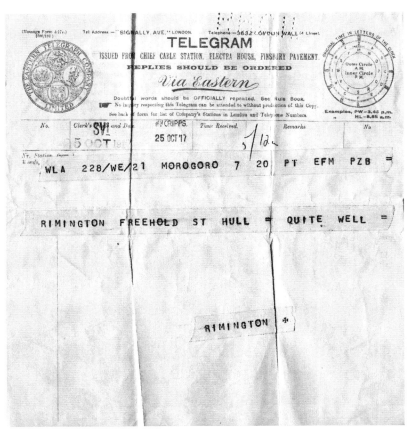

Morogoro Camp was provided with a Telegraph Office (Rimington)

In the May of 1917, with reorganisation of the reformed battery complete, the strength of subsections No. 1 and No. 2, based at Morogoro and on the Rufigi River, was as follows:

Establishment of Subsection No. 2 at Morogoro, May 1917.
1 British Officer – Lt. F. Harrison
1 Battery Sergeant Major – Samuel G. Doyle
1 Sergeant – Harry W. Downs
2 Corporals
1 Bombardier
21 Gunners (five in hospital)
20 Natives
1 Howitzer with gun stores.

Establishment of Subsection No. 2 at Rufigi River, May 1917.
1 British Officer – 2nd Lt. W.W. Adams SR (attached)
2 Gunners
10 Natives
1. Howitzer with gun and signalling stores.
2 Motorcycles (1 Douglas, 1 BSA)

WO 95 Battery War Diary

On the 9th June 1917, the one remaining gun of the former 11th Howitzer Battery, at Morogoro, was handed over to the 134th (Cornwall) Heavy Battery, for operations based from the coastal port of Lindi. Two 5.4-inch howitzers from the 134th (Cornwall) Battery were exchanged, to be used by the battery for training purposes. Until the return from Kimbabwe of the howitzer of the former 13th Howitzer Battery, none of the battery's original complement of guns remained at Morogoro. Jack wrote from Morogoro to his family at home summarising his situation:

> I hope I shall be home for Xmas this year, perhaps we won't be home much before. I am having a fairly good time now. I keep having fever now and again, it lasts a couple of days and I am as well as ever again. I think J. Hawksworth has gone home some time since, he was invalided to the Cape, S. Africa, and several have gone.
>
> Jack Drake, 9th June 1917

On the 19th June, Deventer, now promoted to the command in East Africa, inspected No. 2 subsection at Morogoro. The timing was unfortunate because Sergeant Harry Downs, and a detail of seven gunners, had left Morogoro that morning to join No 1 and 3

A howitzer, two FWD trucks and personnel photographed in 1917. Believed to be at Morogoro (South African National Museum of Military History, Defence Force Archives)

subsections that were operating from the southern port of Kilwa, leaving few able men to constitute the parade.

> Owing to shortage of numbers fell in with RA Details, Morogoro. State of Battery: – 1 British Officer, 1 Warrant Officer, 7 other ranks.
>
> Frank Harrison, 19th June 1917

In 1917, following the rains, illness was rife among the troops in the camps along the Central Railway. Jack had recurrent fever that, apart from his duties as a telephonist and signaller, prevented his joining the battery in the field at Kilwa. On the 24th June 1917, James Moore, from Patrington, near Hull, died of blackwater fever in Morogoro hospital. The following day, his kit and belongings were sold at the regular auction, raising the sum 459.5 rupees for the benefit of his family. The sale of the possessions of those who died had become a common occurrence. Boots, uniforms, tobacco, and other items were still scarce; few men could boast of a decent shirt or pair of trousers that were not threadbare, patched or plain rotten from the sweat and the climate. Personal effects could not be shipped home; the most expedient solution was to raise money for the soldier's family. James Moore is buried in Morogoro Cemetery.

The grave of James Moore, Morogoro Cemetery, Tanzania (author)

June 25th – Another attack of fever; went into Hospital at Morogoro.

Jack Drake

The large Imperial Detail Camp, which spread across slopes and plain below the town of Morogoro, was adjacent to the 15th Stationary Hospital. The camp comprised several sections, each section for an individual unit: it also hosted a large tented area for the convalescence of soldiers recovering from their stay in hospital.

July 5th – Discharged from hospital.

Jack Drake

In the spring of 1917, von Lettow had withdrawn from the Rufigi River to the Matandu valley, inland from Kilwa. The howitzer, which had been left at Kimbabwe on the Rufigi River by the 13th Howitzer Battery, was now withdrawn. Bombardier May, who had

212

joined the battery at Kondoa Irangi, and three gunners were detailed to assist 2nd Lieutenant Adams to return the howitzer to Morogoro. John Silburn, Ernest Young and Jack were detailed to this task, using one of the battery's FWD lorries to tow the gun.

> July 10th – Left Morogoro for the Rufigi River to bring back a gun which had been left there during the rainy season, the rains had finished by the end of May & the ground was fairly dry.
>
> Jack Drake

Driving east from Morogoro, the party passed through the settlement of Mikissi, which lies beside the Central Railway. From Makissi, the road leads south to the Ruvu River crossing. They arrived at Summit Camp following a long ascent from the Ruvu River into the Uluguru Mountains, before descending to Sheppard's Pass. After passing through the villages of Tulo and Dutumi the Mgeta River was reached, and crossed by the newly established pontoon ferry. The party arrived at Kimbabwe on the Rufigi River six days after their departure from Morogoro.

> 17th – Had a day rest before starting on the return journey back to Morogoro. 200 miles away.
>
> Jack Drake

The howitzer and gun stores that Lieutenant Adams and his party had returned to Morogoro, was handed over to the 134th (Cornwall) Battery on the 25th August 1917 for shipment to Lindi. This howitzer, and the one previously transferred in June, provided the Cornwall battery with a two-gun section; they retained one of their original complement of 5.4- inch howitzers. Lieutenant Adams had been attached to the battery following the loss of Lieutenants Maslin and Nannini, having left Morogoro to join the battery at Kilwa. Maslin was invalided to the Cape the previous March, suffering from malaria, appendicitis, and typhoid, a combination that would leave him unfit for further service in the field.

Throughout the summer, fever continued to affect the battery section left by Captain Floyd in Morogoro. Lieutenant Harrison,

213

*The road from Morogoro south to Dutumi on the Mgeta River near Tulo
(IWM Q 15503)*

who had been posted back to Morogoro from the former 158th
Heavy Battery, was admitted to hospital. Number three subsection,
near Kilwa, similarly suffered through fever; its losses were made
good by drafts of men being sent from Morogoro. The return from
hospital of men to the battery subsection at Morogoro provided
replacements for those who were hospitalised from the battery at
Kilwa. Jack's experience is typical of many of the troops who served
in East Africa:

Aug. 21st – Back again in Hospital.

On 29th August 1917, the subsection at Morogoro, commanded
by Lieutenant Harrison, was ordered to Dar es Salaam and there
to embark for Kilwa. In the event, the personnel remained in the
Imperial Detail Camp at Dar es Salaam; Harrison embarked alone.
The troops that remained in camp at Dar es Salaam joined the
battery at Mssindy, inland from Kilwa, some days later. Excepting
those members of the battery who were too ill to be of service, all
available men were committed to the field. All of the subsections
would be amalgamated and their previous designations would cease.
Jack and several other hospitalised men remained at Morogoro,

others that were unfit for the onward journey to Kilwa, remained at Dar es Salaam.

Sept. 3rd – Discharged from Hospital to the Convalescent Camp.

Jack Drake

The German boma at Morogoro viewed from the tented convalescence camp. The boma was used as a hospital but is now the regional government office (IWM Q 15480)

Oct. 1st – Back again in Hospital.
Oct. 12th – Discharged.

Jack Drake

The operations undertaken by the battery from Kilwa would, in brief, entail the battery advancing to the south whilst supporting two mobile infantry columns of General Hannyington's 1st Division. On November 26th 1917, the German forces entered Portuguese territory, present-day Mozambique. At this point heavy artillery was of no further use although the campaign was to continue for another year. Meanwhile, Jack and those who had remained in hospital at Morogoro moved to Dar es Salaam and joined other remnants of the battery convalescing there:

Nov. 11th – Left Morogoro for Dar es Salaam.

Chapter 17

Battery Operations at Kilwa

THE spring rainy season of 1917, which started in January, had prevented any substantial offensive activity by the allied forces assembled at and around Kilwa. Although the 1st Division had secured Kibata to the north-west of Kilwa, and the coastal region, the encircling movement that Smuts had intended, had failed. By May, after continued harrying by Sheppard's brigade from the north, von Lettow had evacuated the Rufigi delta region and moved south to the Matandu River system, inland from Kilwa. By June the Germans held a position stretching from Kimamba Hill, adjoining Kilwa Kisiwani harbour, and westwards to Nahende on the Liwale road. Further detachments of von Lettow's troops faced the allied forces that were based at Lindi. Smuts had, by this time, departed for the Imperial War Conference in London, the command since May 17th being held by Lieutenant General Van Deventer. Major General Hoskins who had commenced operations with the 1st Division at Kilwa departed, left the 1st Division under the command of General Hannyington.

Following Floyd's reformation of the battery, the 11th Hull Heavy Battery concentrated at Kilwa, joining General Hannynton's division. The two remaining howitzers of the former 158th Heavy Battery, and a detachment of men, had been at Kilwa since the previous September. In May, Lieutenant Nannini joined the battery, replacing Lieutenant Harrison as commanding officer. Throughout this period, the battery occupied positions near Chemera, some 40 miles inland from Kilwa.

The difficult nature of the terrain to the south of the Rufigi, combined with the previous experience in the advance from the Central Railway, made divisional organisation impractical. Numerous river crossings, lack of roads and the densely bushed hill country of the interior, suited von Lettow's strategy, but it was a great impediment to his pursuers. In consideration of this, Deventer organised his force into lighter, mobile configurations. To this end, the 1st Division at Kilwa, and those units that occupied Lindi to the south, were formed into flying columns, which would allow them the flexibility and mobility to suit the evolving situation. At Kilwa, No. 1 and No. 2 Columns, under the command of Colonel Orr and Colonel Grant, respectively, were formed; General O'Grady's No. 3 Column, and No. 4 Column commanded by Colonel Tyler, would operate inland from Lindi.

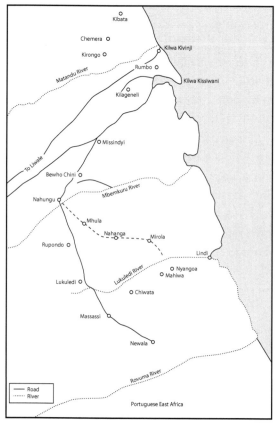

Map showing operations from Kilwa and Lindi

218

Travelling by rail from Morogoro, Captain Floyd, and the personnel for No. 1 subsection, arrived at Dar es Salaam. Here, two new officers were assigned to the battery, 2nd Lieutenant Alan Nevill, and 2nd Lieutenant Edmund William D'Olier. Floyd's party embarked aboard the H.M.T. *Umtata*, en route for Kilwa.

2nd Lieutenant Edmund D'Olier photographed at Summit Camp before joining the 11th Hull Heavy Battery R.G.A. at Kilwa (D'Olier)

2nd Lieutenant Alan Neville R.G.A., aboard H.M.T. Huntsgreen in February 1916 (D'Olier)

All is going on well, we have just landed after a sea trip from Dar es Salaam, we called at Zanzibar and went ashore for a few hours.

Arthur Cowbourne, 2nd June 1917

On the 19th June, Floyd relayed orders to Morogoro, instructing Sergeant Harry Downs and a detail of gunners from No. 2 subsection to travel to Kilwa; they left Morogoro the same day. Upon their arrival at Kilwa they established camp, making themselves as comfortable as their circumstances would allow.

This place looks ripping with plenty of coconut palms all along the shore. Our tent is right bang on the shore, and the sea comes up to the wall (at high tide) about 7 feet from our tent.

Charlie Rimington 25th June 1917

Sergeant Dan Fewster, and twenty-six other ranks, had recently returned to Dar es Salaam, aboard the H.M.T. *Ingoma*, from convalescence in South Africa. On the 23rd January 1917, Dan had been evacuated from the battery position at Kimbabwe on the Rufigi, suffering from the effects of repeated malarial attacks. He had been hospitalised in Cape Town, where several large facilities existed for the treatment of troops that had been sent there from East Africa. Captain Floyd sent orders to Dar es Salaam requesting Sergeant Fewster and his detail to join No. 1 and No. 3 subsections. Embarking aboard the H.M.T. *Salamis* on the 28th June, the reinforcements arrived the same evening, transferring to the camp established at Kilwa.

We arrive at Kilwa Kisiwani, the port of Kilwa Kivinji, commonly called Kilwa. This is another fine harbour with a very tricky entrance. There is no town, not even a village here. I expect the reason for this is that there is no fresh water, all water being carried here from Zanzibar. The town of Kilwa lies on the coast, 16 miles north of this harbour, but Kilwa has no harbour. No ship, with the exception of native dhows can get within a mile of the beach, owing to the water being so shallow. That is the reason this harbour has been opened out, since this part of the country has been in our hands. That the enemy is still in the neighbourhood is proved by the fact that two days ago he brought up his guns and shelled the ships in the harbour.

Joseph Dan Fewster, 1st July 1917

Throughout May, Lieutenant Nannini and No. 3 subsection had been at Chemera. By June they had moved their position to Kirongo, some 12 miles south of Chemera, following the orders of Colonel Grant's No. 2 Column. Upon his arrival at Kilwa, Captain Floyd, and the personnel for No. 1 subsection, joined the battery at Kirongo. Here, Floyd organised the battery, assigning 2nd Lieutenant Nevill to No. 1 subsection, whilst his contemporary from Officer Training School, 2nd Lieutenant D'Olier, was placed with No. 3 subsection.

Towards the end of June, both the battery subsections moved from Kirongo to join No. 1 Column at Rumbo, near Kilwa. Here they joined Colonel Orr, opposing the German positions at Kimamba Hill, close to Kilwa Kisiwani.

> Throughout the month our patrols were in daily touch with enemy patrols, which devoted much attention to harassing our lines of communication. Careful reconnaissance's of the enemy's positions opposite Kirongo, Mnasi, and Rumbo were undertaken, and preparations made for attack on the arrival of reinforcements. These arrived at the end of the month ...
>
> On the 27th the enemy evacuated some of his advanced positions, and on the 28th patrols found that all had been given up, except Kimamba Hill, which was held by a light rear-guard until the morning of the 29th, when our troops drove it off.
>
> Jacob van Deventer

The remaining battery personnel were mobilised from Kilwa to join the battery at Rumbo, where they remained until the end of the month.

> I left Kilwa at 6.00pm. and after a 26 mile ride, I reached my battery at a place called Rombo. The OC seemed pleased to see me but not half so pleased as I was to get back among the old faces, many of which I had not seen for over 12 months.
>
> Joseph Dan Fewster, 2nd July 1917

Charlie Rimington, who arrived from Morogoro in late June, travelled in the same party as Dan Fewster.

> Trekking tomorrow at 6am. It is great to be knocking around again, I can tell you, after the indolent life we have had.
>
> Charlie Rimington 2nd July 1917

The logistics involved to move the two subsections of the battery to Rumbo were formidable. The motor transport for the battery had not yet arrived at Kilwa, it was, therefore, necessary to use porters to undertake this work. Lieutenant Smith of the Army Service Corps, attached to the battery, would take several weeks to assemble sufficient vehicles to make the further use of porters unnecessary.

The Hull Heavy Battery with porters in span moving from Kirongo to Rumbo, near Kilwa, June 1917 (IWM Q 58017)

An indication of the scale of this operation, illustrating the difficulties of the campaign, can be gleaned from the number of porters employed in this operation.

> No. 1 Gun – 130 Porters in Draught
> No. 2 Gun – 150 Porters in Draught
> First Line Loads – 75 Porters
> Second Line Loads – 55 Porters
> Left at Chemera – 260 Loads
> WO 95 Battery War Diary

The move to Rumbo was prescient, Deventer had, by the end of June, assembled a considerable force around Kilwa. His intent was to clear the German positions to the south of his own line near Kilwa, and to facilitate the next phase of his planned advance.

Important operations took place during July in the Kilwa area, where I found myself in a position to initiate operations against the enemy's main forces during the first week of the month... Transport considerations did not yet permit of these operations being pressed beyond a limited distance, but I hoped that I should be able to go far enough to compel the enemy to show definitely whether he intended to retire towards Liwale or Massassi... With these objectives in view I decided, as a first phase, to drive the Kilwa enemy south of the Kiturika Hills. The Lindi force meantime was to contain the enemy opposing it, but to take no action on a large scale pending arrival of reinforcements.

Jacob van Deventer

Von Lettow, however, having observed Deventer's activities, and foreseeing the impending action, evacuated his front line opposite Kilwa. Apart from a rear-guard detachment that remained in position; he retired his troops to the south-west, towards the settlements of Mnindi and Mtschkama, where once more he prepared for the British advance.

On the 4th July 1917, following the German withdrawal from Kinamba Hill, No. 1 and No. 3 subsections of the battery advanced from Rumbo and reached Beaumont's Post the same day, despite snipers hampering their progress. Accompanying the infantry of Colonel Grant's No. 2 Column, the battery reached the crossroads, on the Mnindi to Lindi road, on the 6th July, where a stiff fight was in progress.

There was sharp fighting during the whole of the 6th, No. 1 Column driving the enemy from a position four miles north east of Mnindi and pressing him backwards, while No. 2 Column attacked Mnindi from the west.

Jacob van Deventer

Following early success in driving the Germans from their positions, the enemy counter attacked regaining much of the lost ground. The Hull battery was ordered into action, but before they were called upon to fire, the enemy relinquished its position and withdrew along the Mtschkama road.

We have had a big fight today, and the enemy has been driven out of all his positions on our front.

Joseph Dan Fewster, 6th July 1917

The rapid movement of von Lettow's troops, matched by that of the advancing allied infantry columns, made the work of the battery frustrating. On numerous occasions, severe fighting would occur at each position that the Germans had prepared and occupied. Von Lettow, recognised the limitations of his troop numbers and their irreplaceability, would engage strongly with the British infantry until such time that his position became threatened. At this point the Germans would retire to a new position that had been prepared; the process would be repeated. On each such occasion, the battery would prepare for action, but was often frustrated in their efforts by the withdrawal of Germans.

More "flying column" work but well fed this time. Had quite an interesting week but the infantry etc interfere with our work severely by driving the Germans to blazes when we get ready to chuck them a few reminders that we are still here. It is very satisfactory for the infantry but rotten for us.

Charlie Rimington, 9th July 1917

Porters position a howitzer. June 1917 (IWM Q 15515)

Number three subsection, which had remained at Beaumont's Post, re-joined No. 1 subsection at Kiwatama on the 15th July. The following morning both subsections left Kiwatama, advancing towards Mtschkama to the south.

Nearby Mtschkama, the Germans held the high ridges overlooking the place. Upon the arrival of the battery, an intense firefight was taking place between the infantry of both No. 1 and No. 2 Columns and the entrenched Germans. The dense vegetation and tall grass made observation difficult, but the battery was brought into action, firing eleven rounds without actually seeing anything of the German force.

> We leave Kiwitama before daybreak and after a short run to a place named M'Tchama, we come into action and have a full day of it. I don't think I was ever so tired in my life as I am tonight. I must have lost my stamina.
>
> Joseph Dan Fewster, 16th July 1917

At this juncture the battery received its new complement of motor transport from Kilwa, a mixture of FWD lorries and Napier cars. With improved mobility, the battery was ordered to proceed with all speed to join with the 1st Division. Passing through Migerigeri (N'gere-gere) and Kirongo the battery reached Mtandawala where it re-joined No. 1 Column that was spearheading the right flank of Deventer's advance. The journey was not without incident:

> Last night we received orders to move onto the other flank. This morning we left and I am not feeling well by any means. I had another bad night, with high temperature. We had a splendid run until an hour before dark and then began a full chapter of accidents. We had reached a stretch of really good road and were travelling at about 16 an hour when the tail-pin of the lorry (to which my gun was fastened) broke. The connecting rod of the gun limber dropped to the ground and slid along until it met a small hole in the ground. The gun was travelling at such a rate that the limber was turned completely over with the trail of the gun resting on the top and smashing the limber boxes to matchwood. We had hoped to reach N'gere-gere by dusk but this put the tin hat on it.

I was near beat myself, but it was no use looking at it. We set about it and got the gun clear of the wreckage. Then we put the remains of the limber in another lorry, made fast the trail of the gun to the lorry and away we went. I had aches and pains all over me, with a thirst like a wooden god, but we would make N'gere-gere by 7 o'clock. What a hope! We had travelled some seven or eight miles and we came to a dry river bed. We were crossing by an old wooden bridge when both hind wheels of my three-ton lorry went through, carrying most of the bridge with it. I had a rigor on me and although I had my greatcoat on, my teeth were chattering, but this had to be got out. We worked for hours, and at last got clear and crept into N'gere-gere at 12.30am. I had had nothing to eat all day and wanted nothing now but a drink. After I got that, I laid down and watched the stars all night, until they faded away at sunrise.

Joseph Dan Fewster, 18th July 1917

The roads were very sandy and the following morning, before they had travelled very far, the lorries bogged down. Only the use of ropes and manpower enabled any progress to be made, by the end of the day the men were exhausted. To reach Mtandawala the next day, it required the use of 400 porters. Upon arrival, the battery was posted to the force reserve; it was subsequently transferred to No. 2 Column at Mssindy. Throughout August the battery remained inactive at Mssindy. The infantry, meanwhile, cleared those remaining German forces from areas recently occupied by the allied forces. During this period Deventer strengthened the Kilwa force and concentrated his troops at Mssindy, in anticipation of a renewed advance to the south.

The light rains have started somewhat early and we are doing nothing now but strengthening our position... It is dull and rainy now and has been for some days. Yesterday afternoon the rain swept right through the hut and the trenches were two thirds full before it stopped. The Kings African Rifles in their sunken huts came off very badly for the rain could not get away.

Charlie Rimington, 17th August 1917

Concurrent with the re-assignment of units on Deventer's northern front near Kilwa, operations from the southern port of Lindi commenced in early August. These operations had the intent, once again, of cutting the enemy line of retreat to the south, whilst pressurising von Lettow's forces that were split between Kilwa and Lindi. This operation was, however, short-lived. It became apparent that von Lettow had reinforced his Lindi positions by moving a number of his units south from the Kilwa area. In light of this development, Deventer reduced the activity of both his Kilwa and Lindi forces to active patrolling until his reinforcements had arrived.

The grave of Corporal 290010 Francis William Winter. Dar es Salaam War Cemetery, Tanzania (Fecitt)

The commmemorative plaque of Corporal 290010 Francis William Winter. Dar es Salaam War Cemetery, Tanzania (author)

By the middle of September 1917 the additional troops had arrived. They included, the 25th Indian Cavalry, 55th Coke's Rifles, and the 127th Baluchi Light Infantry, along with the remainder of the Nigerian Brigade. The 7th South African Infantry would join them shortly afterwards. The Kilwa force, including the 11th (Hull) Heavy Battery, renewed their initiative on the 19th September.

> My plan was to make a combined movement southwards from the Kilwa area, and south-westwards from Lindi, engaging the enemy wherever met with.
>
> Jacob van Deventer

From Mssindy, the battery travelled 8 miles to Ndessa, occupying a previously reconnoitred position near the Lungo River. The enemy controlled the opposing bank, their encampments and machine gun positions were well dug in around the hillocks of Ndessa Kati and Ndessa Juu.

By using aeroplanes and wireless communication for ground observation, the battery was able to be ranged, with some reliability, on to targets. Assistance was provided by the 2/ 3rd Kings African Rifles when cloud obscured aerial visibility. On the 20th September in support of the infantry attack the battery fired forty three rounds on the Ndessa Kati before switching to the Ndessa Juu as the advancing infantry approached the latter position. The enemy withdrew with little resistance, the battery moving to the fore upon the enemy retirement to protect the force in the event of an expected counter attack that subsequently failed to materialise.

The infantry column, with cavalry support, fought von Lettow's forces hill by hill, from one defended position to the next, towards the village of Nahungu. Situated on the north bank of the Mbemkuru River; Nahungu was the location of von Lettow's headquarters. It was from here that he directed operations both at Kilwa, and Lindi. His force reserve was held nearby that allowed von Lettow to move his troops to the north or south, through interior lines, as the strategic situation dictated.

The two allied columns advanced on Nahungu and engaged the German forces there. It took Deventer's troops several days to force von Lettow from Nahungu, whereupon he crossed the Mbemkuru River, towards Ruangwa, where he occupied new positions just south of the river. The enemy withdrawal from Nahungu enabled the battery left at Ndessa to move forward to rejoin the main body of No 1 Column. The battery and the 25th Cavalry arrived at Nahungu on the 29th and 30th September 1917 respectively.

> The cavalry have been doing some pretty good work. Their horses are well fed now and look splendid. One thing, they do not keep everlastingly cantering their horses as the South African Horse used to do, they walk them on the march.
>
> Charlie Rimington, 29th September 1917

Early in the morning on the 1st October, in preparation for the resumption of the advance, Captain Floyd, with the assistance of 2nd Lieutenant Nevill, undertook reconnaissance on an enemy occupied position some 8 miles south of Nahungu. Von Lettow had established machine guns and entrenchments on the high ground that overshadowing the road; it had the potential to halt the advance by the Kilwa force along this route. The battery moved to a position selected by Floyd during his earlier reconnaissance. With close support from the Hull battery, the infantry of No. 2 Column, to which the battery was attached, advanced against the enemy positions on the hill forcing the Germans to withdraw.

> From 9:30am 37 rounds were fired at points where machine gun were located and where enemy movement was observed.
>
> Basil Edward Floyd, 1st October 1917

The following morning, the battery, returned to their camp on the north bank of the Mbemkuru River. The close proximity of the enemy and the overlooking hills gave cause for concern; snipers had been a constant danger to the troops and their current camp location would be no exception unless some protection could be offered. To this end the Hull Battery was assigned to night firing at intervals onto the adjacent hillside to prevent the digging in of enemy snipers, twelve rounds of shrapnel were fired in all, no sniper activity was reported. The following day, 3rd October, the battery rejoined No. 1 Column, the right flank of Deventer's advance.

On the 4th October, the battery crossed the Mbemkuru River and took up a position some 3 miles to the south. In an action with similarities to that of No. 2 Column, No. 1 Column was engaged against enemy positions on a hill overlooking the intended line of advance southwards. Supporting the 1 /3rd Kings African Rifles, the battery came into action at a range of 3,500 yards. Throughout the day they fired sixty six rounds of 50-pound shells, on several occasions silencing the enemy's rifle and machine gun fire. The fight continued into the following day, after the Kings African Rifles relieved by the 129th Baluchis. Firing on a reduced range of 2,200 yards, a further forty-eight rounds were fired; the battery's action effectively quashed a German counter attack. The fight for the German position continued and on the October, the 7th South African Infantry forced the enemy withdrawal from their positions.

Throughout the actions described above Deventer had sent the part of the Nigerian Brigade, attached to the Kilwa Force, forward by a circuitous route to join with the right flank of the Lindi force near Mtama. The Germans had already started retiring from below the Mbemkuru River, intending to concentrate around the town of Massassi. Von Lettow remained with his northern force to direct operations to cover his retreat.

Von Lettow was expected to retire from Ruangwa through Rupondo. No. 1 Column in anticipation moved from the Nahungu area, flanking the Mbemkuru River, through Kiperele to Mnero, and reached Rupondo on 10th October. The Germans avoiding Rupondo, instead moved south along interior lines through Ruangwa. Through the combined movements of the German and allied forces, von Lettow was effectively trapped between No. 2 Column to his west, and the Lindi force to the south. The further movement of No. 1 Column to Rupondo, circumvented a juncture between von Lettow's force and those Germans, commanded by Captain Theodore Tafel, who were known to be retiring from the Mahenge plateau to the north-west.

> The situation at this time demanded careful watching, as a strong enemy movement northwards against our long drawn out line of communication to Kilwa was always possible.
>
> Jacob van Deventer

Deventer, conscious of his extended line of communication, ordered the Lindi force inland along the Lukuledi River valley to apply pressure to von Lettow's forces at Mtama. The fight at Mtama was brief: the enemy withdrew to the west reaching Mahiwa, near Nyangoa, on the 15th October. Von Lettow, now at risk that his line of retreat would be severed by the allied advance from Lindi, marched his reserve troops south from the Mbemkuru River, joining the battle at Mahiwa. The battle was particularly fierce, and after four days of intense fighting the casualties on both sides were high. The arrival of No. 2 Column, at Lukuledi, that threatened the German flank from the west, forced von Lettow to order the withdrawal from Mahiwa on the 19th of October.

The Hull Battery moved to Rupondo and continued south to join the main force of No. 1 Column at Lukuledi Mission some twenty three miles distant towards Massassi. No. 1 Column had moved from Rupondo on the 17th October with a view to preventing von Lettow moving either to join with the German force retiring from Mahenge, or his moving west to Massassi. No. 1 Column had been attacked at Lukuledi by three companies of the enemy troops on the 18th: on that occasion they were repulsed. Three days later, bolstered by an additional three companies, the Germans attacked again. The attack was countered, with heavy loss to the German force, when the Hull Battery was brought into action. Twenty-seven rounds of shrapnel and high explosive shells were fired against the German line; the infantry captured two machine guns with several prisoners taken. In the early evening, three further rounds were fired against enemy troop concentrations that were seen to be forming up to counter attack. The enemy subsequently withdrew, No. 1 Column and the Hull Battery moved back to Rupondo on the 23rd October, remaining there for the rest of the month whilst awaiting developments with respect to von Lettow's movements.

The allied general advance resumed on the 6th November 1917. The Kilwa force passing back through Lukuledi, crossing the Massassi to Lindi road and arrived at Jumbe Mminanwa south-west of Chiwata Hill on 10th November and found that the Germans occupied the latter and the settlement of Chiwata beyond. The Lindi force pushed westwards and secured the Mahiwa district before continuing to Nangoo and there finding that the Germans had retired to Chiwata, south-west of Nangoo. The Lindi force pursued the enemy and by the 14th was overlooking the settlement of Chiwata from the heights of the Makonde plateau.

The Lindi and Kilwa forces were now in contact with each other, a situation that allowed for their combined operation. Mounted troops occupied the town of Massassi, there a field gun and a sizable number of German and askari troops were captured, further prisoners were taken at Ndanga Mission, and significantly the majority were German.

I decided to attack it [Chiwata] from the North with the Lindi force and from the west with the bulk of the Kilwa force, while mounted troops, supported by infantry, operated towards Kitengari against the enemy line of retirement.

Jacob van Deventer

Accompanied by the battery forward observation party, the 127th Baluchi Light Infantry attacked Chiwata Hill on the 11th November. Just after noon the Hull Battery was called upon to support the infantry. Rapidly going into action, the battery fired twelve rounds, in quick succession at the enemy trenches. Four direct hits were scored which caused the Germans to hurriedly evacuate their trenches. In the following hour eight more rounds were fired at several machine gun crews that were observed to be digging into the hillside. Battery operations continued in the following days, targeting German patrols and positions with shrapnel and high explosive charges.

Moved out on new road to Chiwata, camped on roadside. Guns in action against Chiwata position. Telephone line still maintained with F.O.O. on Chiwata Hill, this, the only line continuously open between Column HQ and Chiwata Hill.

Basil Edward Floyd, 14th November 1917

A gun of the Hull Heavy Battery firing near Chiwata, November 1917 (IWM Q 15508)

Moved about 1 1/2 miles on road to Chiwata, guns in action against Chiwata Positions. Telephone line still maintained.

Basil Edward Floyd, 15th November 1917

Signaller Arthur Cowbourne was the telephone operator in the Forward Observation Post on Chiwata Hill.

290070 Serjt A. Cowbourne R.G.A. (Hull)
For conspicuous gallantry and devotion to duty and marked ability in taking charge of battery observation post. During an attack he maintained telephonic communication between battery and observation post (six miles) for four days, this being the only line kept open between the column commander and the forward elements of the column.

London Gazette, 3rd October 1918

Sergeant Arthur Cowbourne who awarded the D.C.M. for his actions at Chiwata Hill (Cowbourne)

With Deventer securing a shorter line of communication through the port of Lindi, and an increase in troop numbers, von Lettow now faced a formidable opponent. Under such pressure, he withdrew from Chiwata, meeting with little opposition. He headed for Lutshemi, where for several days Deventer's mounted troops engaged him. His hopes for the arrival of the Tafel's force from Mahenge were frustrated. The juncture of the two German forces would have provided von Lettow with sorely needed men and ammunition.

Von Lettow, abandoning the juncture with Tafel's force, marched for the town of Newala, situated on a plateau north of the Rovuma River near the border with Portuguese East Africa. Continually engaged by Deventer's mounted troops and desperate to secure rations for his troops due to the widespread famine south of the Rufigi, von Lettow crossed the Rovuma into food-rich Portuguese East Africa on the 26th November 1917.

"Moved out on new road to Chiwata, camped on roadside". Officers (seated) and men take a rest during the fight at Chiwata, November 1917 (IWM Q 15486)

Tafel, unaware that von Lettow's troops had retired from the Makonde Plateau, clashed with mounted patrols from Deventer's force. Outnumbered, with increasing losses and contact with von Lettow lost, Tafel realised his predicament; he surrendered his force to Deventer on the 28th November 1917. German East Africa was finally clear of German forces. It would take another year and the armistice in Europe before von Lettow surrendered.

The continuation of Deventer's campaign throughout 1918 was to be exclusively pursued by native troops. To this end, all European troops were demobilised from Lindi. With no further contribution possible by the artillery, the Hull Battery were demobilised. They arrived at Mtama on the 26th November having left Chiwata on the 16th.

Fetched 2 guns from Nyangao recently loaned to 134th Cornwall Heavy Battery RGA, also their equipment.

Basil Edward Floyd, 27th November 1917

Having recovered their complement of guns, the battery headed for Mingoyo, a town at the mouth of the Lukuledi River, and there went into camp. The estuary and its shallow waters, would only allow for lighter boats to be used for transport. On the 5th December 1917, the battery loaded its four howitzers, limbers and the remaining ammunition on to the lighter boats using block and tackle that was established alongside. The battery reached Lindi the following day. The following morning, leaving the loaded lighters at the quayside at Lindi, the battery personnel embarked on the H.M.T. *Umtata*, sailing for Dar es Salaam at seven o'clock in the morning of the 7th December.

Chapter 18

Illness and Convalescence

THROUGHOUT the campaign in German East Africa, malaria, dysentery, relapsing fever, and typhoid were contracted by thousands of the troops who served there. To suffer any of these diseases once would be sufficient for most healthy people, but, in many cases, a man would have each of them on several different occasions. Their plight was compounded by the undernourishment caused by the frequent shortage of rations.

The Hull Battery was not immune to these ailments, Lieutenant Farley of the 38th Brigade ammunition column contracted dysentery aboard H.M.T. *Huntsgreen* before his arrival in East Africa. Once ashore at Mombasa, many of the battery contracted this debilitating disease, officers and men alike were stricken. Typhoid, or enteric fever as it was contemporaneously known, resulted from drinking contaminated water. Many water sources in the tropical areas become infected with human and animal waste. On many occasions water was in short supply, especially when all the troops were on the march. Under

The grave of Gunner 159 Francis Charles Lucop. Dar es Salaam War Cemetery, Tanzania (Fecitt)

these conditions, the men would drink any available water that they came across; it was rarely purified before consumption.

> Landed and was sent to Wynberg Hos.
>
> Alec Robertson, January 7th 1917

The overriding and constant affliction was malaria; there are several types of malaria one of which, cerebral or falciparum, is a killer.

> Custom has sharpened our clinical instinct, and where, in civil life, we would look for meningitis, now we only write cerebral malaria, and search the senseless soldier's pay-book for the name that we may put upon the "dangerous list." As this name is flashed 12,000 miles to England, I sometimes wonder what conception of malaria his anxious relatives can have… For there is no aspect of brain diseases that cerebral malaria cannot simulate; deep coma or frantic struggling delirium. A drop of blood from the lobe of the ear and the microscope reveals the deadly "crescents"—the form the subtertian parasite assumes in this condition. No time this for waiting or expectant treatment. Quinine must be given in huge doses, regardless of the danger of blackwater, and into the muscles or, dissolved in salt solution, into the veins. The Germans have left me some fine hollow needles that practice makes easy to pass into the distended swollen veins. Through this needle large doses of quinine are injected, and in six hours usually no crescent remains to be seen. As a rule, conscious life returns to these senseless bodies after some hours; but, unhappily, such success does not always crown our efforts.
>
> Robert Dolbey

The less serious strains of malaria, such as vivax, whilst still debilitating, affect the liver. To treat malaria, the troops in East Africa were provided with large doses of quinine. The combination of the excessive quinine and malaria caused the kidneys of a man to become infected. This was known as blackwater fever, a potentially fatal affliction that, if not treated promptly caused the death of many.

There was no need to seek the cause in the scrap of paper that was the sick report. All who ran could read it in the blanched lips, the grey-green pallor of their faces, the jaundiced eye, the hurried breathing... At first, if there was no vomiting, it was easy to ply the hourly drinks of tea and water and medicine. But once deadly and exhausting vomiting had begun, one could no longer feed the victim by the mouth. Then came the keener struggle for life, for fluid was essential and had to be given by other ways and means. Into the soft folds of the skin of the armpits, breast and flanks we ran in salt solution by the pint. The veins of the arms we brought into service that we might pour in this vitalising fluid. Day and night the fight goes on for three days, until it is won or lost.

Robert Dolbey

Less frequent, but not unknown within the battery, was relapsing fever or tick fever:

More commonly known as "relapsing fever," this illness attacks men who have been sleeping on the floor of native huts, which in this country are swarming with these parasites. Once in seven days for five or seven weeks these men burn with high fever—higher and more violent even than malaria—but sooner over. As you may imagine, it leaves them very debilitated for no sooner does the victim recover from one attack than another is due. The ticks that are the host of the spirillum, the actual cause of the disease, live in the soft earth on the floor of native huts at the junction of the vertical cane rods and the soil. Here, by scraping, you may discover hundreds of these loathsome beasts in every foot of wall. But they are fortunately different from the grass ticks that, though unpleasant, are not dangerous to man. For the tick that carries the spirillum is blind and cannot climb any smooth surface. So to one sleeping on a bed or even a native "machela" above the ground, he is harmless. But woe betide the tired soldier who attempts to escape the tropical rain by taking refuge on the floor. In sleep he is attacked, and when his blind assailant is full of blood he drops off; so the soldier may never know that he has been bitten.

Robert Dolbey

Persistent diseases progressively weakened the troops. Initially, treatment would be given at the field and base hospitals that were established close to the areas of operations. As the campaign developed and shipping became readily available, men were sent to recuperate in Wynberg near Cape Town in South Africa. At Wynberg, their afflictions could be treated more effectively than in the field hospitals, they could be fed properly and rested with a welcome respite from re-infection and the tropical heat of East Africa.

The grave of Gunner 290219 George Ledrew. Cape Town (Plumstead) Cemetery, South Africa (James White)

Troops that were sent to South Africa would embark upon a hospital ship at Dar es Salaam. There were many such ships pressed into service, amongst them the transport vessels *Ebani, Oxfordshire, Commonwealth, Ingoma,* and the *Karoola.* The voyage from Dar es Salaam to Cape Town could take up to ten days but longer if an additional call was made at Durban en route.

Dar es Salaam photographed by John McBain from the Hospital ship Ebani, en route for Cape Town, March 1917 (McBain)

Upon their arrival at Cape Town, the patients would be entrained at the dockside for the short trip to Maitland Railway Station, a few miles outside central Cape Town. Private motor cars were then used to transfer the men to the Princess Alexandra Hospital where upon arrival they handed in their service kit and were issued with a blue hospital uniform to wear throughout their stay.

Standing; Piercy (Hull), Milns (South Africa), Wright (South Africa). Kneeling; John McBain, John Fisher, Arthur Frost wearing their hospital blue uniforms at Princess Alexandra Hospital, 1917 (McBain/ Frost)

Most of the patients were suffering from malarial fever. Apart from the continued prescription of quinine, daily measures of wines and ports were given. Each patient received a daily inspection by their doctor, and if considered sufficiently fit, could request a day pass that allowed for them to roam freely in and around Cape Town.

Saw Wainright, King, Pinder and host more of our boys.
Alec Robertson, February 5th 1917

Princess Alexandra Hospital, Maitland, South Africa (McBain)

The corporation of Cape Town had gone to some lengths to accommodate the needs of the hundreds of troops passing through the hospitals in and around the city. Trams were made available freely for three days a week, and at the Feather Market, free teas were available to all men wearing hospital blue uniforms.

> Sports held in the ward at night, blanket tossing, scrap with tomatoes, pillows etc followed by a clean up of the place by the belligerents. This took place about 10pm. the proceedings ended with the presentation of prizes, the first prize being a bedpan.
>
> Jim Dixon, 6th Feb 1917

The concerts that were held at the end of the pier, and the church services at Cape Town Cathedral proved popular destinations. Regular musical salons, smoking parties and theatre productions provided additional recreation. The townsfolk of Cape Town proved especially generous to the troops, inviting individuals for dinner at home, or arranging day trips to Camps Bay, Sea Point or via motorcar over the mountain to Hout Bay.

> Dan Fewster arrived Wynberg from GEA looking very thin.
>
> Alec Robertson, February 15th 1917

Newlands House, Kennilworth, South Africa (McBain)

The ladies of the nearby district of Claremont provided regular dinner evenings, whilst Lady Buxton, wife of Viscount Buxton the governor general of South Africa, provided entertainment and dinner parties at their home with special trains provided to transport the patients to and from Maitland Hospital. Lady Buxton, sportingly hosted cricket matches against the patients, with her own team composed of ladies of her acquaintance.

> Dan and I met Syd [Wainright] and went to town.
>
> Alec Robertson, February 19th 1917

Many of the men from the Hull Heavy Battery had been sent to the Cape from East Africa at different times. Invariably a group from the battery would be found together meeting up in Cape Town to share the entertainment and meals so generously provided by their hosts.

> Dished out with striped blue and white blues. Look like a pork butcher.
>
> Jim Dixon, 26th February 1917

Their busy social life continued, with the additional attraction of visiting Kalk Bay, where time could be spent bathing and flying kites. A particularly pleasurable pastime and obviously popular, was promenading the seawall accompanied by the young ladies of Cape Town. Any relapse or return of fever would see the man returned to Maitland Hospital for continued treatment.

Bernard Berry (rear left), Jim Dixon (rear Centre) Newlands House, 1917 (Chandler/ Dixon)

Gnr. E. Jones died in this block this morning.

Jim Dixon, 11th May 1917

As the health of the patients improved they were successively moved to Newlands House in Kennilworth, or the Victoria Cottage Hospital in Wynberg. Upon attaining a reasonable degree of fitness and bodily strength, the troops would hand in their hospital blue

Promenading near Cape Town docks, McBain, Miss Gould, Frost, Miss Smith and Fisher in July 1917 (McBain/ Frost)

The grave of Gunner 169 Edward Jones, Cape Town (Maitland) Cemetery, South Africa (Colyn Brookes)

uniforms and be reissued with their army uniform before being transferred to the Palace Barracks at Simonstown to undertake garrison duties.

It was from Simonstown that, following further medical examination, troops were discharged for returning to the battery in East Africa. When their health would not allow, they were embarked upon a hospital ship bound for England, considered unfit for further service in that theatre of war.

Palace Barracks, Simonstown (McBain)

"Dear Clara, – This is the vessel I am coming home by. I should like you to keep this; it is a good picture of Table Mountain", Robert Colbridge, October 3rd 1916 (Colbridge/ McKinder)

Those soldiers who remained at Simonstown were entrained to Durban, and there embarked for the voyage to Dar es Salaam or Zanzibar to rejoin the battery.

Robert Colbridge. After leaving East Africa he was transferred to the Royal Engineers (Colbridge/ McKinder)

Chapter 19

Homeward Bound

THE completion of operations by Deventer's forces at Kilwa and Lindi, and the future use of native troops in East Africa, initiated a demobilisation of several European army units. The Hull Heavy Battery was one such unit that was to leave the country. Jack and the remnant of the battery that had remained at Morogoro, travelled by train to Dar es Salaam.

> Nov. 12th – Arrived at Daresalaam.
>
> Nov. 29th – Back in Hospital recommended for invaliding to South Africa.
>
> Dec. 9th – Battery returned from the Lindie Area, and I was given the choice of rejoining the battery for home or wait for the hospital ship, I choose the battery.
>
> Dec. 10th – Discharged from hospital to rejoin the Battery for sailing home.
>
> Jack Drake

Following von Lettow's evasion of Deventer's forces near Newala on the Rovuma River, and his crossing into Portuguese East Africa, the Hull Heavy Battery, with no further contribution to the campaign possible, sailed from Lindi; it landed at Dar es Salaam on the 8th December 1917.

> We are expecting to leave this country in a day or two for S.A. I suppose we shall stay there a while before going

anywhere else, we may come home or it may be Egypt. I hope it will be home and before long too. We are back in Dar es Salaam again, we arrived here from Lindi two days ago, I do not think there are any German forces left in GEA but there is still a few roaming about over the border.

Arthur Cowbourne, 10th December 1917

With all of the battery personnel now in Dar es Salaam, they loaded their remaining kit and stores aboard their transport vessel.

13th – Left Daresalaam on HMT. *INGOMA*
19th – Disembarked at Durban spent a good Xmas.

Jack Drake

The battery was accommodated at Congella Camp on the outskirts of Durban.

Congella Camp, Durban (author)

The weather here is simply glorious and Durban is really a fine place, it is just like being at some seaside place in summer at home.

I went down to a YMCA this morning for breakfast given to us troops in Durban and it was a first class affair, the people of Durban will do anything for us troops. I have just heard that we are leaving here on the 27th, I think we are going on to Cape Town and stay there a while, from there I think we should come on home.

Arthur Cowbourne, 25th December 1917

UNION-CASTLE LINE TO SOUTH AND EAST AFRICA

INTERMEDIATE STEAMER "DURHAM CASTLE."   8,239 TONS.

The RMS Durham Castle *that transported the remaining officers and men of the Hull Heavy Battery from South Africa in January 1918 (author)*

27th – Embarked for England on the RMS *Durham Castle* called at East London, Port Elizabeth, Mossall Bay.

Jack Drake

We left Durban on the 27th Dec. and expect reaching Cape Town today, it has been a rather longer journey than usual as we called at East London, Port Elizabeth and Mossel Bay, as far as we know we are putting into Cape Town but we know nothing as to how long we shall stay.

Arthur Cowbourne

1918/ Jan. 1st – Reached Capetown, went on shore.

Jack Drake

Just having a run round Cape Town, it is a glorious day and we are making the most of the chance.

Arthur Cowbourne, 3rd January 1918

4th – Left Capetown HMS *Kent* escorting us to Sierra Leone.
Jack Drake

Freetown Harbour, Sierra Leone (author)

On the 6th January 1918, Corporal Alfred White died of typhoid in No. 3 General Hospital, Durban.

Corporal 290235, Alfred White and Bombardier 43, Frederick Elmer Hagestadt commemorated on the Dar es Salaam British and Indian Memorial, Tanzania (Fecitt)

15th – Sierra Leone.

Jack Drake

Freetown, the capital of Sierra Leone, provided fresh water and was a Royal Navy coaling station. Many ships returning from the Cape would call here or alternatively Dakar on the Gold Coast (Ghana).

16th – Left Sierra Leone with a convoy, HMS *Kent* left us and we were escorted to England by the Armadale Castle an Auxilliary Cruiser. All smoking was prohibited on deck after 6pm. A strong guard was kept on the look out for submarines.

Jack Drake

Gunner Arthur Batchelor, from Cherry Burton, died from blackwater fever on the 19th January and was buried at sea the same day.

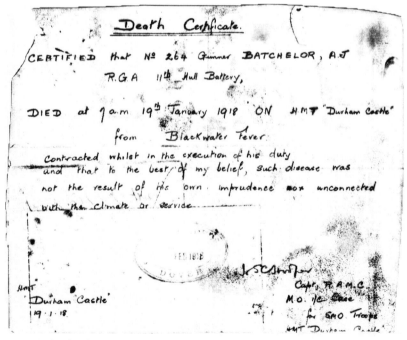

The death certificate of Arthur Batchelor, from Cherry Burton (National Archives)

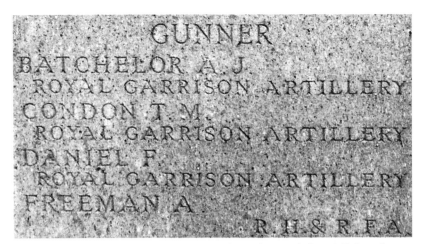

The memorial to Gunner 290254 Arthur John Batchelor Hollybrook,
Southampton, England (British War Graves Photographic Project)

Jan 24th – Strange ship sighted she did not answer the signal.
The Armadale Castle fired 2 or 3 shells at her and pulled
her up. After duty officer had seen the ships papers she was
allowed to proceed on her course. We were now 1,320 miles
west of Gibralter & 1200 from England.

Jan 30th – Arrived at Plymouth lost my kit bag and all it
contained.

Jack Drake

Of the original 274 ranks of the 38th Howitzer Brigade R.G.A.
that had departed from Devonport in February 1916, only sixty-
one returned aboard the RMS *Durham Castle* to Plymouth. Of these
sixty-one, many were collected from Cape Town en route. Charlie
Rimington and Jack, despite his many bouts of illness, were amongst
a handful of men from the battery who had continuous service in
German East Africa throughout the campaign.

Jan 31st – Arrived at Aldershot.

Jack Drake

At Aldershot the battery was billeted in Lille Barracks, now long
since demolished. Captain Floyd granted all men of the battery five
weeks leave.

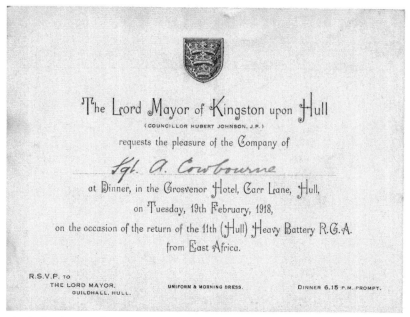

An invitation to a homecoming dinner given by the City of Hull (Cowbourne)

Feb 7th – Went to a dinner given by the City of Hull at the Grosvenor Hotel.

Jack Drake

The Hull Heavy Battery at their homecoming dinner at the Grosvenor Hotel, Carr Lane, Hull, on the 19th February 1918. Captain Floyd (uniformed) stands next to the Mayor of Hull (Rimington)

Gunner Maurice Boyd, a former student, and the last man to enlist in the Hull Heavy Battery upon its formation, died on the 16th February in the 3rd Northern General Hospital, Sheffield from a fractured skull sustained when knocked from his bicycle.

Those troops of the Hull Heavy Battery who were too seriously ill to join the battery for the voyage home aboard the *Durham Castle* to England remained in hospital in Cape Town. They eventually departed South Africa aboard the S.S. *Ulysses*, outbound from Melbourne, Australia, docking in Hull in March 1923.

Part 2

Chapter 20

The 545th Siege Battery R.G.A.

THE 545th Siege Battery R.G.A. was amongst the last group of artillery batteries to be formed during the course of the war; it resulted from the renaming of the 11th (Hull) Heavy Battery R.G.A. to meet its new role in France. It was established on the 1st March 1918, with recently promoted Major Basil Floyd as its commanding officer. Floyd, keen to build on the esprit de corps he had previously fostered within the Hull Heavy Battery whilst in East Africa, went to some lengths to ensure he filled the ranks of his new command with as many men from his original battery as was possible. The ranks who had returned with him from East Africa the previous January returned from leave to rejoin their unit, as Jack notes:

> March 7th – Returned to Aldershot. The Battery was renamed the 545 Siege Bty. RGA.

Of those men from the original battery, many had been invalided home from East Africa, some had died, others, upon their recovery, had been posted to other artillery batteries or regional depots.

Floyd set out to find the men who were available and fit enough to serve with him again. Lieutenant Maslin, the former section officer with the 13th Howitzer Battery whilst in East Africa, was now employed at the R.G.A. Records Office in Dover. The severe nature of Maslin's illnesses that he contracted in East Africa ensured

| *The grave of John William Alexander who was killed in action whilst serving with 90th Siege Battery R.G.A. in Belgium (author)* | *The grave of Allan Lawson who was killed in action whilst serving with the 16th Heavy Battery R.G.A. in Belgium (author)* | *The grave of William Turner, who was killed whilst serving with the 136th Heavy Battery R.G.A in France. (author)* |

that he was sent to hospital in South Africa. Following a period of convalescence at Wynberg hospital, Maslin was repatriated to England for further specialised treatment.

Eventually Maslin was discharged from hospital, but his medical category was such that he was unfit for further service in any theatre of war. Maslin was, therefore, posted to the records office, an administrative role which gave him and therefore Floyd access to the records of the men from the Hull Battery and enabled them to locate the scattered remnants of the battery.

Dan Fewster, who as a stretcher case had left Dar es Salaam in September 1917, landed in England before spending several months at the specialist malarial hospital in Oxford. His experience is typical of how Floyd orchestrated the formation of the new battery.

> I arrive at Avington Park, Winchester from Oxford and report myself discharged from hospital, when the first thing I see lying on the desk is a telegram from Major Floyd asking when he may expect me. After the orderly room clerk had taken down my particulars, I put in my application for transfer to my battery. "Oh" said the clerk "I have a wire here from your OC, your transfer will be through tomorrow."
>
> Joseph Dan Fewster, 13th March 1918

Dan arrived at Aldershot to rejoin the battery on the 30th March where he was reunited with his former comrades. Avington Park, Winchester was the base for No. 1 and No. 2 Reserve Heavy Brigades R.G.A. from where, had it not been for Floyd and Maslin's connivance, under normal circumstances as a returning soldier, he could be re-posted to any artillery unit rather than his own battery. Dan was not the only man to receive a telegram.

British Columbia-born, insurance company clerk, William Brocklehurst, was upon his arrival in England from South Africa, first sent to hospital in Manchester. Upon his discharge from hospital, he, similarly, was posted to No. 1 Reserve Heavy Battery where Floyd quickly found him; he joined the 545th Siege Battery on the 17th April 1918.

William Brocklehurst photographed upon his return to England in 1917 (Brocklehurst)

Tom Boswell from Lockington, near Beverley was formerly a railway porter for North Eastern Railways. He was repatriated from Wynberg, South Africa in November 1917 and admitted into hospital at Oxford. When discharged he was sent to No. 2 Depot at Preston, Lancashire. When he was fully recovered, Tom was posted to No. 1 Reserve Heavy Brigade R.G.A. where, upon arrival, he was posted directly to 545th Siege Battery. He joined the battery on the 25th April whilst it was at the Siege Artillery School, Lydd.

The establishment of the new battery was enlarged to 170 men by a complement of signallers posted from Catterick, Yorkshire. The additional men were a mixture: they included several miners from Wales, some Scots and a number of Londoners; men from differing backgrounds and regions. The battery numerically, and due to their previously shared experience and esprit de corps, essentially remained, in all senses, the Hull Heavy Battery.

The first month back at Aldershot was taken up with drill where the instructors took particular pleasure in criticising the battery, despite it being equal, if not better than others in both smartness and competence. It was with some relief that, at the end of the month, they received orders to attend the Siege Artillery School at Lydd.

> April 2nd – Left Aldershot for Lydd.
>
> Jack Drake

Upon their arrival at Lydd, the battery became part of B Training Brigade for the duration of their course, quickly settling into their camp and falling into the daily routine of the school. The harsh regime of the Aldershot instructors was soon forgotten, and the battery found themselves, much to their own surprise, to be one of the most competent batteries under training at that time.

> We have a fair selection of guns here including 18 pounder field guns, 60 pounder, 6" howitzers and 9.2 inch howitzers. The other morning while we were on the 6" howitzers the OC of the camp was watching our work. I heard him ask our OC if we always did our work like that. Our OC told him we did. The colonel then said we need not be kept on the guns after 12 noon so we are being favoured.
>
> Joseph Dan Fewster, 12th April 1918

The battery demonstrated both its professionalism and consistency when executing the course work. This brought the battery praise and reinforced their esprit de corps whilst raising their morale. Major Floyd, a career artillery officer and somewhat a perfectionist, had ensured he would not be disappointed by the performance of his battery. Throughout the long campaign in East Africa, Floyd had ensured that the battery continued gunnery training; the benefit of this training was now proven.

> We again come out top in the criticism this morning. Our gun drill came out as near perfect as possible. I was pleased about this because a detachment gets messed about a good deal in these tests. The GI's are walking about in the battery during

the course, putting various parts of the gun mechanism out of action and making casualties in ones detachment with a ruthless hand. One starts with a detachment of ten men and probably finishes with four or five. At the same time the sight clinometer and the quick release may be put out of action. During some part of the course you are sure to be attacked by gas and have to work in box respirator. Still the rate of fire must go on the same.

Joseph Dan Fewster, 1st May 1918

The battery's gun drill was good; soon they proved themselves on the firing ranges, responding to aeroplane observation, something not altogether unfamiliar to them, having experienced this in East Africa. Their previous work, and in particular the achievements of the 3rd of May, won the battery the honour of having a Complimentary Order issued in the Brigade Orders for the 4th May 1918.

We have had a proud day today. Our course included an S.O.S. target. When marching on to the battery, the No 1 receives the necessary angle, elevation, projectile and charge required for this target. The switch to the S.O.S. target is always such that the gun requires to be run up, to get the trail spade out of its bed, so that it is possible to lay on the new target. The S.O.S. order is always given during the firing of another course, with the idea of getting a spark into the work and training units to expect it at any time. One round is fired from each gun and then the detachment stands by for further orders. The record time for getting an S.O.S. target and firing one round is two minutes. Today we have broken that record with ease. The longest time taken was 55 seconds and the shortest 37 seconds. My detachment was 39 seconds in getting the round off. The battery received congratulations from the staff at Lydd for this work.

Joseph Dan Fewster, 3rd May 1918

On the 14th May 1918, Lord Nunburnholme, who it may be recalled instigated and financed the formation of the original Hull Heavy Battery, joined it at Lydd. From May 1918, he was an Honorary Colonel with the East Yorkshire Regiment. In order for him to join the 545th Siege Battery in action abroad, it was required that he undertake an artillery battery officer's course. Nunburnholme was granted the rank of Temporary Captain in the R.G.A..

Tintown Camp, Lydd.

Lydd, Siege Artillery School, Tintown Camp (author)

Many of the battery now present at Lydd had, until a few months previously, been in East Africa. During their service there, all had succumbed to malaria and other afflictions on multiple occasions. Major Floyd and his officers had similarly suffered and, because of this experience, took a lenient approach to the absences caused by the occasional bouts of fever the men continued to suffer. He did not insist on them reporting sick, but he allowed them to lie up for the day until recovered.

Some cases were more serious; whilst at Aldershot several of the battery had a recurrence of malaria. Amongst others, Bombardier James Birch, one of the sixty-one ranks that had arrived home aboard the *Durham Castle* from Cape Town in January, was admitted to the Connaught Hospital at Aldershot with malaria. After thirty-seven days in hospital he was discharged to rejoin the battery that had, since his hospitalisation, moved to Lydd. The battery, already proving efficient and in good spirits from their previous success, found further favour at Lydd.

During the last three weeks we have had a rather busy time shooting a series of experimental shoots, as well as some exhibition shooting for Sir William Robertson who has been paying a visit here. Altogether we have fired twenty-three courses, which is far in excess of the normal requirement.

Joseph Dan Fewster, 24th May 1918

When the battery had completed its retraining on the larger and more modern weapons than their previous experience in East Africa had allowed, it prepared to mobilise for France.

May 29th – Hear we are leaving Lydd on Friday for Hilsea.

Jack Drake

One hundred and fifty eight ranks of the battery left Lydd on Friday 7th June, reporting at Portsmouth the following Monday and going into billets at Hilsea Barracks. With each day's first parade at seven in the morning, and the working day finishing at four in the afternoon, the men considered it a bit of a holiday following their recent intense training activities. The battery was, however, required to provide a camp guard and undertake occasional duties as the town piquet.

Unfortunately, after his arrival at Hilsea, Jack did not make any further entries in his pocketbook. The war the battery was now to join would be very different to that they had experienced in East Africa. Henceforth, the battery would be involved in almost continuous action; the men with little time available, and much stricter censoring of letters home than had been the case in East Africa, has ensured that little detail has survived of this period. Similarly, the requirement for Major Floyd to maintain a unit war diary was withdrawn for Siege Batteries; this responsibility was now taken at Brigade level. However, to some extent, and despite this order, Floyd did maintain a skeleton of a battery diary, enabling their activities to be established throughout the following period.

Upon its arrival at Hilsea, the 545th Siege Battery was designated as a 12-inch railway howitzer battery. Major Floyd objected strongly to this proposal. Having personally gone to great lengths to rebuild the ranks from the remnants of the Hull Heavy Battery, he was in no mood to see his men reduced and dispersed. Railway batteries had one gun only; they required fewer ranks to service them. The designation as a railway battery would have resulted in his battery being split with some men dispersed to other batteries.

With similar determination to that he had demonstrated whilst rebuilding the Hull Battery from the scattered remnants of the 38th Brigade R.G.A., Floyd managed to achieve a change of position. With some effort, he secured for the new battery four 6" Mark XIX field guns, as replacements for the railway gun. After settling the new establishment of the battery, and receiving their mobilisation stores on the 13th June, the battery proceeded on four days' embarkation leave in two sections.

On their return to Hilsea, the first section of the battery's four new 6-inch guns was received on the 5th July. The day was met with some excitement by the men, but was, however, marred. Captain Frank Harrison (previously Lieutenant) who had served with the battery throughout the East African campaign was admitted to hospital with a recurrence of fever. Captain Harrison never rejoined the battery due to his continued and severe illness. The remaining section of two guns arrived on the 9th July, with the addition of the firing platforms and four Holt caterpillar tractors to tow the guns.

The 6-inch Mark XIX, gun entered service in 1916. The War Office requested Vickers, its manufacturer, specifically for a gun design capable of firing a charge 13,000 yards, much further than existing 6-inch weapons. Vickers responded quickly to their requirement by matching a newly designed longer barrel, to an existing but improved howitzer carriage that was utilised on their own 8-inch howitzer. The latest model of this gun, with which the battery was equipped, was capable of firing deep behind the enemy lines. Compared to previous models, it had improved elevation and the advantage of a thirty-degree lateral swing facilitated by the purpose designed firing platform. Upon their receipt by the battery, the guns were christened; they were each named after an engagement of the battery's previously experience in East Africa. Two guns are known to have been named Duthumi and Kondoa.

At this later stage in the war, less reliance was made on the use of horses for pulling heavy artillery pieces, although many of the heavy batteries continued to use draught animals. The entry of America

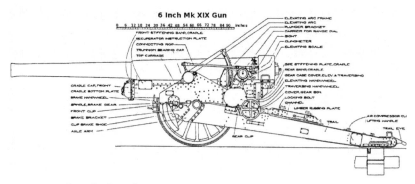

Detail of a Mk XIX Gun – Side Elevation (Wikipedia)

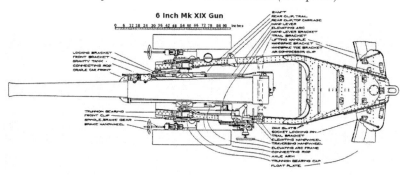

Detail of a Mk XIX Gun – Plan View (Wikipedia)

into the war and the increased flow of war materials across the Atlantic saw the greater use of tracked vehicles to tow the guns.

Holt & Best of California had bought the patent for continuous tracks from Richard Hornby of Grantham in Lincolnshire. They had developed the concept and produced a range of agricultural and industrial tractors incorporating this innovation. The outbreak of war found a ready use for these machines. Interestingly the continuous track design returned to Lincolnshire when the Landships Committee applied it in their designs for the first armoured vehicles. The first tanks were made by William Foster & Company in Lincoln. Their works were adjacent to that of fellow engineers, Ruston and Hornsby, Ruston having merged with the original patentee. The tractors assigned to the 545th Siege Battery were the latest 120-horsepower models. Unlike earlier models that employed a forward single ground wheel for steering, the new model was steered by slewing with the tracks. Holt & Best eventually became the Caterpillar Tractor Company: CAT.

On the 12th July 1918, outside of their barracks at Hilsea, the battery sections had their photographs taken. On the 16th July the remaining stores were issued and loaded into the mechanical transport company of the Army Service Corps that was attached to 545th Siege Battery. This transport company consisted of sixteen Thornycroft lorries commanded by Lieutenant Geoffrey Rackham.

Officers and N.C.O.s of the 545th Siege Battery, Hilsea Barracks, 12th June 1918. Dan Fewster (centre, back row) Arthur Cowbourne (third from left, middle row), Thomas Reaston (centre, middle row), James Allenson (front row, left) (Hopkin)

Later that day the guns and the transport drove to Portsmouth docks. The tractors and lorries were handed over for loading onto the transport ships. The following day the battery personnel left Hilsea and travelled by train from Cosham station to Southampton West station, then marched in pouring rain to the docks for embarkation. Once aboard it became apparent that by wearing their lifebelts, which were compulsory, there was only room to stand. The ship was packed with troops, and the battery appeared to be the only British contingent aboard. America had joined the war in

Europe and thousands of their young men had crossed the Atlantic to England before they were shipped to the war in France.

Men of the Left Section, D Subsections of 545th Siege Battery R.G.A., Hilsea, 12th June 1918. John McBain (back row, second from left), John Burnham (back row, third from left), Harold Masterman (fourth row from front, second from left), George Saul (fourth row from front, second from right), Charlie Rimington (third row from front, second from left), Dan Fewster (front row, second from right (Hopkin)

Landing in Le Havre on the 18th July 1918, the battery went into camp where they receive a welcome meal. Until that time the men had sustained themselves on the very familiar East Africa diet of bully beef and biscuits. The battery equipment was landed ashore three days after their arrival. The town was full of American troops.

> There are five or six thousand Americans passing through here daily, physically they are a fine body of men, but then they have not had four years of war. Perhaps the most noticeable thing about them is their boasting. One gets tired of continually hearing what we ought to have done and how they will do it and finish the job. This swanking does not strengthen the friendliness between the two parties and little scraps are frequent.
>
> Joseph Dan Fewster, 23rd July 1918

The battery marched from their camp to Le Havre, Maritime station to entrain for the battlefront. The boredom of waiting for the train, whilst stood in full kit, was assuaged by the men singing songs that were popular at that time, and by smoking. The train arrived after a six-hour wait and, after departure, travelling through the night making painfully slow progress. Non-commissioned Officers and men were packed thirty- to forty into ordinary railway boxcars; the officers enjoyed less crowded but no more salubrious accommodation. At daybreak they passed through Calais, reaching St. Omer, a short distance, many hours later. They continued to Aire Sur la Lys where the train halted, and the battery was ordered to disembark; it was eleven o'clock in the evening. Before the men were marched to their billets at St. Quentin, a village some two miles or so from Aire, the tractors and guns were unloaded. Lieutenant H. A. Hounsell, a new officer to the unit, had left Hilsea some days earlier than the batterywith a forward party consisting of fourteen men. This party had made the local arrangements and acquired billets for the battery, a mixture of farm buildings, barns, and houses. The motor transport of the A.S.C. travelled by road from Le Havre and joined the battery at the village of St. Quentin.

Holt & Best tractor towing a Mk XIX Gun somewhere in France (I.W.M. Q 8608 IWM)

Chapter 21

The Lys Salient

IN March 1918, the German Army commanded by Erich von
Ludendorff, conscious of the impending build-up of American
troops, launched an offensive, Operation Michael, in the Somme
region of the Western Front. Its aim was to finish the war by dividing
and the subsequent defeat of the British and French armies. The
recent collapse of Russia, due to the revolution there, had allowed
many German divisions to be transferred from the Eastern Front,
giving Ludendorff a numerical advantage on the Western Front at
this time. The British Third and Fifth Armies opposing the offensive
were forced to fall back before the onslaught. It was several days
before British reinforcements would enable the momentum of the
German offensive to be stayed.

Having not succeeded in his original plan Ludendorff launched
a second major offensive during April in Flanders to the north,
intending a breakthrough to the channel ports, capturing the allied
lines of communication and thereby causing the allied armies to
collapse. This second offensive known as Operation Georgette
resulted in the rapid advance along the valley of the River Lys to
the south of the Ypres Salient. German intelligence had correctly
identified a weakness in the British Line; this sector, whose
defences had been neglected, was in part manned by a Portuguese
contingent of conscript troops who had little experience and whose
morale was poor. Under the full onslaught of the attacking German
divisions, this part of the line was breached resulting in the British
withdrawing rapidly to a new line further west. The German attack

was halted, leaving the Germans in possession of a large salient from which, due to exhaustion and lack of further supplies, they were never able to continue the advance.

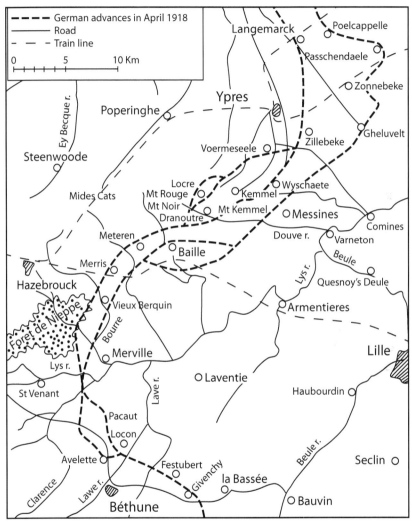

Map showing the Lys Salient formed during the German Spring Offensive of April 1918

This salient proved very costly for the Germans, just as had the British Salient at Ypres to the north. The ability of the heavy artillery to target every road, bridge, stores dump, hostile battery, and billet made it a killing ground for the German army. It was to this sector that the 545th Siege Battery was deployed. Within a few days of the battery establishing their positions, on the 8th August, the Battle of Amiens would start some fifty miles to the south. It was the beginning of what is now known as the Hundred Days, during which time the allied forces would repeatedly attack and finally breach the German lines and, in so doing, instigate the mass withdrawal and eventual collapse of the German Army.

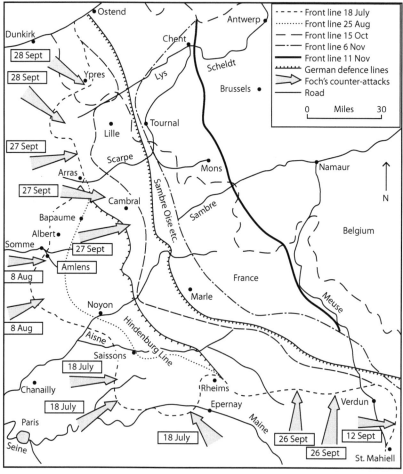

Map showing the Allied advance from July to November 1918

With their guns consigned to the Army Ordinance Corps for final adjustments, calibration and equipping, detachments from the left section took forward the gun platforms to the position recently vacated by 521st Siege Battery R.G.A. and prepared gun pits for their expected arrival.

We arrive at our destination and at once start digging in. We have taken a fine position for our two guns in an orchard alongside a farmhouse at Haverskerke. We are just to the right of the main road running through Haverskerke to Merville. On the right is the Lys Canal, about a quarter of a mile away on our left is the great Nieppe Forest, while in our rear is the village or small town of La Foret.

Joseph Dan Fewster, 30th July 1918

New billets were procured nearer the gun positions, a convenient barn at a farm some half a mile to their rear making a comfortable if precarious dwelling. The barn was well within the range of enemy artillery but miraculously never received a direct hit during their stay there although many rounds landed in close proximity. The two guns of the left section were taken into position on the night of the 1st August and manhandled from the road into the gun pits concealed in the orchard of the farm. Whilst the men struggled to manoeuvre the fifteen-ton weight of their guns over the soft yielding ground, the German artillery commenced a blanket bombardment with gas shells in the immediate area of the battery forcing the men to wear their box respirators. In order to avoid the risk of being hit by shrapnel from the continual harassing artillery fire from the German artillery, the men returned to their billets in ones and twos. No casualties resulted from the enemy action but George Saul was severely injured with a broken spine when a dugout they were building collapsed.

We were making a dug out in the battery position. Gnr Saul was working inside and the rest of us heaping earth on top. The crossbeam supporting the corrugated iron suddenly broke and the lot fell in with Gnr. Saul still inside it.

Robert Raleigh

I was working inside the dug out with Gnr Saul. I asked those outside if anybody was on top as I heard some creaking. The beam then fell in and as only one side was covered in earth nothing touched me but it all fell on Gnr Saul.

E. Lowther

George had served throughout the East African campaign, in civilian life he had worked for Reckitts in Hull having joined them in January 1912 at their Morley Street, Stoneferry works.

> My father only came home the once, I remember him bringing home a piece of ivory 9" long and 3" wide. My mother used it to prop open the door in summer. He also brought home six ostrich feathers and a pod of what he called "lucky beans" each was 2" long, black and red at the top. I remember him lying down in front of the fire, shivering yet covered with blankets. I asked my mother what was the matter and she told me he had malaria fever.
>
> George Saul Jnr., 2001

George Saul never recovered from his injuries and died at No. 8 General Hospital, Carniers on the 10th October 1918, his grave was made in Etaples Miltary Cemetery close to where he died.

The grave of Gunner 290306
George Henry Saul,
Etaples Military Cemetery (author)

Gunner 290306 George Henry Saul
(Saul/Dinsdale)

On the night of the 7th August, the enemy artillery fired a barrage of gas shells in the immediate area of the battery's guns and the two anti-aircraft batteries that were positioned adjacent. The attack was accompanied by heavy air raids that necessitated the men from the battery taking to their trenches for protection. Suffering no casualties during the night, at daybreak, the battery commenced the bombardment of German positions: part of the preparations for an attack on the salient by the infantry. The German artillery, knowing the approximate location of the battery probed the area in an attempt to silence the battery guns but without success.

Major Floyd established the battery headquarters at the hamlet of Tannay, some distant behind where the battery sections were positioned. He took time to organise his command and split the men into three shifts of duty, each to be of twenty-four hours' duration. The first period would be spent by a detachment at the guns, followed by a day's rest. Finally a day was to be spent on battery fatigues and ammunition duties. Each gun required a ten-man gun crew in attendance for each spell of duty.

The guns of the right section, subsection A and B, were returned to the battery from the Army Ordinance Corps' depot in the second week of August. At this point, a new gun position was established to the south of the Lys Canal, near the hamlet of Bas Hamel. During these operations, the battery came under the command of the Fifth Army as Army Troops, nominally attached to the 11th Army Heavy Artillery Brigade.

In August and early September the British Second and Fifth Armies, assisted by the 27th and 30th Divisions of the American II Corps, reduced the Lys salient. The German withdrawal had started as early as the 10th August, and by the 19th August, Merville, a previous target for the battery, had been captured. The enemy withdrawal, which continued, left the battery less active than it had previously been during early August. Men from the battery, particularly those from the rural districts, found recreation in helping the local farmers with their harvest. The rapid German advance during the spring had coincided with the sowing season and, despite the war being in close proximity, had left the growing crops relatively unscathed. By the 31st August, huge fires were seen burning in front of the battery positions: the Germans were burning their remaining stores to prevent their capture. Infantry patrols reported that there were no live Germans within two miles of the frontline, but German air raids against allied targets and artillery persisted.

The success of the British attack at Amiens had a profound effect on the German situation, summarised here by Sir Douglas Haig, the Commander in Chief of the British armies:

> The exhaustion of the enemy's reserves resulting from the Allied attacks made the shortening of the German line imperative. The obvious sector in which to affect such a shortening was in the Lys front. The enemy had only maintained himself in the salient under the constant fire of our guns at the expense of heavy casualties, not only to his infantry line, but also to his artillery and troops in back areas. With the abandonment of his projected offensive against the Channel Ports all reason had gone for remaining in so costly a salient, while the threat, carefully maintained by us, of a British attack provided an additional reason for withdrawing.

Lord Nunburnholme, who had remained at Lydd, had now completed his battery officer's course and rejoined the battery on the 14th September. Thoughtful for the men's needs, he brought them each a small tablet of soap, which was much appreciated as it was a scarce commodity. It was still late summer in France; the men had become accustomed to bathing in the nearby Lys canal. Unfortunately, as can happen in peacetime, Gunner William Shackleton drowned there. Shackleton, from Tyneside, had been posted to the 545th Siege Battery upon its formation in March.

The grave of Gunner 89508 William Shackleton, who drowned in the Lys Canal. Tannay British Cemetery, Thiennes (author)

The enemy had now withdrawn beyond the useful range of the battery which instigated a move to new forward positions. The left section, passing through Merville and Estaires, repositioned at Doilieu; the right section moved some two and a half miles forward of their previous position, close to the village of St. Floris. It was during the move to Doilieu that the gun of C subsection left the narrow track, plunging deep into the ditch adjacent the road. It took the power from two of the Holt tractors, coupled by chains in tandem, to retrieve the gun. The recovery operation caused the front end of the forward tractor to rear skywards in an alarming manner.

Now back within range of the enemy, action commenced from the new positions on the 20th September and was soon spotted by one of their observation balloons. The left section of the battery came in for a hot time. After only having fired three or four rounds from the new position, the German artillery bombarded the battery heavily with shrapnel and high explosive.

> Fragments of shrapnel were whistling and shrieking so that it was almost impossible to hear anything else. After a while he slackened down a bit so then we started again. But the Boche had not finished his argument. He started again with renewed vigour. We had been having it hot for some time when the OC bawled out for us to take cover. We had no dugouts made so we had to scatter.
>
> Joseph Dan Fewster, 20th September 1918

The following day, both sections of the battery were ordered to withdraw and concentrate on the small railway village of Berguette. This town had remained relatively unscathed by the war that raged nearby and safe, if crowded, billets were found for the battery in the YMCA building. The early risers from the battery had the opportunity to have a brief tour of the village before the arrival of their railway wagons in the sidings. The afternoon was spent loading their guns and tractors along with the battery stores onto the wagons ready for their evening departure. The motor transport travelled onward by road, whilst the battery left Berguette at 8 p.m. the evening of the 22nd September 1918 southbound for Peronne, where they would join General Rawlinson's, Fourth Army.

Chapter 22

The Battles of the Hindenburg Line

UPON their midday arrival at Peronne the battery went briefly into the rest camp placed some three miles out of town, receiving orders later that day to join 47th Brigade R.G.A. assigned to III Corps' artillery of the Fourth Army. Their new position would be between the villages of Villers Faucon and St. Emilie where several other batteries of 47th brigade were already in position near the sunken road and the open ground close by, the battery finding billets in Villers Faucon. The brigade had as recently as the 18th September been involved in supporting the III Corps' attack at Epehy and Ronssoy, preliminary attacks for the assault on the main Hindenburg Line positions.

The current allied offensive by the Fourth and Third Armies had commenced along the line Amiens – Albert – Arras on the 8th of August.

Following up this success in the following weeks they were now poised to assault the main Hindenburg defensive system from a starting position roughly that following the German Spring offensive of the previous March. In this advance, matched by similar gains to the right and left by the French and British First Army, the line was shortened, releasing men and allowing important railheads and communications to be recovered. In the forthcoming battles the Fourth Army would play the major role having its front such that the St. Quentin Canal defences, part of the Hindenburg Line would be

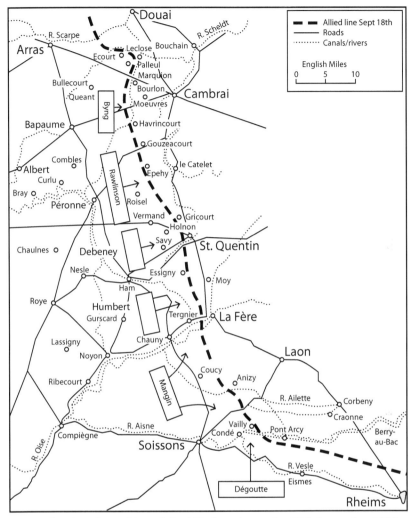

Map showing the position of the Allied armies on the 18th September 1918

to its fore. It was at this juncture that the 545th Siege Battery joined the Fourth Army.

Leaving their camp near Peronne the battery took their firing platforms forward to their new position on the night of the 24th September in readiness for positioning their guns. Unable to find suitable locations in the dark and hampered by shellfire the task was abandoned for the night, the platforms being left beside the road with a guard from the battery until morning. During the night the German artillery was active, firing on the roads in an effort to prevent the movement of troops and materials to the forward positions, which resulted in the guards having to take cover under the platforms as protection from shrapnel. One of the platforms received a direct hit which destroyed it completely, but, miraculously, it did not harm the badly shaken men beneath it. The guns towed by their tractors finally took up their position on the night of the 25th September and fired nine rounds the following morning to establish range.

> We take up position and I think we are in for a warm time. We are in full view of 7 or 8 enemy observation balloons and we have no cover of any kind.
>
> Joseph Dan Fewster, 25th September 1918

In the growing barrage for the forthcoming assault on the Hindenburg Line, 309th and 109th Siege Batteries, some distance forward from 545th Siege Battery, were firing gas shells. Observed from the enemy balloons they were targeted by enemy artillery, and sustained numerous casualties as a result of counter battery fire. The Hull boys who by this date in the war considered themselves lucky with respect to casualties had a reminder of their mortality that was reinforced later in the day.

> We have two cooks who go up with the guns to cook for the detachments on duty with the guns. Today when "dinner up" was called, the whole crowd rushed up with their mess tins. Just then Jerry dropped a whiz-bang in the midst of them. Fortunately it was a dud, but filled our dixies with mud, so we had to go without any dinner… An Aussie horse convoy pulled up about 100 yards in our rear to snatch a midday meal. This drew enemy fire and before one knew what was happening, half the convoy was up in the air. Fragments of horses, wagons and men were all over the place.
>
> Joseph Dan Fewster, 26th September 1918

The Hindenburg Line that was now the obstacle facing the Allied Armies and was to absorb much of the 545th Siege Battery's attention in the coming days was a formidable defensive system. Established at relative leisure by the Germans in 1916 behind its previous front line positions and occupied by withdrawal to it in 1917 it had been constructed with great military and engineering skill. Utilising the natural terrain to create a deep defensive system of trenches, dugouts, and machine gun emplacements further protected by dense belts of barbed wire gave the Germans a formidable advantage in defence, their position dominating the higher ground and commanding the approaches to it. Typically the

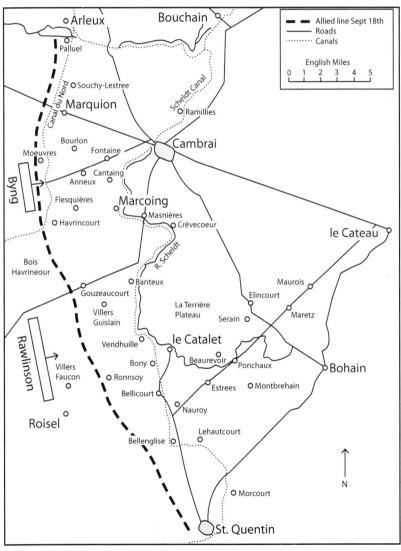

Map showing the position of the British Third and Fourth Armies before the assault on the Hindenburg Line of the 27th September 1918

defences consisted of an outpost line forward of the main trench system, the latter backed by a support line from which reserves could be mobilised. To the rear was a second support line, which in the sector of the Fourth Army would become known as the Beaurevoir Line. It was less formidable but had the added threat of numerous machine gun positions beyond. Each trench system was protected by barbed wire, strategically placed machine gun emplacements, and mine fields, some positioned forward of the outpost line.

The impending renewal of the offensive by the British intended to secure the approaches and eventually breach through the strongly defended Hindenburg Line saw the battery commence firing on the 27th September. On this day the American II Corps (30th & 27th Divisions) attacked the Knoll, a ridge overlooking a broad valley and the Bellicourt canal tunnel beyond. This, from the German perspective, overlooked the Allied lines from the western bank of the St. Quentin Canal. This attack was a precursor to a main attack on the Hindenburg Line that would commence on the 29th September but failed to achieve its intended objective. The 47th Brigade R.G.A. acted as a reinforcing brigade during this attack but in line with orders issued by GHQ on the 22nd September was employed in counter battery fire to the rear of the German line. The 545th Siege Battery fired 377 rounds that day at roads and hostile batteries in the areas around Villers Outreaux.

> We have a very heavy day, and I shall be pleased when I have chance of a rest.
>
> Joseph Dan Fewster, 27th September 1918

The following day whilst the actions continued around the Knoll, the Germans having partially re-occupied it, 545th Siege Battery continued its work with a further 276 rounds fired, four calls for support being received from the American and Allied infantry.

The momentum of the Allied armies was now such that major attacks could be undertaken in quick succession. The supply of manpower and materials were available in sufficiency to maintain the pressure on the German Army that was showing signs of weakening. The artillery that had learned much throughout the war was never more effective, better equipped, or as technically advanced as now: it was formidable and was at last able to achieve the responsiveness required for the infantry to succeed. The 29th of September would see the Fourth Army make its main attack on the Hindenburg Line.

> Big attack on whole front from Cambrai to St Quentin, we support Americans and 12th & 18th Division who attack Vendhuile.
>
> 47th Brigade R.G.A. (Unknown: WO 95 War Diaries),
> 29th September 1918

The old Hull battery was now an important part of this colossus, firing day and night targeting roads, dumps and the enemy lines of communication, their long-range guns enabling distant targets to be engaged to great effect, disrupting movement, silencing hostile artillery and demoralising the enemy wherever he could be found.

> There is a great battle raging along this front and the thunder of guns is beyond description. The Boche must be having a terrible time, judging by the metal that goes over. We have had it hot enough, but we must have it cushy by comparison.
>
> Joseph Dan Fewster, 29th September 1918

The attack of the 29th September saw the Hindenburg Line breached. During these momentous events 545th Siege Battery fired 739 rounds between 01:00 on the 29th and 12:00 hrs on the 30th September: a combination of counter battery work, road, and bridge targets and infantry calls for support. A further 213 rounds were fired from noon on the 30th to noon on the 1st October.

> During the past 5 days batteries have fired constantly without rest, carrying out bombardment, harassing fire and counter battery work.
>
> 47th Brigade R.G.A. (Unknown: WO 95 War Diaries),
> 30th September 1918

The Commander in Chief of the British Army, Sir Douglas Haig, later wrote:

The heavy and continuous bombardment opened on the morning of the 27th September, had been maintained by the Fourth Army along its whole front without intermission for two days. The intensity of our fire drove the enemy's garrisons to take refuge in their deep dugouts and tunnels, and made it impossible for his carrying parties to bring food and ammunition.

On the 1st October, III Corps was relieved by XIII Corps and the 47th Brigade R.G.A. and 545th Battery affiliation were transferred to the latter.

The days following the successful attack saw the infantry consolidate ground already captured whilst continuing the attack on sections of the line still occupied by the enemy. Meanwhile the IX Corps and Australian Corps were to press on with the advance in order to gain advantageous positions before the Hindenburg support line (Beurevoir), the next major objective of the Fourth Army. To frustrate any German intent to reinforce their front or to organise for a counter attack the 545th Siege Battery fired on key roads and concentration areas to the enemy rear. On the 1st October the battery targeted Usigny Dump some six or so miles distant from their position at Ronssoy, beyond Beurevoir and to the north of the village of Ponchaux. This depression had been used extensively for storage by the enemy and so was a likely place for reinforcements to concentrate for any potential counter attack and, due to the number of machine guns positioned there, it would pose a threat to the planned advance. Villers Farm, another strong point, commanded their attention, as did the fortified villages of Elincourt and Serain, well behind enemy lines but potential strong points that could inflict substantial casualties on the Allied infantry. Roads in the Villers Outreax and Malincourt areas were also heavily shelled to further disrupt German movement and re-supply.

Between the 3rd and 5th of October the IX and XIII Corps of the Fourth Army resumed the offensive and attacked the Hindenburg support or Beaurevoir Line. Physically a less formidable obstacle than the main Hindenburg positions it was crossed, but not without considerable trouble caused by the many machine gun posts ranged behind the line. The howitzers of 47th Brigade R.G.A. had been moved forward progressively from St. Emilie to just east of Ronssoy where their best effect could be employed. The 545th Siege Battery, whose guns were capable of firing much further than the howitzers, joined them at Ronssoy. The right section moved on the 1st October and was joined by the left section during the night of the 3rd October; firing commenced on the morning of the 4th October.

> The fight here has been raging for days and shows no sign of slacking. Our troops are making a big attempt to breach the Hindenburg Line, which lies less than a mile in front of us. When daylight came we found ourselves in the midst of batteries of all kinds; 18pdrs, 4.5s, 6in, 8in, 9.2 howitzers, 6in Mk VIIs and 6in Mk XIXs all in less than a quarter of a square mile. The ground is strewn with mangled bodies and derelict tanks, but I don't think it possible for anything to stand the bombardment which we have put up.
>
> Joseph Dan Fewster, 4th October 1918

To give some perspective of the firepower of the Fourth Army artillery during this period, the ammunition expenditure is indicative. From the 26th September when the barrage operation for the assault on the Hindenburg Line commenced, until midday on the 4th October the heavy artillery fired in the order of 365,000 rounds. Over 11,500 rounds of this were fired by the 6-inch guns, mainly Mark XIX models, with 545th Siege Battery firing 1638 rounds or over 14 percent of that figure. The 6-inch Howitzers, which were more numerous, would expend eighteen times more shells than the equivalent-sized guns. The total expenditure including the lighter guns of the Field Artillery was a colossal 1,300,000 rounds.

> Batteries cooperate in operations at Beaurevoir.
> 47th Brigade R.G.A. (Unknown: WO 95 War Diaries), 4th October 1918

One of the critical factors that was addressed by the British army once production issues had been resolved, was the choice of its artillery weapons. Until the end of trench warfare, commencing with the breakthrough at Amiens in August and a return to a mobile form of warfare on the Western front, the war had in many respects resembled a siege. The shorter barrelled howitzers that could lob a shell onto the enemy positions were very useful weapons in these circumstances and had a very good longevity when compared with the longer-range 6-inch guns. The muzzle velocity of a 6-inch gun was much higher than that of a howitzer of similar size. This combined with the higher firing pressure to achieve the required velocity resulted in higher wear rates in the barrel with subsequent loss of accuracy when it became acute. Typically, a howitzer could fire six times as many rounds for similar barrel depreciation as a gun and thus for strategic and practical reasons howitzers far outnumbered guns.

With the Beaurevoir Line crossed, preparations were put in hand by the Fourth Army to exploit its recent success. Reports had indicated weakness in the German army, with a general withdrawal underway along many parts of the front. The howitzers were again moved forwards in stages, 47th Brigade establishing its headquarters in the village of Nauroy, astride the old roman road that heads north eastwards towards the town of Le Cateau. The howitzer batteries of the brigade were deployed around the village of Estrées just a few hundred yards away from the recently captured Beaurevoir line, whilst the longer-range guns followed some days later.

On the 8th October, the British attacks continued, the left section of the battery moved forward from Ronssoy passing through Bony where some days before the American divisions had attacked.

> Just before Bellincourt I saw the American Field Ambulance collecting the dead. There were five rows, with about a hundred in each row, and they were still hard at work bringing more in.
>
> Joseph Dan Fewster, 8th October 1918

Leaving Bellincourt and passing through Nauroy and Estrées, the left section of the battery took up positions just to the west of the hamlet of Ponchaux and the right section, still at Ronssoy, targetted the village of Elincourt. The right section joined the left section near Ponchaux on the 9th October but some distance in advance of the latter's existing position.

Very successful attack on 4th Army front.
47th Brigade R.G.A. (Unknown: WO 95 War Diaries), 8th
October 1918

The brigade again moved forward establishing its HQ in the environs of the recently captured village of Beaurevoir. Battery positions were found at Sonia Farm, Bronx Farm, and Usigny Dump. Here the effect of the previous bombardment by 545th Siege Battery and other 6-inch guns was apparent when over 100 German corpses were found there: the men had been killed as they effected a withdrawal. The German Army was now retreating but still a fighting force. The artillery maintained constant fire throughout the advances by the Fourth Army and whilst the German infantry would leave the line rather than fight, the machine gunners would hold out to the last with resulting casualties in the attacking allied infantry.

The 3rd Cavalry Corps attempted to exploit the situation but were driven back by the still numerous machine guns forcing their retirement to near Nauroy where some cover was afforded. Throughout the afternoon and into the night the German air force sought out and attacked the cavalry with their bombers. The rapid advance caused a problem for the artillery; by the 9th October it was not found possible to keep sufficient ammunition supplied to the batteries of the brigade due to the congested roads and the increasing distance from the dumps. To reduce their logistical requirement and increase the effectiveness of their weapons in what was

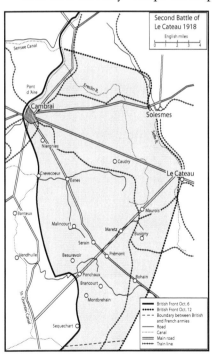

Map showing the Second Battle of Le Cateau, showing the advance of the British Fourth Army between the 6th and 12th October 1918

now a very mobile war some 6-inch Howitzers of the Brigade were to remain behind. The nucleus of the 47th Brigade went forward under the title of Andrews Brigade and comprised of 1 section of 189th Siege battery, the right section of 545th Siege Battery, 1section of 143rd Siege Battery and 189th Siege Battery: the latter coming into action at Serain the same day.

The right section of 545th Siege Battery, which had moved from Ronssoy to Ponchaux during the night of the 8th October, joined Andrews Brigade, an ad hoc artillery formation, to pursue the British infantry advance. They established their section at Maurois railway station, where the embankment of the cutting on the east of the railway line protected the level ground on the western side of the track. From this position, on the 10th October, the battery resumed its barrage of German positions. The left section of the battery had remained at Ponchaux, their billets in a large barn of a small chateau at the crossroads, at Geneve, a hamlet adjacent to Ponchaux and straddling the road to Le Cateau.

The German air force continued its aerial attacks on the troop concentrations which were confined to the long straight roman road, and the shallow valleys that bisected it that the undulating countryside affords. During the night of the 9th of October the battery billets of the left section in the barn at Ponchaux, were severely bombed.

> During the night the battery billet was severely bombed– no casualties.
>
> Basil Edward Floyd, 9th October 1918

The lack of casualties was fortunate, the proverbial luck of the battery seemed to be holding despite their billet receiving a direct hit from the German bombers; others were less fortunate.

> It is a sickening sight this morning. There are dead men lying as thick as leaves in autumn. Just outside our door a bomb had been dropped alongside an ambulance convoy of six light cars. All the lot went west, patients, drivers and cars, which were reduced to scrap iron. Further down the road one of our ammunition lorries was unlucky and had a bomb

dropped plumb on it. There was enough left of the first driver to recognise him but there wasn't a vestige left of the other driver.

Joseph Dan Fewster, 9th October 1918

With the Cavalry again in action well to the fore of their position and the German Army heading full out for Le Cateau and the River Selle, the left section guns still positioned at Ponchaux were stood down from action.

Before dark I had some of the dead to be cleared to one side so that we had clear paths round the gun. After dark, the first time I moved 5 yards I stumbled over one body and my outstretched arms plunged into another.

Joseph Dan Fewster, 9th October 1918

The right section at Maurois remained active, it was further forward and still in touch with the enemy. The left section personnel were sent forward to the village of Maretz to form a brigade ammunition dump. They remained at Maretz until the 19th October in anticipation of the crossing of the River Selle near Le Cateau, the right section moved forward and transferred to 73rd Army Brigade R.G.A.. Throughout the battle, the battery came under direct orders of XIII Corps.

My section goes up again, so today I am relieved at the dump… We proceed through Maurois, where the right section of my battery is in action, Honnechy, St Benin, and take up a position at Le Cateau. I expect the enemy has taken up a strong position in Mormal Forest at the other side of the town.

Joseph Dan Fewster, 19th October 1918.

In the XIII Corps' area, the 50th and 66th British Divisions spearheaded the attack. Corps and Divisional artillery was positioned, and detailed barrage plans had been estblished for both the heavy and the siege artillery. The V Corps, to the north of XIII Corps, would provide counter battery support throughout the operations.

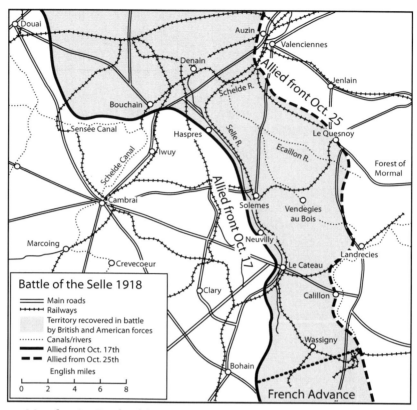

Map showing Battle of the River Selle, showing the advance of the British Fourth army between the 17th October and the 25th October 1918.

This morning our artillery gave the biggest bombardment I have yet heard. All watches had been synchronised at midnight. At 1:30am all guns opened fire. There must have been hundreds of guns round us. The thunder was terrifying. We were switching from one target to another without a stop. This continued for 5 hours. Then the infantry went over.

Joseph Dan Fewster, 23rd October 1918

The attack was successful and captured all of the planned objectives. The River Selle formed one of the last natural defensive obstacles on the Fourth Army front. The Germans, their lines of communication and military infrastructure now in disarray, were effectively in retreat although their artillery remained active for some days in the area of the 545th Siege Battery's position. On the 4th November, the British infantry pushed forwards again, crossing the Sambre–Oise canal and continuing through the Forest of Mormal beyond. For the battery, the continuous firing of their weapons throughout the advance had taken its toll. Unable to maintain accurate fire due to barrel wear, the guns of the battery were condemned on the 27th October and sent to the Ordinance Depot at Amiens for new barrels to be fitted. The battery personnel of both sections moved forwards to Le Cateau.

The ammunition column joined the battery at Le Cateau, but during the night of the 27th October came under heavy fire from German artillery, which was still active. Two of the seven lorries of gun cotton and ammunition were ignited by the enemy action and, being only 30 yards away from the battery personnel, placed the men at great risk. Second Lieutenant Geoffrey Rackham of the Army Service Corps, attached to the battery, was awakened by the alarm and sped to the scene, finding flames issuing from the petrol tank of one vehicle. Replacing the cap on the tank he mounted the driver's seat, and after starting the lorry, drove it to a place of safety despite charge canisters exploding to his immediate rear. Sergeant Goodwin (A.S.C.) and Lance Bombardier Frank Dickens R.G.A. of the 545th Siege Battery, showed great gallantry in throwing the shells from the burning lorry, both were subsequently awarded the Meritorious Service Medal. Two days later, another of the battery ammunition column lorries drove into no-mans-land in error, it was abandoned until the Germans had retreated. The battery guns were returned from Amiens in time for the renewal of the advance.

> Bde took part in operation for capture of Mormal Forest.
> Batteries in Brigade taking part. 189, 312, 449, 504, 545.
>
> H. Adams, 73rd Brigade, 4th November 1918.

At the battery, and in the infantry ranks, rumours were rife with the prospect of the German government suing for peace. President Woodrow Wilson, of the United States, had proposed terms to Germany but, in the preceding weeks, the terms had been rebuffed. The retreat of the German forces, still pursued by the tanks and infantry of the British army on all fronts, was becoming a rout. Germany's once formidable army was, to all intents and purposes, finished.

Chapter 23

The Victory

FROM the 5th November 1918, all artillery batteries in the XIII Corps' area were stood down out of action, and ordered not to move forward but to remain in their positions. Personnel were withdrawn from their guns and billeted in the town of Le Cateau. On the 6th November, Major Floyd took temporary command of the 73rd Army Brigade R.G.A., but left the 545th Siege Battery for England the following day to attend the Senior Officers Siege Course at Lydd.

> Shortly after 11am our wireless operator reported that the Germans had signed the armistice terms. Well let us hope the politicians make a good job of it. According to the papers obtained, the terms of the armistice are such that the Hun will not have a kick left in him, but to my mind, we are in a better position to argue in the field than at the table.
>
> Joseph Dan Fewster, 11th November 1918.

Within a few days of the armistice, artillery batteries were being allocated to new duties. Some were designated to form part of the Army of Occupation on the Rhine; others were to remain for the present time in France. The armistice, it was felt, did not guarantee the end of the war, and could possibly be used by Germany to reorganise its army and resume hostilities should the final terms of the armistice agreement be rejected. To this end 189th Siege Battery, being one battery for the proposed army of occupation, was

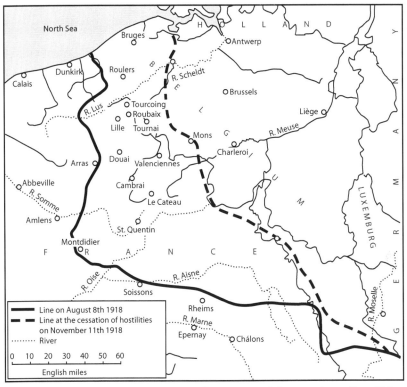

Map showing the Allied line between 8th August and the cessation of hostilities on 11th November 1918

Signallers from the 545th Siege Battery aboard a Sunbeam motorcycle outfit, with one of the battery's Mk XIX Guns (D'Olier)

rearmed with three of the Mk XIX guns of the 545th Siege Battery that had recently returned from Amiens ordinance workshops. In exchange, 545th Siege Battery took over the Mk VII howitzers belonging to the former. The remainder of November was spent at Le Cateau, where the battery personnel, along with thousands of other men from different army units, were put to salvage work in the old battlefield areas. For the battery and its ammunition column, this was predominantly collecting ammunition from the numerous dumps and former battery positions for transport back to the railhead and disposal.

> We leave Le Cateau today, and passing through Inchy, we arrive at Beauvois or Fontaine au Pire, both places being joined together. The whole of the 73rd Brigade of Artillery are mustering here. We are billeted in a large house in one of the main streets, while the right section is in a house further down the street.
>
> Joseph Dan Fewster, 30th November 1918

During their stay at Beauvois, the battery had a quiet time: only one parade a day, some physical exercise, and an hour's route march each morning. Each soldier was given a thorough medical examination and injuries, ailments and disabilities duly recorded by the examining medical officers. This was to establish if such conditions were war related and to determine the severity of the disability, which they quantified in percentage terms. If found to be war related, the condition recorded would in future be reviewed: and if the condition persisted there was the possibility of an award of a pension. Notably, the majority of the battery, those who had served in German East Africa, was recorded as having had malaria, consistent with their previous experience. On the 13th December,

The old cloth factory in Saulzoir where the 545th Siege Battery spent the winter of 1918. The postcard dates from 1907 and the photograph from 2006 (author)

when the medical examinations were completed, the battery moved north to the large village of Saulzoir. Billets large enough to accommodate the whole battery, as was the wish of the commanding officer, were found in a derelict cloth factory. The battery settled down in their new surroundings and prepared for Christmas.

> It is Christmas day and we have had a rare day. We bought a pig out of battery funds, and although the cost worked out at 4/2d a pound, we forgot that when we ate it. We also had a barrel of beer, which we were able to sell at 2d a pint, and very decent stuff it turned out to be. Each man was allowed two pints. We had plenty to drink and eat so under the circumstances, what more did we want?
>
> Joseph Dan Fewster, 25th December 1918

Near Saulzoir, the battery was allocated an area to carry out salvage. In keeping with their experience, they recovered artillery ammunition that had been left in their allotted area. The material when found was transported to the nearest roadside, where dumps were established, later to be collected by lorries for removal to the larger dumps and railheads to the rear. These activities occupied the morning hours, the afternoons were devoted to sports. All of the army favourites were indulged, with leagues established to add some competition to the proceedings, tug of war, soccer, rugby, cross country running, and boxing were popular. Gunner Voysey, a regular army soldier, who had been attached to the battery at Charlton Park in late 1915, won the brigade middleweight boxing championship held in the theatre in the nearby town of Caudry on the 28th December. He also won the Corps' artillery middleweight title at the same venue on January 5th 1919. He was no amateur: a few days before leaving Denham for East Africa in January 1916 he had won the Army and Navy welterweight championship at the National Sporting Club in London. There is little evidence of him pursuing this vocation after the war.

Apart from the obvious benefits of organised sport in keeping the men occupied and in good physical condition, the Army also provided trade classes in mechanics, electrics, driving and languages for those with ambitions for the civilian street where they were likely to return in the months to come. Provided that a sufficient number of interested soldiers could be mustered for a course, one was invariably provided; the choice of subjects was diverse.

The army now with less constraints imposed by the exigencies of war, allowed the battery to be reasonably well catered for: they received a regular supply of rations, based upon their manpower, or ration strength. However, with many thousands of soldiers still in the field there was little surplus capacity.

> By being exceedingly careful with our rations since Christmas we have been able to save a little bread, margarine and tea. We have bought some currant bread with money raised by subscription. We issued invitations, through the Mayor of this town, to all children under 5 yrs old, to have tea with us today. We collected tables, forms, etc from all over the place. The schoolteachers started bringing them in at about 4pm and what a procession it was! What pleasure it gave us to wait upon them! How they did eat. The civilian ration is only very meagre here. I really think that for the children it was the first unlimited meal they had had for many a long day. Many of them were so small that the mothers carried them here, and after tea carried them home again. After tea, the Mayor and the teachers made speeches, which we did not understand, but we did understand the heartiness of the children's singing of the Marseilles and the hearty cheer they gave the battery.
>
> Joseph Dan Fewster, 1st January 1919

In the New Year of 1919, the battery was preoccupied with their impending demobilisation. A few of the men, who had joined the battery prior to embarkation for France in July, were demobilised between Christmas and New Year. This, understandably, did not get a good reception from the Hull men who considered it fairer if a first in, first out, basis was applied. It became less palatable when it was realised that a few of those demobilised had achieved this through the influence and efforts of their families back in England.

The army of course thought differently to the Hull men. It had established a scale of categories to apply to each soldier in order to demobilise the men in the fairest possible way whilst fulfilling its own immediate needs. Therefore, those whose peacetime occupation was deemed more important to the national interest than remaining with the army in the field were classed as Pivotal. Guaranteed men were those who could produce a letter from an employer guaranteeing their immediate employment once they were demobilised. The government was very conscious of the risks of thousands of soldiers arriving back in England with no employment. The potential for political agitators to offer a platform for the soldier's grievances offered the prospect of the communist elements gaining support, and the prospect of mob rule.

Length of service was also used as a measure. Many of the Hull men had been engaged since 1914, which boded well for early demobilisation when compared against those en and conscripts whose service commenced later in the war. Finally the soldier's age played a part in the decision to demobilise. The army had little requirement for older men now that the likelihood of hostilities resuming had declined. Men that were just below the 45 years of age cut off upon enlistment in 1914 were by now four years older, so logically they could be released.

Sergeant Dan Fewster, whose diary and letters I have had the privilege to use throughout this narrative, met all four criteria. He was issued his demobilisation papers by the R.G.A. Records Office, Dover on the 10th January 1919. Jack, being twenty years younger than Dan, would wait until early March before his release, whereas Charlie Rimington, a schoolteacher with the guarantee of a job, but only three years older than Jack, received his demobilisation papers the day after Dan. It was very much a lottery despite some attempt by the army to provide a fair system.

> I leave the battery for the dispersal centre at Cambrai. I felt more despondent at leaving the boys than I care to admit. We have gone through a lot together and quite a lot are still here who were in the battery when it was first formed. All the officers of the battery came to the mess and wished me the best of luck on my return to civilian life.
>
> Joseph Dan Fewster, 22nd January 1919

As the battery was successively disbanded, the men were sent via Cambrai to Rouen, where they were placed in the rest camp that was filled with thousands of men from other army units, all shortly to be sent home. Discipline had deteriorated somewhat, men fought over food, rations were insufficient and the meals comparably small; there was a threatening air either through frustration or impatience about the place. Eventually, the mixed groups of soldiers would be formed into marching columns and directed to Rouen railway station. At Le Havre they were embarked on a steamer bound for Southampton. Upon their disembarking, and in the absence of any catering arrangements since leaving Rouen, each man was issued a mug of tea or coffee and some sandwiches. French money could be exchanged on the quayside platforms of the railway station and a further issue of a bag of sandwiches, polony, and sausage rolls was given to each man for the onward journey. John Silburn, a shepherd from North Newbald, had served with the battery throughout the East African campaign. En-route for Clipstone dispersal camp, following his demobilisation, he died of Spanish influenza in Gravesend hospital on the 15th February 1919.

The grave of John Silburn at North Newbald, Yorks (author)

Clipstone Camp near Mansfield, Nottinghamshire, was the main dispersal camp designated for the majority of the men from the original Hull Battery. Upon their arrival each man was served a hot meal followed by a medical inspection. There followed the issue of a demobilisation certificate that informed of his demobilisation class, based upon his age and current fitness for rejoining in the event of further hostilities. In addition it informed the soldier of his base depot for rejoining in that event.

Finally, a Protection Certificate was issued, enabling the soldier to draw from his local post office a set number of payments of his final army pay. This provided some security until he was able to find employment when once more back in civilian life. The final group of men of the original Hull Heavy Battery were demobilised from Clipstone camp on the 31st July 1919.

Certificate of Transfer to Army Reserve for James Robinson Skern. As a farrier he was transferred from the Hull Heavy Battery to the Royal Field Artillery in January 1916 and served in Salonika (Skern)

The Protection Certificate given to George Sprowson at Clipstone Camp upon his demobilisation (Sprowson)

Chapter 24

The Old Comrades Association

WHILST the battery awaited demobilisation in Saulzour, the Hull men contemplated their return home, and to the future remembrance of those of the battery who had died. It was a core of the battery members, who lived in Hull who organised an Old Comrades Association.

Initially, this was an informal arrangement that revolved around a small group, meeting regularly, in one of Hull's numerous public houses. The formation of the British Legion in 1921 gave impetus to formalising the arrangements. By the mid 1930s the association had grown to be a significant fund-raiser and through its social enterprise was able to support its members, when the need arose.

Remembrances were held every November, close to the anniversary date of the armistice. By 1934 the association had grown its membership and was able to host the first of many annual reunion dinners. This first dinner took place at Wenlock Barracks on the 28th November 1934; it was repeated at the same venue in November 1935.

The association held social meetings on a fortnightly basis at The Society Tavern on Dagger Lane, their now regular venue; committee meetings were held twice a year. By 1937, the membership had grown significantly and the Grosvenor Hotel, a venue familiar to them, hosted the reunions for the following two years.

OLD COMRADES REUNION.— ifth annual dinner of the First Hull Heavy Battery, R.G.A., Old Comrades' Association was held at the Grosvenor Hotel, Hull. This "Mail" picture shows Sergeant Fewster, Mr H. T. Walker, Mr J. Masterman, Mr Oliver Wright (president), Mr J. C. Bland, and Captain G. Gosnold, M.C.

The annual reunion dinner held at the Grosvenor Hotel, Carr Lane in November 1938 (Hull Daily Mail)

Fundraising was an important activity as the association had costs to cover, but also increasingly needed funds for its benevolent work. As the members of the battery grew older, some became less able to care for themselves and two members had lost their eyesight. The funds raised enabled the association to care for their own. Music concerts and smoking parties were employed to help with this requirement.

The outbreak of war in 1939 curtailed the activities of the association somewhat. The fortnightly meetings continued (as did the benevolent work and fundraising), but the annual reunion dinner was cancelled due to the imposition of food rationing. It was not until 1946 that the association was able to restore the annual dinner to the social calendar.

On every occasion of the annual reunion dinner, the association would send an invitation to Floyd. Invariably, due to his commitments, he would not be able to attend, but he would always send a telegram conveying his best wishes for the association, and

Hull Heavy Battery, Old Comrades Association annual reunion dinner at Troxler & Stanley's Café c. 1946 (Hopkin)

its members. In 1948, Floyd was at last in a position to accept the invitation, which he confirmed by telegram.

On the 24th November 1948, Floyd arrived at Paragon Station, Hull. To meet him from the train waited Charlie Rimington, and his daughter Mary. His acceptance of the invitation gave the association a dilemma; where to accommodate him? Eventually, by additional individual subscription by the members, they were able to offer quite comfortable accommodation at one of Hull's better hotels.

Following the meal and speeches and the several toasts, the association presented Floyd with a handcrafted miniature chest of drawers. It was specifically to accommodate his medals, which, following the Second World War, were now numerous. Charlie, who had retained his love of handicrafts, had designed and then made the drawers in the outhouse of his home. On the top of the chest was inlaid a small brass plaque, and thereon inscribed:

Presented to
Brig. B.E. Floyd M.C. R.A.
by the
1st (Hull) Heavy Battery, R.G.A.
1914 – 1918 "Old Comrades" Association
November 1948

Floyd, never known within his family for his domesticity ended the evening by assisting the wives of the association members by washing dishes. The men who formed the Hull Heavy Battery may be long gone, but the little chest of drawers that Charlie so carefully crafted remains.

The final reunion dinner was held on the 24th November 1950, informal social meetings continued for many more years amongst the city dwellers. With most of the surviving members of the battery now over sixty years of age, it was the logical end of the Old Comrades association.

Postscript

BASIL Floyd remained a career soldier in the Royal Artillery. During the Second World War he served in Malta and Egypt before his retirement, with rank of Honorary Brigadier, in 1942. Jim Dixon, who was evacuated from East Africa with cerebral malaria, rejoined the family firm of solicitors, Jacobs Dixon & Co. Joseph Fewster returned to his previous civilian occupation at Hull Breweries, he retired in 1935. Charlie Rimington resumed his teaching career, Frank Ledran, who had helped restore the locomotives destroyed by the Germans in East Africa, immigrated to Australia. Arthur Cowbourn, a printer, returned to his home town of Bradford, and Ernest Morison went to settle in Mombasa in British East Africa.

I was born when Jack was seventy years of age, by which time many men of the battery had already passed away. Jack lived until he was nearly ninety-three years of age, one of the last survivors of the battery. The fortune of his longevity, and consequently what he could tell me has allowed the story of Jim, Dan and Charlie and that of the other men of the Hull Heavy Battery to be told. Through this small book we remember the Hull men of that forgotten war in East Africa, and their heroic service in France during the Great War 1914–1918.

Appendix 1
Nominal Roll of Battery Officers

7th February 1916

38th (BL Howitzer) Brigade RGA.

Officer Commanding Lieutenant Colonel Piercy Neville Graham Reade.[1]
Brigade Adjutant Lieutenant Francis Thomas Galloway.[2]
Headquarters Lieutenant Edward Kenneth Biggs.
2nd Lieutenant Guybon Ebden Fitzgerald Boyes.[3]

11th (Hull) Heavy Battery RGA.

Officer Commanding Captain Basil Edward Floyd.
Lieutenant Anthony James Nannini.[4]
2nd Lieutenant Harry Tayler.[5]
2nd Lieutenant Thomas Macartney Nicholson Guilford.

158th (Hull) Heavy Battery RGA.

Officer Commanding Lieutenant Frank Harrison RGA.[6]
2nd Lieutenant Walter Henry Maslin.[7]
2nd Lieutenant Edward Charrington Mackenzie.

38th (BL Howitzer) Brigade Ammunition Column RGA.

Officer Commanding Lieutenant Frederick Farley.[8]

11th (Howitzer) Battery RGA.

17th May 1916

Officer Commanding Lieutenant Anthony James Nannini.[4]
2nd Lieutenant Harry Tayler.[5]

13th (Howitzer) Battery RGA

Officer Commanding Captain Basil Edward Floyd MC.
2nd Lieutenant Walter Henry Maslin.[7]
2nd Lieutenant Thomas Macartney Nicholson Guilford.

14th (Howitzer Battery) RGA

Officer Commanding   Lieutenant Colonel Piercy Neville Graham Reade.[1]
Lieutenant Frank Harrison RGA.[6]
2nd Lieutenant Edward Charrington Mackenzie.
Lieutenant Frederick Farley.[8]

Reformed 11th (Hull) Heavy Battery RGA
30th April 1917
Officer Commanding   Captain Basil Edward Floyd MC.
Lieutenant Frank Harrison.[6]
No 1& 2 Subsections:
2nd Lieutenant Wilfred Adams RFA S/R (attached)[9]
Lieutenant Anthony James Nannini.[4]
No 3 Subsections:
2nd Lieutenant Edward Charrington Mackenzie.

31st October 1917
Captain Basil Edward Floyd MC.
Lieutenant Frank Harrison.[6]
2nd Lieutenant Alan Nevill.[10]
2nd Lieutenant Edmund William D'Olier.
2nd Lieutenant Guybon Ebden Fitzgerald Boyes.[3]

ASC Officers Attached to the Battery
Lieutenant G. Carter, ASC.

Lieutenant C. H. Dale, ASC.

Lieutenant William Cuthbert Smith, ASC: MC (LG 27 Jul 18).
Medical Officer
Lieutenant J. Cameron., RAMC.

Officers Disembarking *RMS Durham* Castle at Plymouth
30th January 1918
Officer Commanding   Major Basil Edward Floyd MC.
Captain Frank Harrison.[6]
Lieutenant Edward Charrington Mackenzie.
Lieutenant Thomas Macartney Nicholson Guilford.
Lieutenant Edmund William D'Olier.

545th Siege Battery RGA

July 17th 1918

Officer Commanding Major Basil Edward Floyd MC.
Captain Gordon Douglas Coe.[11]
Lieutenant Edmund William D'Olier.
Lieutenant Edward Charrington Mackenzie.
Lieutenant Thomas Macartney Nicholson Guilford.
Lieutenant Harold Andrew Hounsell.
Lieutenant Claude Henry Garred.

30th September 1918

Officer Commanding Major Basil Edward Floyd MC.
Captain Rt. Hon. Lord Nunburnholme CB. DSO.
Lieutenant Edmund William D'Olier.
Lieutenant Edward Charrington Mackenzie.
Lieutenant Thomas Macartney Nicholson Guilford.
Lieutenant Reginald Laurence Tribe.
Lieutenant Harold Andrew Hounsell.
Lieutenant Claude Henry Garred.

1. Invalided to England in January 1917.
2. Posted from battery 4th May 1918 at Lydd.
3. Later to become a Pilot Officer in the RAF.
4. Admitted to hospital at Kilwa in July 1917. Did not rejoin battery.
5. Invalided from East Africa.
6. Admitted to hospital at Hilsea in July 1918. Did not rejoin battery.
7. Invalided from East Africa in March 1917, posted to RGA Records, Dover.
8. Invalided from East Africa in October 1916.
9. Admitted to hospital at Morogoro in August 1917. Did not rejoin battery.
10. A.D.C to G.O.C Brig. Gen. Hannyngton's force, November 1917.
11. Posted to 544th Siege Battery on the 21st September 1918.

Appendix 2
Officers' Awards

Captain Rt. Hon. Lord Nunburnholme:
    Orders:
        Companion of the Bath – 1918
    Medals:
        Distinguished Service Order – *London Gazette* 27th
        September 1917
Captain Basil Edward Floyd:
    Medals:
        Military Cross – *London Gazette* 1st January 1918
        Croix de Guerre – *London Gazette* 31st August 1917
    Mentioned in Despatches:
        France – *London Gazette* 22nd June 1915
        East Africa – *London Gazette* 8th February 1917
        East Africa – *London Gazette* 6th August 1918

Lieutenant Francis Thomas Galloway:
    Medals:
        Military Cross – *London Gazette* 27th July 1918
    Mentioned in Despatches:
        East Africa – *London Gazette* 7th March 1918

Lieutenant Anthony James Nannini:
    Mentioned in Despatches:
        East Africa – *London Gazette* 6th March 1918
        East Africa – *London Gazette* 6th August 1918

Harrison, Lieutenant Frank:
    Mentioned in Despatches:
        East Africa – *London Gazette* 6th August 1918

2nd Lieutenant Walter Henry Maslin:
    Mentioned in Despatches:
        East Africa – *London Gazette* 8th February 1917
        Secretary of State for War (Class B) – *The Times* 27th
        March 1918

Appendix 3

1st (Hull) Heavy Battery RGA

Rank[1]	Reg. No.	Renumber	Surname	Christian Name	Age	DOE[2]
	1					
	2					
	3					
	4					
Gunner	5	290003	Pearson	Frederick William		11-Sep-14
Gunner	6	290004	Clay	Arthur	24	11-Sep-14
	7					
Gunner	8	290006	Hawksworth	John Thomas	20	11-Sep-14
Gunner	9	290007	Stone	Fred		11-Sep-14
	10					11-Sep-14
Gunner	11	290009	Parry	John Henry Naylor		11-Sep-14
Act. Corporal	12	290010	Winter	Francis William		11-Sep-14
Gunner	13		Flint	Arthur Thomas	34	11-Sep-14
	14					11-Sep-14
Gunner	15		Dawson	Frank	28	11-Sep-14
Gunner	16		Claxton	George Henry	35	11-Sep-14
Gunner	17	290015	Cartwright	Harry		11-Sep-14
Gunner	18	290016	Myers	James		11-Sep-14
Corporal	19	290017	Redpath	Francis George		11-Sep-14
Bombardier	20	290018	Peacock	John Robert		11-Sep-14
Gunner	21	290019	Collinson	George Marrows	21	11-Sep-14
Gunner	22	290020	Kemp	Ernest		
Gunner	23	290021	Daubney	Fredrick	41	12-Sep-14
	24					12-Sep-14
Gunner	25	290023	Lockwood	William H.		12-Sep-14
Gunner	26	290024	Roydhouse	Tom	20	12-Sep-14
Act. Sergeant	27		Harrison	Frank	21	12-Sep-14
Corporal	28	290025	Wilkinson	John		12-Sep-14
Gunner	29	290026	Markham	John William	22	12-Sep-14
Sergeant	30	290027	Fewster	Joseph Daniel	40	12-Sep-14
	31					12-Sep-14
Gunner	32	290029	Medforth	Oliver		12-Sep-14
Gunner	33	290030	Wright	Oliver	36	12-Sep-14
Gunner	34	290031	Wilkinson	John Henry		
Gunner	35	290032	Thompson	Charles Ernest		
Gunner	36	290033	Spencer	Thomas Hunter		
Gunner	37	290034	Miller	Richard James	31	14-Sep-14
Gunner	38	290035	Clayton	Harry		14-Sep-14
Boy	39		Boyd	Hubert Douglas	16	14-Sep-14
Corporal	40	290037	Howlett	Frederick		14-Sep-14

Rank[1]	Reg. No.	Renumber	Surname	Christian Name	Age	DOE[2]
Corporal	41	290038	Barnett	Frederick		14-Sep-14
Sergeant	42	290039	Bland	James Clifford Waldemar		14-Sep-14
Bombardier	43	290040	Hagestadt	Frederick Elmer	28	14-Sep-14
Gunner	44	290041	Alexander	John William	34	14-Sep-14
Gunner	45	290042	Nottingham	George Edward		14-Sep-14
Gunner	46	290043	Lydon	Matthew	25	14-Sep-14
Gunner	47	290044	Marr	Arthur		14-Sep-14
	48					14-Sep-14
Gunner	49	290046	Marshall	Edmond		14-Sep-14
Gunner	50		Miller	Samuel	35	14-Sep-14
Gunner	51	290048	Hocknell	George		14-Sep-14
Gunner	52	290049	Iveson	Thomas William		14-Sep-14
Sergeant	53	290050	Adlard	Gilbert E.		14-Sep-14
Gunner	54	290051	Butler	Thomas		14-Sep-14
Gunner	55	290052	Wilby	John William	40	14-Sep-14
Gunner	56	290053	Meritt	George	36	14-Sep-14
Gunner	57	290054	Manning	James		14-Sep-14
Gunner	58	290055	Walker	Thomas Charles Henry		14-Sep-14
Gunner	59		Batty	William Neville	23	14-Sep-14
Gunner	60		Codley	Arthur	34	14-Sep-14
Gunner	61		Bilsdon	Arthur	34	14-Sep-14
Gunner	62	290058	Taylor	Henry		14-Sep-14
Sergeant	63	290059	Watts	Mathew Hays	28	14-Sep-14
Gunner	64	290060	Sprowson	George Everitt	24	14-Sep-14
	65					
Gunner	66		Newton	Thomas		
Sergeant	67	290063	Geater	Frederick Thomas		
BQMS	68	290064	Robertson	Alec		
BSM	69	290065	Doyle	Samuel Greenwood		
	70	290066				
Gunner	71	290067	Curtis	Gerrard	19	15-Sep-14
Gunner	72	290068	Shea	Alfred Thomas	55	15-Sep-14
Corporal	73	290069	Tweddell	Archibald John		15-Sep-14
Sergeant	74	290070	Cowbourne	Arthur		15-Sep-14
Gunner	75	290071	Wise	Herbert		15-Sep-14
Gunner	76	290072	Robson	William Henry		15-Sep-14
Gunner	77		Dick	Alfred	24	15-Sep-14
Corporal	78	290074	Smith	William Leonard		15-Sep-14
Bombardier	79	290075	Birch	James	24	15-Sep-14
Gunner	80	290076	Lundy	Matthew		15-Sep-14
Gunner	81	290077	Hodgson	Robert		15-Sep-14
Gunner	82	290078	Wood	Harold John		15-Sep-14
Bombardier	83	290079	Sharp	Harold Hyde		15-Sep-14
Gunner	84	290080	Franter	Reuben		15-Sep-14

Rank[1]	Reg. No.	Renumber	Surname	Christian Name	Age	DOE[2]
Sergeant	85	290081	Wainwright	Sydney		15-Sep-14
Gunner	86		Yeaman	William		15-Sep-14
Gunner	87	290083	Hurd	Ernest		15-Sep-14
Gunner	88	290084	Potter	Charles Henry		15-Sep-14
	89					15-Sep-14
	90					15-Sep-14
Gunner	91	290086	Lowther	Alfred Ernest	28	15-Sep-14
Gunner	92	290087	Jebson	Charles Henry		
Gunner	93	290088	Darby	Henry Maiden		
Gunner	94	290089	Hall	Matthew Tyas		
	95					
Gunner	96	290091	Young	Ernest	30	16-Sep-14
Bombardier	97	290092	Pearson	George Ellis		16-Sep-14
Gunner	98		Collingwood	Charles	21	16-Sep-14
Gunner	99	290094	Marshall	Thomas	39	16-Sep-14
Gunner	100	290095	Woodall	George Henry		16-Sep-14
	101					16-Sep-14
	102					16-Sep-14
Gunner	103	290098	Hart	George Norman	26	16-Sep-14
Bombardier	104	290099	Redshaw	Jack		16-Sep-14
Gunner	105		Cummins	George	27	16-Sep-14
Gunner	106		Harrison	William Algernon	32	16-Sep-14
	107					16-Sep-14
	108	290103	Smart	Robert Cyril	23	16-Sep-14
Gunner	109	290104	Stewart	James	20	16-Sep-14
Saddler	110	225445	Ruston	George	19	17-Sep-14
Gunner	111	290106	Wilson	George		17-Sep-14
Gunner	112	290107	Appleton	Thomas	42	17-Sep-14
Gunner	113	290108	Collins	Frederick John		17-Sep-14
Gunner	114		Shanks	Albert Edward		17-Sep-14
Gunner	115	290109	Barnett	Fred		
Corporal	116	290110	Reaston	Thomas Edward	22	18-Sep-14
Gunner	117		Cunningham	Alexander Lang	27	18-Sep-14
Gunner	118	290112	Stevenson	John Henry		18-Sep-14
Gunner	119	290113	Forrester	James	28	18-Sep-14
Gunner	121	290115	Brockwell	Joseph	41	18-Sep-14
Bombardier	122	290116	Marshall	Thomas Page		18-Sep-14
	123					18-Sep-14
Bombardier	124	290118	Landen	Alfred	31	18-Sep-14
Gunner	125	290119	Herberts	John		18-Sep-14
BQMS	126	290120	Gill	Norman Francis	27	18-Sep-14
Gunner	127	290121	Fisher	John		
	128					
Gunner	129	290122	Rudkin	William		

Rank[1]	Reg. No.	Renumber	Surname	Christian Name	Age	DOE[2]
Gunner	130	290123	Wiles	John		
Bombardier	131	290124	Burras	Albert		
Gunner	132		Walker	William	27	19-Sep-14
Gunner	133	290126	Elsom	Lindsley		
Corporal	134	290127	Danby	Kay		
Sergeant	135	290128	Dewey	Arthur Henry		
Gunner	136	290129	Tipple	Robert		
Corporal	137	290130	Fox	Francis		
Gunner	138	290131	Brown	Reginald E.		
	139					
Gunner	140		Holdorf	George	22	21-Sep-14
Bombardier	141	290134	Ryder	Arthur		21-Sep-14
Gunner	142	290135	Masterman	Harold Hyde	19	21-Sep-14
Gunner	143		Robinson	Charles Fredrick	23	21-Sep-14
Act. Sergeant	144	290137	Jackson	Frank Leach		21-Sep-14
Gunner	145		Dale	Tom	37	21-Sep-14
	146					21-Sep-14
	147					21-Sep-14
Gunner	148	290141	Thornham	John Henry	19	21-Sep-14
Sergeant	149	290142	Harrison	Harry		
Gunner	150	290143	Willison	John Thomas		
BSM	151	290144	Allanson	James Duncan	40	22-Sep-14
Gunner	152	290145	Boswell	Tom	27	22-Sep-14
	153					
Gunner	154	290146	Warrener	William Pease		
Gunner	155	290147	Revill	Albert		
Gunner	156	290148	Bell	Alfred		
Gunner	157	290149	Norfolk	John Henry Raymond	18	
Gunner	158	290150	Burton	Henry Arnold		
Gunner	159	290151	Lucop	Francis Charles		
Gunner	160	290152	Stephenson	Arthur Ernest		23-Sep-14
Sergeant	161	290153	Boanas	Samuel		
Gunner	162	290154	Chapman	Denby		
Gunner	163	290155	Harrison	Harold Edward		
	164					
Gunner	165		Sibley	Walter Henry	19	24-Sep-14
Gunner	166	290158	Traynor	Alfred		
Bombardier	167	290159	Dalton	Andrew McPherson		
Bombardier	168	290160	Foster	Joseph		
Gunner	169	290161	Jones	Edward		
Gunner	170	290162	McBain	John James	19	26-Sep-14
Gunner	171	290163	Roper	Henry Arthur		26-Sep-14
Gunner	172	290164	Woodhall	Percy		26-Sep-14
Gunner	173		Cooper	Thomas	32	26-Sep-14

Rank[1]	Reg. No.	Renumber	Surname	Christian Name	Age	DOE[2]
Boy	174	290166	Elgey	Harold	16	
	175					
Gunner	176	290167	Franklin	George Crighton Wiles	25	28-Sep-14
Bombardier	177	290168	Frost	Arthur		28-Sep-14
Gunner	178	290169	Garnham	Harry	24	28-Sep-14
Gunner	179	290170	Parkin	Joseph	22	28-Sep-14
Gunner	180	290171	Taylor	Arthur		
Corporal	181	290172	Ward	William		
Sergeant	182	290173	Downs	Harry William		
Gunner	183	290174	Hornby	John Edward		
Gunner	184	290175	Prynn	Leslie Thomas		
Gunner	185	290176	Rooms	John	22	29-Sep-14
Gunner	186	290177	Stamper	Cyril	19	29-Sep-14
Gunner	187	290178	Hornby	Robert	34	30-Sep-14
	188					
Gunner	189	290180	Darley	George William		01-Oct-14
Gunner	190	290181	Frazer	George	22	01-Oct-14
Gunner	191		Hepworth	Vernon	27	01-Oct-14
	192					01-Oct-14
Gunner	193	290184	Raleigh	Robert		01-Oct-14
Corporal	194	290185	Tharratt	John Robert	27	01-Oct-14
Gunner	195	290186	Taylor	George Richard		
	196					
Gunner	197	290188	Webster	Thomas		
Corporal	198	290189	Dove	Sidney		
Gunner	199	290190	Hopper	Ernest		
Gunner	200		Bell	George	35	03-Oct-14
Gunner	201		Midgely	Albert Scott	32	03-Oct-14
Sergeant	202	290193	Pinder	Herbert George		03-Oct-14
	203					
	204					
Corporal	205	290196	Whiley	Ernest Arthur		
	206					
Gunner	207	290198	Elliott	Thomas Edward		
Gunner	208	290199	Jickells	John		
Corporal	209	290200	Johnson	Edward		
	210					
Gunner	211	290202	Yates	John George Wallis		
Corporal	212	290203	Smith	Augustus William	32	19-Oct-14
2nd Lt	213		Maslin	Walter Henry		20-Oct-14
	214					
Gunner	215	290206	Morison	Ernest		
Sergeant	216	290207	King	Harry Edward	31	16-Nov-14

Appendix 4

1st (Hull) Heavy Battery (1st Depot Company) RGA

Rank[1]	Reg. No.	Renumber	Surname	Christian Name	Age	DOE[2]
Bombardier	217	290208	Gibson	John	37	08-Dec-14
Gunner	218	290209	Magee	James William		
Gunner	219		Le Mawer	Fred	25	11-Dec-14
Gunner	220	290211	Reynolds	George Frederick		12-Dec-14
Gunner	221	290212	Taylor	Leslie		12-Dec-14
Gunner	222	290213	Brown	Albert Ernest		
Gunner	223	290214	Drake	John William	24	14-Dec-14
Gunner	224	290215	Dearing	Harold Edwin	28	14-Dec-14
Gunner	225	290216	Ford	John William	19	14-Dec-14
Gunner	226		Gibson	Frank	23	14-Dec-14
Gunner	227	290218	Kirby	John Leonard		14-Dec-14
Gunner	228	290219	Ledrew	George		14-Dec-14
Gunner	229	290220	Moore	James Billany		14-Dec-14
Gunner	230	290221	Roydhouse	Harrison		14-Dec-14
Gunner	231		Staniforth	George William		14-Dec-14
Gunner	232	290222	Teeney	James Frederick		
Gunner	233	290223	France	Tom Hartley		
Gunner	234	290224	Allison	John Herbert		
Gunner	235	290225	Jacobson	Arthur Reginald		
Gunner	236	290226	Turner	William		
Gunner	237	290227	Johnson	Joe		
Sergeant	238	290228	Folkard	George Frederick		
Gunner	239	290229	Towers	Alfred Henry	19	18-Dec-14
Act. Sergeant	240	290230	McKee	George		
Gunner	241	290231	Abbott	John Edwin	37	19-Dec-14
Gunner	242		Hughes	Andrew	26	19-Dec-14
Bombardier	243	290233	Masterman	Jesse	17	19-Dec-14
Gunner	244		Wharram	Ernest	32	19-Dec-14
Corporal	245	290235	White	Alfred	42	19-Dec-14
Gunner	246	290236	Shanks	Percy		
Gunner	247	290237	Tong	William Harold		
Gunner	248	290238	Heathcote	Joe		
Gunner	249	290239	Hill	Ernest		
Gunner	250	290240	Wardle	Thomas Barker	35	24-Dec-14
Gunner	251	290241	Lazenby	Charles William		
Gunner	252	290242	Burnham	John Edward		
Gunner	253	290243	Day	Thomas Edward	19	26-Dec-14
Bombardier	254	290244	Garton	George		26-Dec-14
Gunner	255	290245	Hodgson	Fred		26-Dec-14

Rank[1]	Reg. No.	Renumber	Surname	Christian Name	Age	DOE[2]
Gunner	256	290246	Perry	Herbert		26-Dec-14
Gunner	257	290247	Silburn	John William		26-Dec-14
Gunner	258	290248	Witham	Robert	31	26-Dec-14
Gunner	259	290249	Ablett	George Kemp	19	28-Dec-14
Gunner	260	290250	Jarvis	Wilfred Wyndham		
Gunner	261	290251	Harness	Leonard		
Gunner	262	290252	Hudson	Ernest		
Act. Sergeant	263	290253	Richardson	Fred		
Gunner	264	290254	Batchelor	Arthur John	26	30-Dec-14
Gunner	265	290255	Dixon	Henry Alvin		
Gunner	266	290256	Fox	John H		
Gunner	267	290257	Wiles	George Frederick		
Gunner	268		Sanderson	George Edward		
Gunner	269	290259	Williams	Nicholas Charles Francis		
Gunner	270	290260	Bilton	Charles		
	271					
Act. Sergeant	272	290262	Varey	William		
Bombardier	273	290263	Berry	Bernard		
Gunner	274	290264	Clarkson	Charles	30	04-Jan-15
Bombardier	275	290265	Colbridge	Robert Seaton	35	04-Jan-15
Bombardier	276	290266	Garrod	George Arthur	24	04-Jan-15
Gunner	277	290267	Marshall	George	27	04-Jan-15
Sergeant	278	290268	Skern	James Robinson		25-Jan-15
Gunner	279		Boswell	Harry	20	16-Mar-15
	280					
Gunner	281		Hopper	Ellis Flower	29	30-Mar-15
Gunner	282	290271	Rimington	Charles Townend		04-May-15
Gunner	283	290272	Guest	Thomas Richard		06-May-15
Gunner	284	290273	Romans	Harry Freemantle		
	285					
Gunner	286		Acey	James	24	11-May-15
Gunner	287	290276	Dickens	Frank		
Gunner	288	290277	Chapman	William Thomas		
Gunner	289	290278	Hunter	Fred		
Gunner	290	290279	Johnson	Frank		
Gunner	291	290280	Johnson	Harry		
Act Bombardier	292		Habbershaw	Lichmere William	28	17-May-15
Gunner	293	290281	Freeman	George		17-May-15
Gunner	294	290282	Pike	Henry	35	17-May-15
Gunner	295		Blood	Herbert	20	17-May-15
Gunner	296	290284	Garbutt	Frederick William Parkinson		17-May-15
Bombardier	297	290285	Webster	Sydney	24	17-May-15
Gunner	298	290286	Webster	Charles Laughton		17-May-15
Bombardier	299	290287	Brocklehurst	William Geoffrey	21	20-May-15

Rank[1]	Reg. No.	Renumber	Surname	Christian Name	Age	DOE[2]
Gunner	300		Longman	Joseph Sanderson	36	20-May-15
Gunner	301	290289	Hill	Arthur		20-May-15
Gunner	302	290290	Etheridge	Frank	27	20-May-15
Gunner	303	290291	Hilton	James Thompson		
Gunner	304	290292	Jones	Alfred Ernest	20	21/05/914
Gunner	305	290293	Lawson	Allen		21-May-15
Gunner	306	290294	Walker	Albert Thomas		21/05/915
Gunner	307	290295	Wright	Thomas William	30	21-May-15
Sergeant	308	290296	Gardiner	George		
Bombardier	309	290297	Holmes	Herbert A.		
	310					
Gunner	311		Beadle	Arthur	22	25-May-15
Gunner	312	290300	Britton	James		25-May-15
Gunner	313	290301	Fox	Tom	23	25-May-15
Gunner	314	290302	Grey	Charles Henry		25-May-15
Bombardier	315	290303	Ledran	Frank Felix		25-May-15
	316					25-May-15
Gunner	317	290305	Rodmell	Henry	35	25-May-15
Gunner	318	290306	Saul	George Henry		25-May-15
Gunner	319	290307	Spackman	Arthur		25-May-15
Gunner	320	290308	Tate	Arthur M.		25-May-15
Gunner	321	290309	Walker	Ernest	38	25-May-15
Gunner	322	290310	Walker	George	23	25-May-15
Gunner	323	290311	Binley	John Robert	19	26-May-15
Gunner	324	290312	Cartwright	Joseph H.		26-May-15
Gunner	325		Feeton	Garnet	19	26-May-15
Gunner	326	290314	Forth	Ernest	18	26-May-15
Gunner	327		Mail	Norman	19	26-May-15
	328					
Gunner	329		Hird	Albert	26	27-May-15
Bombardier	330	290318	Dixon	James Maurice	24	28-May-15
Gunner	331	290319	Mann	William Henry		31-May-15
Gunner	332	290320	Storry	William	21	24-Jul-15
Gunner	333	290321	Tuton	Reginald Thomas	23	24-Jul-15
Gunner	334	290322	MacKay	Donald		
Gunner	335	290323	Wiles	Thomas Herbert	21	08-Feb-15
Gunner	336	290324	Boyd	Maurice Bradley Parker	19	02-Oct-15

Appendix 5

Men Discharged from 1st (Hull) Heavy Battery RGA

Rank[1]	Reg. No.	Surname	Christian Name	Age	DOE[2]	DoD[3]
Gunner	15	Dawson	Frank	28	11-Sep-14	12-Feb-15
Gunner	16	Claxton	George Henry	35	11-Sep-14	26-Mar-15
Gunner	50	Miller	Samuel	35	14-Sep-14	29-Oct-15
Gunner	60	Codley	Arthur	34	14-Sep-14	26-Mar-15
Gunner	71	Curtis	Gerrard	19	15-Sep-14	26-Jun-15
Gunner	77	Dick	Alfred	24	15-Sep-14	25-May-15
Gunner	98	Collingwood	Charles	21	16-Sep-14	26-Mar-15
Gunner	105	Cummins	George	27	16-Sep-14	03-May-15
Gunner	117	Cunningham	Alexander Lang	27	18-Sep-14	19-Oct-14
Gunner	132	Walker	William	27	19-Sep-14	01-Mar-15
Gunner	143	Robinson	Charles Fredrick	23	21-Sep-14	02-Jul-15
Gunner	145	Dale	Tom	37	21-Sep-14	30-Apr-15
Gunner	165	Sibley	Walter Henry	19	24-Sep-14	02-Jul-15
Gunner	173	Cooper	Thomas	32	26-Sep-14	23-Mar-15
Gunner	191	Hepworth	Vernon	27	01-Oct-14	03-Aug-15
Gunner	200	Bell	George	35	03-Oct-14	14-Nov-14
Gunner	201	Midgely	Albert Scott	32	03-Oct-14	30-Apr-15

Appendix 6

Men Discharged from 1st (Hull) Heavy Battery
(1st Depot Section) RGA

Rank[1]	Reg. No.	Surname	Christian Name	Age	DOE[2]	DoD[3]
Gunner	226	Gibson	Frank	23	14-Dec-14	25-Mar-15
Gunner	244	Wharram	Ernest	32	19-Dec-14	28-May-15
Gunner	279	Boswell	Harry	20	16-Mar-15	14-Jan-16
Gunner	286	Acey	James	24	11-May-15	19-May-15
Act Bombardier	292	Habbershaw	Lichmere William	28	17-May-15	04-Mar-16
Gunner	295	Blood	Herbert	20	17-May-15	28-May-15
Gunner	300	Longman	Joseph Sanderson	36	20-May-15	27-May-15
Gunner	302	Etheridge	Frank	27	20-May-15	28-May-15
Gunner	311	Beadle	Arthur	22	25-May-15	28-May-14
Gunner	325	Feeton	Garnet	19	26-May-15	04-Jun-15
Gunner	327	Mail	Norman	19	26-May-15	29-May-15
Gunner	329	Hird	Albert	26	27-May-15	04-Jun-15

Appendix 7

Men Discharged to Officer's Commission 11th (Hull) Heavy Battery RGA

Rank[1]	Reg. No.	Renumber	Surname	Name	Age	Corp	DOE[2]	DoC[3]
Act. Sergeant	27		Harrison	Frank	21	RGA	12-Sep-14	22-Dec-14
Gunner	39		Boyd	Hubert Douglas	16	RFA TF	14-Sep-14	7–Dec-15
Corporal	73	290069	Tweddell	Archibald John	21	RNVR	15-Sep-14	14-Mar-18
Sergeant	202	290193	Pinder	Herbert George	38	RASC	3-Oct-14	26-Jul-18
BQMS	213		Maslin	Walter Henry	25	RGA	20-Oct-14	13-Jul-15
Gunner	281		Hopper	Ellis Flower	29	DLI	30-Mar-15	7-Sep-15
Sergeant	308	290296	Gardiner	George		KAR		

Appendix 8

Mentioned is Despatches

Rank[1]	Reg. No.	Renumber	Surname	Christian Name	Age
Gunner	29	290026	Markham	John William	22
Sergeant	30	290027	Fewster	Joseph Daniel	40
BQMS	68	290064	Robertson	Alec	
BSM	69	290065	Doyle	Samual Greenwood	
BQMS	126	290120	Gill	Norman Francis	27
Corporal	134	290127	Danby	Kay	
Sergeant	135	290128	Dewey	Arthur Henry	
BSM	151	290144	Allanson	James Duncan	40
Gunner	169	290161	Jones	Edward	
Bombardier	217	290208	Gibson	John	37
Bombardier	254	290244	Garton	George	
Gunner	269	290259	Williams	Nicholas Charles Francis	
Gunner	304	290292	Jones	Alfred Ernest	20
Bombardier	315	290303	Ledran	Frank Felix	

Appendix 9
Roll of honour of those who died

Rank[1]	Reg. No.	Renumber	Surname	Christian Name	Cause	Died
Act. Corporal	12	290010	Winter	Francis William	Blackwater Fever	22-Aug-17
Bombardier	43	290040	Hagestadt	Frederick Elmer	Malaria	16-Feb-17
Gunner	44	290041	Alexander	John William	Pneumonia	24-Jan-18
Gunner	47	290044	Marr	Arthur	Pneumonia	12-Nov-18
Gunner	61		Bilsdon	Arthur	Dysentery / Malaria	02-Jun-16
Gunner	86		Yeaman	William	Malaria	08-Jun-16
Gunner	103	290098	Hart	George Norman	Natural Causes	24-Sep-18
Gunner	114		Shanks	Albert Edward	Natural Causes	25-Feb-18
Gunner	129	290122	Rudkin	William	Died of Wounds	19-Oct-18
Bombardier	141	290134	Ryder	Arthur	Malaria	19-Dec-16
Gunner	159	290151	Lucop	Francis Charles	Malaria	21-Dec-16
Gunner	169	290161	Jones	Edward	Malaria	11-May-17
Gunner	199	290190	Hopper	Ernest		28-Mar-17
Gunner	207	290198	Elliott	Thomas Edward	Dysentery	13-Sep-17
Gunner	228	290219	Ledrew	George	Malaria	3-Jun-17
Gunner	229	290220	Moore	James Billany	Blackwater Fever	24-Jun-17
Gunner	230	290221	Roydhouse	Harrison	Killed in Action	26-Apr-18
Gunner	236	290226	Turner	William	Killed in Action	25-Aug-17
Corporal	245	290235	White	Alfred	Malaria	06-Jan-18
Gunner	257	290247	Silburn	John William	Influenza	15-Feb-19
Gunner	264	290254	Batchelor	Arthur John	Blackwater Fever	19-Jan-18
Gunner	305	290293	Lawson	Allen	Killed in Action	11-Sep-18
Gunner	318	290306	Saul	George Henry	Died of Injuries	10-Oct-18
Gunner	336	290324	Boyd	Mawrice Bradley Parker	Died of Injuries	16-Feb-18

Appendix 10
Hull Rolls of Honour

Hull Grammar School
> Norman Francis Gill
> James Maurice Dixon
> John George Wallace Yates

Staniforth Place
> Edward Jones

Portland and Garden Street
> Alfred Landen

Blenheim Street
> James Myers

Clifton Street
> Fredrick Daubney

Campbell Street
> James Manning

Blaydes Street
> Arthur Cowbourne

Saint Charles Roman Catholic Church
> Mathew Lydon

Appendix 11

Men released from military service

Rank[1]	Reg. No.	Surname	Name	Age	Trade	Released to
Gunner	21	Collinson	George Marrows	21	Fitter	Armstrong Whitworth & Co. Ltd. Newcastle upon Tyne
Gunner	140	Holdorf	George	22	Marine Engineer	Armstrong Whitworth & Co. Ltd. Newcastle upon Tyne
Gunner	219	Le Mawer	Fred	25	Driller	Armstrong Whitworth & Co. Ltd. Newcastle upon Tyne
Gunner	242	Hughes	Andrew	26	Labourer	Babcock & Wilcox & Co. Ltd. Renfrew, Scotland

Resources and Further Reading Matter

Books

Armstrong, H. C. *Grey Steel: J. C. Smuts: A Study in Arrogance* (Harmondsworth: Penguin Books, 1939)

Barnes, Barry S. *Known to the Night* (Hull: Hull University, Sentinel Press, 2002)

Becke, Major A. F. Order of Battle. Part 4 The Army Council, G.H.Q.s, Armies, and Corps, 1914–1918 (London: H.M.S.O, 1945)

Blake, Robert. *The Private Papers of Douglas Haig, 1914–1919* (London: Eyre & Spottiswoode, 1952)

Bonsor, N. R. P. *North Atlantic Seaway, Volume 2.* (Jersey: Brookside Publications, 1978).

Buchanan, Capt. Angus. *Three Years of War in East Africa* (London: J. Murray, 1920)

Doebold, Holger. *Mounted Schutztruppe Units in East Africa, 1914–16* (January 2002)

Dolbey, Capt. Robert V. *Sketches of the East Africa Campaign,* (London: J. Murray, 1918)

Edmonds, Brigadier-General Sir James E. and Maxwell-Hyslop, R. *Advance to Victory, Military Operations. France and Belgium, 1918: Volume V.* (London: H.M.S.O, 1947)

Hogg, I. V. and Thurston, L. F. *British Artillery Weapons & Ammunition 1914–1918* (London: Ian Allen, 1972)

Hordern, Charles. *Military Operations East Africa, Vol. 1* (London: H.M.S.O, 1941)

Jones H. A. *The War in the Air Volume IV: being the story of the part played in the Great War by the Royal Air Force* (Oxford: Clarendon Press, 1934)

Leipoldt, John, *et al. Official History – The Union of South Africa and the Great War 1914–1918* (Pretoria, Government Printing and Stationary Office, 1924

Lettow-Vorbeck, General Paul von. *My Reminiscences of East Africa: The Campaign for German East Africa in World War One* (London: Hurst and Blacken, 1920)

Marble, Sanders. *The Infantry Cannot do with a Gun Less; The Place of the Artillery in the British Expeditionary Force 1914–1918.* (Columbia University Press, 2002)

Mosley, Leonard. *Duel for Kilimanjaro: The East African Campaign 1914–18* (London: Weidenfeld and Nicholson, 1963)

Pullen, Richard. *Chasing Von Lettow Vorbeck: The Story of Harold Downs' Great War Service with the 11th Hull Heavy Battery, Royal Garrison Artillery by Sergeant Harold Downs DCM.* (Lincoln: Tucann Press, 2013)

Rutherford, Alan. *KAPUTALA, The Diary of Arthur Beagle & The East Africa Campaign 1916–1918* (Bishops Cleeve: Hand Over Fist Press, 2001)

Young, Col Michael. *Army Service Corps 1902–1918* (London: Leo Cooper, 2000)

Young, Francis Brett. *Marching on Tanga.* (London: W. Collins, 1917)

London Gazette and War Office

Smuts, Lieutenant General J. C. Despatch to the War Office (London: H.M.S.O, *London Gazette,* 20th June 1916)

Smuts, Lieutenant General J. C. Despatch to the War Office (London: H.M.S.O, *London Gazette.* 27th October 1916)

Smuts, Lieutenant General J. C. Despatch to the War Office (London: H.M.S.O, *London Gazette.* 17th January 1917)

Smuts, Lieutenant General J. C. Despatch to the War Office (London: H.M.S.O, *London Gazette.* 18th April 1917)

Van Deventer, Lieutenant General J. L. Despatch to the War Office (London: H.M.S.O, *London Gazette,* 5th April 1918)

Van Deventer, Lieutenant General J. L. Despatch to the War Office (London: H.M.S.O, *London Gazette,* 16th December 1918)

Van Deventer, Lieutenant General J. L. Despatch to the War Office (London: H.M.S.O, *London Gazette,* 26th April 1919).

Supplement to the *London Gazette* – 29th December 1914

Supplement to the *London Gazette* – 15th March 1915

Supplement to the *London Gazette* – 19th July 1915

Supplement to the *London Gazette* 30932 – 1st October 1918

Supplement to the *London Gazette* – 23rd February 1916

Supplement to the *London Gazette* – 18th February 1918

Supplement to the *London Gazette* – 5th March 1918

Supplement to the *London Gazette* – 14th May 1918

Supplement to the *London Gazette* – 6th August 1918

Supplement to the *London Gazette* – 10th August 1918

Supplement to the *London Gazette* – 1st October 1918

Supplement to the *London Gazette* – 3rd October 1918

Supplement to the *London Gazette* – 31st October 1918
Supplement to the *London Gazette* – 19th November 1918
Supplement to the *London Gazette* – 16th December 1918
Supplement to the *London Gazette* – 7th July 1919
Supplement to the *London Gazette* – 3rd October 1919

National Archive Resources

WO 95/5314 – War Office: First World War and Army of
Occupation War Diaries
WO 293 – War Office: Army Council: Instructions; 1914–1964
Army Council Instruction – L. 20/Gen. No/3485; A.G. 1.
WO 363 – British Army: WWI Service Records; 1914–1920
WO 364 – British Army: WWI Pension Records; 1914–1920
WO 372 – War Office: Service Medal and Award Rolls Index
WO 374 – Officers Services

Private Diaries and Correspondence

Dixon, James. Private Diary (Unpublished: 1916 –1917). Courtesy
of Hillary Dixon and Jean Chandler
Fewster, Joseph. Diary and letters. (Unpublished: 1916–1918).
Courtesy of Denis and John Hopkin. http://www.jfhopkin.karoo.
net/DanFewster/
1. Jackson, Captain Frederick E. Diary of the East African
Campaign. (Unpublished: May 1916–August 1917). Courtesy
of Major J. L Keene, South African Museum of Military History,
Johannesburg, South Africa
Rimington, Charles T. Private letters (Unpublished: 1916–1917).
Courtesy of Mary Rimington
2. Thompson, E. S. Private diary – A Machine Gunner's Odyssey
Through German East Africa. (Unpublished: January 1916–
February 1917). Courtesy of Major J. L Keene, South African
Museum of Military History, Johannesburg
Wainwright, Sydney. Hull Boys in East Africa, correspondence with
the Hull Daily Mail. (Hull: *Hull Daily Mail*, 1916)

Articles, Papers and Miscellaneous Resources

Allen, Jim. Article regarding Four Wheel Drive Auto Company:
Off Road Adventures Magazine (oramagazine.com, March 2005
Issue)
Bulmer's History and Directory of East Yorkshire (1892)
Kivaisi A. K. and Mtui G. Tanzanian Mushrooms with Medicinal

Potential Value. Applied Microbiology Unit, University of Dar es Salaam

McWatters, Cheryl S. and Foreman, Peter. Reaction to World War I constraints to normal trade: The meat-packing industry in Canada and Australia. University of Alberta and Deakin University (extension.ualberta.ca/faculty/publications.aspx)

The *Snapper*. Journal of the East Yorkshire Regiment. January 1915 (Reckitt Benckieser Archives)

War Office. Locally Raised Unit. List of Units raised by Communities and Individuals, who undertook to clothe,house, and feed them at the public expense until such time as the military authorities were prepared to assume these duties. (London: H.M.S.O, 1916). Courtesy of Graham Stewart

Web Resources

Boxing History Org. Information on the boxing career of Gunner Voysey provided from records compiled by Miles Templeton and Richard Ireland of www.boxinghistory.org.uk.

Commonwealth War Graves Commision. www.cwgc.org

Great War Forum. www.1914-1918.invisionzone.com

History of Hull. www.hullwebs.co.uk

National Archives. www.nationalarchives.gov.uk

The British Newspaper Archive. www.britishnewspaperarchive. co.uk

1. The Long Long Trail: The British Army in the Great War of 1914-1918. www.1914-1918.net

The Soldiers Burden. www.kaiserscross.com

Copyright and Permissions

37. Ronald Tuton
38. D'Olier family (Kenya)
39. Author
40. Author
41. John McBain
42. Denis Hopkin and John F. Hopkin
43. Hull History Centre (formerly Hull City Archive)
44. Author
45. Hull History Centre (formerly Hull City Archive)
46. John McBain
47. John McBain
48. John McBain
49. J. Stancliffe and J. P. Roydhouse
50. Author
51. Hillary Dixon and Jean Chandler
52. Author
53. Author
54. Author
55. Author
56. Author
57. Hillary Dixon and Jean Chandler
58. D'Olier family (Kenya)
59. D'Olier family (Kenya)
60. Author
61. Author
62. Lewisham Local History and Archive Centre
63. Author
64. South African National Museum of Military History
65. Hillary Dixon and Jean Chandler
66. Author
67. Author
68. Author
69. Richard Pullen
70. Author
71. Author
72. Author
73. Hillary Dixon and Jean Chandler
74. Richard Pullen
75. Lewisham Local History and Archive Centre
76. John McBain
77. Hillary Dixon and Jean Chandler

78. John McBain
79. John McBain
80. John McBain
81. John McBain
82. Author
83. John McBain
84. Mary Rimington
85. Mary Rimington
86. Mary Rimington
87. Mary Rimington
88. Mary Rimington
89. Author
90. Author
91. Author
92. Author
93. Author
94. Author
95. Imperial War Museum Photographic Archive
96. Imperial War Museum Photographic Archive
97. Imperial War Museum Photographic Archive
98. D'Olier family (Kenya)
99. D'Olier family (Kenya)
100. Mary Rimington
101. Harry Fecitt MBE TD
102. Harry Fecitt MBE TD
103. D'Olier family (Kenya)
104. Imperial War Museum Photographic Archive
105. Mary Rimington
106. Mary Rimington
107. South African National Museum of Military History
108. Author
109. Imperial War Museum Photographic Archive
110. Imperial War Museum Photographic Archive
111. D'Olier family (Kenya)
112. D'Olier family (Kenya)
113. Imperial War Museum Photographic Archive
114. Imperial War Museum Photographic Archive
115. Harry Fecitt MBE TD
116. Author
117. Imperial War Museum Photographic Archive
118. Derek, Donald and John Cowbourne

119. Imperial War Museum Photographic Archive
120. Harry Fecitt MBE TD
121. James White. Great War Forum
122. John McBain
123. John McBain and Geoff Frost
124. John McBain
125. John McBain
126. Hillary Dixon and Jean Chandler
127. John McBain and Geoff Frost
128. Colyn Brookes
129. John McBain
130. Robert S. Colbridge and Lynda McKinder
131. Robert S. Colbridge and Lynda McKinder
132. Author
133. Author
134. Harry Fecitt MBE TD
135. National Archives
136. British War Graves Photographic Project
137. Derek, Donald and John Cowbourne
138. Mary Rimington
139. Author
140. Author
141. Author
142. John Brocklehurst
143. Author
144. Wikipedia
145. Wikipedia
146. Denis Hopkin and John F. Hopkin
147. Denis Hopkin and John F. Hopkin
148. Imperial War Museum Photographic Archive
149. Author
150. George Saul jnr. Reckitt's Archives. Courtesy of Charles Dinsdale
151. Author
152. D'Olier family (Kenya)
153. Author
154. Author
155. Fred, Phil, Brenda and Betty Skern
156. P. Sprowson
157. *Hull Daily Mail*, British Newspaper Archive
158. Denis Hopkin and John F. Hopkin

Other Contributors and Individuals to whom thanks are due:

Major J. L. Keene, of the South African National Military Museum of History, for the provision of the diaries of Captain F. E. Jackson, and C. S. Thompson

Staff at the James Cavell Library, Woolwich

Staff at the Imperial War Museum Photographic Archive

Charles Dinsdale, for providing research material from Hull City Archives and Hull Local Studies Library

Richard Flory, for providing information with respect to artillery officers

Ben Masterman, for identifying individual soldiers in some of the photographs

Chris Baker and the members of the Great War Forum, for information and support

Bob Hutchison for proof-reading and editing assistance

Karen Dyer and Steve Mwenda at African Eden Safaris, Arusha, Tanzania

Edward Nannini, Garner and Kenneth Ledran, Maurice Lydon, Elsie Jacobson, Elsie Binley and David Elsom for correspondence